HOW SCIENCE and RELIGION HAVE FAILED HUMANITY

Who you are and why you are here!

by

Rodger Christopherson

CONTENTS

<u>ORIGINS & MEANING</u>

Who you are and why you are here

How Science and Religion Have Failed Humanity

Comments and questions---

intercept777@centurylink.net

The ego is a jealous god. Its primary purpose is to interpret the world and protect the individual. It wants it's interests served and is often reluctant to admit the reality of anything except that which it can understand and feel comfortable with, the truth included.

"We are not human beings on a spiritual journey, we are spiritual beings on a human journey." **Pierre Teilhard de Chardin**

QUESTIONS

In the evening after the day was done, our three little children would cuddle close around their mother on the couch as she read bedtime stories before tucking them in with hugs and kisses. It was an everlasting, perfect picture. They were five, six and seven at the time. Less than a year later, however, they were motherless.

Melanoma, stated the doctor, and carved a hand sized amount of flesh off her back which included the tiny lump that had suddenly appeared there. But it was already too late. Its heedless growth had encompassed a blood vessel and sloughed malignant cells into the blood stream where they found their way throughout the body. Lumpectomy after lumpectomy, chemotherapy, pulsed laser radiation, x-rays, I don't think she wanted any of it but subjected herself to it in the interest of science and out of response to the desperation felt by those around her. Then, one day my oldest daughter, then eight, called me at work. "Mommy fell down and can't get up," she said.

Even in the hospital, totally without complaint, she did her best to smile and cheer those who came to see her. The dreadful pain, impossible as it must have been near the end, was never too much and she was alert and in control, accepting of her fate, always graceful. Finally, however, less than eight months from the initial onset, only thirty one years old, at four in the morning, she slipped away. By the time I left the hospital the sky was graying in the east. Lost, I went into a nearby coffee shop and sat down. Customers came and went, cars moved in the street, people went to work, the sun came up just as it had the day before, the rest of the world was unconcerned and unaware. It was dreadful, confusing and impossible to understand, made even more so by what had happened previously.

Five months earlier there was a bright young secretary at work who always seemed to know everyone's birth date and baked a special cake for the occasion. She drove an old car she could barely afford and the men would help her with repairs to keep it running. At break time she would often come into my office, sit on the desk and tell me about her boyfriends, her life, the girlfriend she shared an apartment with. One day her roommate's father evicted her sixteen year old brother from the house and he moved into the apartment with the two girls. On the weekend she baked another birthday cake for someone at work and the brother purposely ruined it with his fingers. In trying to stop him he went into a rage and brutally murdered her with a kitchen knife. She was only twenty two. Then, within less than a year of the others, my best friend died of heart failure, also at far too young an age. They were all exceptional people. Kind, caring, generous, involved, self sufficient and necessary.

Shortly after my wife's funeral the minister of the church she occasionally attended, stopped by in a fumbled attempt to console but spent most of his time pathetically expressing his personal fear about the small, benign growth that had been removed from his own neck. Even the surgeon himself, the one who had carved away on my wife so desperately all those months, told me of his own deeper concern. He was going to have his partner remove a small mole on his own cheek, too. Then, a few days after the funeral some stranger had clipped the obituary notice out of the paper, laminated it in plastic and sent it to me in the mail along with an inane Biblical quote and a request for twenty dollars. And for weeks after that it was shallow condolences of "God works in mysterious ways" and other trite attempts to provide consolation which were totally incapable of giving even the smallest bit of necessary comfort. Even worse, in spite of assuming they were all put forth with good intent, in that lost and desperate time where neither modern medicine or religion was able to extend her life, they came across as stupid, superficial and meaningless, as indeed they were.

And, so what, some may say. Look at what else is going on in the world. War and genocide. millions of innocent people caught up in the havoc, maimed and slaughtered simply because they were in the wrong place at the wrong time. Nothing more, just victims of other people's madness. What about them? Where is justice when so often there is not one single family member or friend left alive to even mourn them? Tough questions for sure, questions that often make life seem even more meaningless than it already appears to be, especially when personal tragedy strikes.

Then too, on the other side of it, what I was supposed to tell my children? That somehow their mother's death was "God's will?" Was that supposed to make it all right? How could it? For me, simply dumping the blame on God was much too irresponsible and unsatisfying. I loved and respected my children more than that. Regardless of the proportions of our personal situation, however, their world and mine had changed irrevocably. And even though rational answers appeared to be unavailable, my sanity still demanded more.

But while (for me) religion was bad enough, science was even worse. There was absolutely no solace to be found in the predominant views of contemporary science. The official position of science in the matter was that the universe was an accidental happening and therefore, so was life. And if life is nothing more than an accident, then there is no higher, inherent meaning to it or to anything else. You live subject to pure chance alone, and then you die. Dead is dead. It doesn't get any more dismal than that.

At the same time, however, I still had a job I couldn't do without and three small children who still needed parenting, now more then ever. So, best as I could at the time, I came to terms with it enough to keep what remained of my life together. But the memories of that beautiful person and the questions that arose from her death at such a young age never went away, even though the many years passed. Questions, always, as my mind reached out in search of some larger explanation to it all. Something even more difficult to find because I insisted that the answers had to not only explain the good things life has to offer, but the bad as well, in all of their proportions, along with everything in between. Indeed, there were times when it might have been easy to compromise, or even to end it all. Or, as a therapist once told me, sometimes there are just holes that exist in the mind, little psychological voids that can't be filled up no matter what but that if it ever became too difficult, there were medications one could take. Like lithium, for example, which smoothed things and made life bearable. But I didn't want things to be smoothed out and bearable. Not with hand-me-down answers, nor with drugs (prescriptive or otherwise), or alcohol, or muddled mysticism, or Jesus, or ultimately, suicide.

Then, in there somewhere along the time line of my life, as I read more and searched farther, I found that there was a philosophy called existentialism. This philosophy emphasized the uniqueness and isolation of the individual's experience in an indifferent or hostile universe which regarded human existence as unexplainable.

Where else could this lead then but to a feeling of alienation of the self from the universe?

Edward Edinger, analytical Jungian psychologist, said that "One of the symptoms of alienation in the modern age is the widespread sense of meaninglessness. Many patients seek psychotherapy because they feel that life has no meaning.... Accompanying the decline of traditional religion there is increasing evidence of a general psychic disorientation. We have lost our bearings. Our relation to life has become ambiguous." And while it is probably true that, for many, there may well seem to be be no other options but to just try and accept that and let it go, I wasn't ready to do that at that point. Perhaps it was as Edinger also said, "Alienation is not a dead end. Hopefully it can lead to a greater awareness of the heights and depths of life." At the time I certainly hoped so because I was most definitely feeling alienated from the universe, even at thirty six. Then, becoming more aware, it also became apparent that such feelings do not always have something to do with personal tragedy. They just seem to happen at some point in life.

Psychologist, William James, cites the case of Leo Tolstoy, the author of such great works as War and Peace, and, Anna Karenia whose outlook on life began to disintegrate when he was about fifty. As he stated at the time, he had a good wife, good children, lots of property and was quite famous as a writer and philosopher. He was also sane and in good health and "possessed a physical and mental strength which he had rarely seen in persons his own age. Up to that point life had been enchanting. Then suddenly it was flat sober, more than sober, dead. Things were meaningless whose meaning had always been self evident" and he could give no reasonable meaning to any actions of his life. What would be the outcome of what he did today or tomorrow? What would be the outcome of his life? Why should he live? Why should he do anything? Did life have any purpose which death did not undo and destroy?

What happened to Tolstoy also happens fairly frequently in modern society. Middle-aged people in particular suddenly find themselves sinking into massive depression, something we find to be fairly common as people open up and become willing to talk about it. It also occurs at all levels from rich to poor but it seems particularly perplexing when it happens to those who seem, "to have it all." Fame, fortune, the good life, everything it would seem that anyone could ever ask for. But then.... Why? Obviously it is because something of even greater importance is missing. Higher meaning. Without that, the rest all becomes nothing more than a silly game to be played out. In spite of its limitations, some people become very good at keeping up the facade, however, indulging in ego boosting power games, hiding from themselves, hoping dearly that they haven't gotten it all wrong but afraid to take a closer look at what might be more important than what. And so, with that thought in mind, we come back to asking the same basic questions as Tolstoy and all the rest of the questioning population. Where did we come from and what is it all about? In this regard the critical issue is this. If life is purely accidental then, by definition, it has no inherent, built-in meaning in and of itself. If, on the other hand, it had any other causal beginnings then there would be an intrinsic purpose and meaning behind it all.

ORIGINS

So, did life on earth evolve by pure chance out of pond scum or was it created and sent on its course by some omnipotent being? While this may have been a debatable issue at one point, it has degenerated into a very heated exchange along the way and, at present, the arguments over these two diametrically opposed possibilities still rage. Divine creation or accidental happening, and for those who have made a choice between these two very limited-in-scope possibilities, it has become a situation where both sides are left feeling threatened by the other side's view and continue to respond to it, often severely. Present day religious fundamentalism is, in many respects, a direct reaction to the barren edicts of modern science that challenge their belief systems and way of life. In the far extreme it leads to a disconnected, grotesque form of insanity where people who are mentally incapable of opposing this over-exaggerated threat with reason are driven to terrorism and war to make their point. Those scientists devoted to Darwinian evolutionary theory, however, still continue their efforts to prevail in the classrooms of America, regardless of the flaws in their thinking and the negative impact their statements have on the rest of humanity, preventing any open discussion of opposing views as to how it all began,

There are other creation stories out there too, and some of them are very bizarre. Meanwhile, other people of religious persuasion continue to add to the confusion by voicing an opinion that could only come from a complete misunderstanding of what Darwinian evolution is fundamentally all about. Whether it is an attempt to appear up to date and informed or a misguided and impossible attempt to resolve the controversy between science and religion, it fails badly. Even the Pope has fallen into this trap by stating that he, personally, doesn't have a problem with evolution theory. Such people don't have a problem with it because they believe that everything from the Big Bang on was all part of God's plan. God caused the Big Bang. God created the universe and put everything into motion, the evolution of life forms included and they don't see why there should be any controversy regarding the subject. God, in his wisdom, also created scientists who were put here to investigate such things and provide the rest of us with the interstitial details and where is the difficulty in that? After all, it doesn't take a great deal of awareness to see that most livings things change and evolve over time. So what are all the arguments about?

These people are serious when they say such things too, even though the disconnected logic of such an explanation completely misses the most basic point of all. First and foremost, there is no God, or creator, in the scientific explanation of things. It seems to be especially true for the evolutionists. For these individuals there is no God, period. Nor is there one for most physicists and a whole lot of other scientists in general. And even if there were, as far as they are concerned, God had nothing to do with the Big Bang or evolution. Regardless of what triggered the beginning, everything that happened since came together by pure chance.

God did not wave his arms and put the universe together. It happened the way it did simply because all the basic particles that came out of the initial explosion had certain defining characteristics and were compelled to act and react in certain ways and not others. Then, as a result of everything that happened since, it accidentally created the universe. And that most definitely includes the appearance of biological life. So, here we are, we humans, having also accidentally evolved because purely random mutations, and only purely random mutations, produced variants which were sorted out by "survival of the fittest" selectivity. This is not to say that the survival of the fittest part of it does not have some validity because it can be a factor in the process. This has been seen clearly enough in recent years in at least two major areas.

One of these is in insect populations which have changed to survive the use of pesticides in agriculture. The other is harmful bacteria which have become drug resistant and pose a direct threat to human health. Neither of these events should have come as a surprise, however. They should have been anticipated and taken into account before tampering with nature and should serve as a warning before blindly trying to control those things which humans find annoying or threatening. Regardless, the fact that the strong survive is not in question. The question is, what actually brought about the necessary mutations to begin with? And were those mutations purely random as theory dictates, or were other factors involved?

This is where evolutionary theory is lacking the most. Theorists accept the fact that mutations occur, but no comprehensive studies seem to have been done to explain those mechanisms in detail. Why do living things seem to be threat sensitive to start with? Obviously they are, or they wouldn't be here. Additionally, when threat does not exist, they, like those crocodiles and cockroaches, do not change because they do not need to. But, as pointed out elsewhere, if random mutation goes on all the time, then change would be apparent and mandatory and all living things would physically change over time. But since they do not, then mutation is not purely random and therefore mandatory. It is something else instead. But what? There is, as we hope to show, more to the story than meets the eye.

Regardless, the mistake comes in accepting random mutation as the entire story and attempting to extrapolate this singular phenomenon backwards in time, declaring that all life has a purely accidental, meaningless beginning. Thus, when it comes to the question of origins, anyone who professes a belief in a divine creator but is still willing to accept evolution as presently put forth has either been badly misled or glossed over the technicalities and come away with a very superficial idea of what has been said. At the same time, however, on the other side of the issue, there are still droves of people who also "have religion," but see the corner science has backed them into and are "mad as hell" about it because science has deprived them of the opportunity to express their views on the subject of origins in that most vital of places. The public school system. Regardless, while both ideological extremes exist, there are still a vast number of other individuals left in the middle, unconvinced about the correctness of either view, as indeed they should be.

These people, finding neither creationism or strict science to be very satisfying, are left adrift, intuitively and intellectually, which creates its own unique set of difficulties. **As a result, <u>the lack of a cohesive, unifying philosophy of life that serves to give human existence a clear, positive meaning is at the top of the list of serious problems facing the modern world</u>.** Interrelated but caused by this lack, there is not only the disparity between science and religion already stated but there are also extreme religious differences amongst the multitude of religious factions themselves, much of which contributes to the ideological insanity of various political systems and forms of government which manifests in oppression, nationalism and war.

Just as important in countries such as the U.S., a place which has less than five percent of the world's population but uses eighty percent of the world's prescription narcotics, there is also massive, widespread depression, lack of purpose and focus, perversity, self destructive behavior and suicide, along with an outward lack of consideration and feeling for those less fortunate. While all of these are secondary effects, they still trace back to a massive confusion and a deep misunderstanding as to why we are here on the planet to begin with.

Therefore, religion has failed humanity because

religions have not come together in any cohesive, significant way to provide guidance and meaningful answers to people but have created immense, ongoing conflict instead. Science, on the other hand has failed humanity because it hasn't yet found any ultimate truths and has <u>prematurely</u> stated that life is purely accidental and therefore meaningless, in and of itself, leaving people psychologically and morally adrift.

With this in mind, let it be said here that the purpose of this book is not to find some common ground of compromise between science and religion but to take issue with both as necessary in order to get to larger concepts. Knowledge, information, discussion and an on-going, open-minded search for the truth is the only real answer to the problem. As will hopefully be seen as we progress in the discussion, part of that truth is that life on the planet is not accidental and therefore inherently meaningless, but has great purpose and reason. While this may sound as if it were coming out on the side of religion, it is not. Not only is the ongoing search for objective truth mankind's highest and noblest goal as Einstein stated but finding that objective truth is the only thing which will allow the human race to evolve into some greater potential.

Objective truth for the scientist lies in the ability to formulate theory and experimentally verify that the physical world obeys certain postulates and mathematical laws. Unfortunately, however, whatever these theoretical hypothesis and mathematical formulations turn out to be in the end, it is still a substitute for reality, a profile of sorts, but never the real thing. Like all the holy books, the scientific view is just another story, also very incomplete and in many respects, incorrect. Therefore:

"The outstanding achievement of twentieth century physics is not the theory of relativity..., or the theory of quanta..., or the dissection of the atom....; it is

15

the recognition that we are not yet in contact with the ultimate reality." This statement was made by Sir James Jeans, British scientist in 1931, almost a century ago. The significant thing about it is that, whether it is recognized or not, we are definitely not in contact with some ultimate reality. The greater reality existing behind what we consider physical reality to be. Instead of continuing the search in earnest, however, most scientists still take the easy way out by almost unanimously declaring life on earth to be the result of, and only the result of, some stupendous cosmic accident. What you see is what you get. That's all there is. No greater meaning, no life after death, nothing. A statement with serious overtones and consequences wherein, once the implications of such a conclusion are accepted as truth, everything changes dramatically.

Lacking any larger concept of life, it is now up to the individual to seek out and come to terms with this dismal hypothesis in a world of limited choices. The easy way is to simply embrace religious edict or turn one's thinking over to others by adopting the skewed philosophy of some of the many self serving, errant groups in existence. Other than that, one is left trying to sort this issue out individually. If they are in any way still capable of doing so, of course, after having to deal with all the other more immediate and wearing concerns necessary for survival in every day life.

For those with more time and energy on hand, however, they can still simply decide to just not worry about it. Instead, purposely ignore the entire issue, stay distracted and see where life takes them. For what seems to be the majority, however, it is not that simple. They flounder back and forth, not completely sure as to what they should devote their energy to, or why. If life is an accident, it has no point and if one is born into sin and dies in sin, what is the point? Either way it becomes a no-win situation. With that as a baseline, what difference does it matter what a person does or how irresponsibly they behave?

Among other things, there is solace in over eating, especially in eating all the wrong food. And in alcohol and drugs. One can also escape into other forms of mind numbing trivial behavior, meaningless escapades, virtual reality, overt depredation and anti-social destructive extremism. Then, if one is still feeling despicable and valueless, they can still turn it around in self righteous justification and abuse the other people in their life because, somehow, all the misery must be those other people's fault. That may even justify getting an automatic weapon and shooting up a school, a shopping mall, an office building or whatever else craziness drives them to do. Other than that they can join a hate group or go off to war, anything at all that seems to give them purpose, right or wrong, or do whatever else it takes to avoid the larger issue. Last but not least, there is always suicide, the ultimate escape and a growing trend in the United States, especially amongst teens and military veterans.

These things happen because there is also a fragility to life. For some it is far more difficult than for others. Some are the victims of others, some of themselves. In too deep, the pain too great. Nothing compelling to believe in and meaningful enough to give guidance. Tragic that life should turn out to be so horrible that extreme choices seem to be the only way out.

The other choice for the individual, however, the most difficult of all for those of an inquiring mind, is to observe, learn and keep seeking the truth without regard for what either religion dictates or the direction in which the majority opinion of the contemporary scientist leans. Things are what they are because religion is stuck in the past while modern science has severely restricted itself in terms of what it will allow itself to investigate and has made harsh judgments about almost everything else that does not strictly conform to the predominant views about whose views get to be recognized.

As an example of this selectivity and prejudice, consider the following. Taking a series of scientific articles that had already been published in major science journals, the names of the authors and the name of their countries or places where the work was done were changed to some previously unrecognized location and then resubmitted to the very same journals that had originally published them. Out of a hundred such resubmissions, eighty percent were summarily rejected with statements saying that the work was not good science or the method was bad, the interpretation of the data was bad, and so forth. Therefore it would seem that much of what is determined to be scientific truth is decided more by who said it rather than by what was actually said.

When it comes to dissension, however, religion is even more intolerant. In that regard, the Pope also went on record by saying that freedom of speech should have limits, especially when it comes to religion. It does not matter what he said it in regard to, whether it was aimed at French cartoonists drawing pictures of Allah or someone blasting the holy trinity, it was still a very dogmatic statement. Fortunately, however, a modern day Pope does not have the over riding power to enforce such an edict and for the most part his comment was largely ignored. Nevertheless, modern world or not, there are still places on earth where such freedom does not exist and it is ominous in its own way because where would the rest of us be if we were deprived of the right to speak freely? Certainly we would not be allowed to publicly make the following harsh statement.

Religious dogma is the sign of death, one of mankind's greatest enemies. It keeps people frozen in the past and inhibits human spiritual development, preventing individuals from reaching their highest potential. Scientific dogma is equally debilitating and prevents mankind from reaching a clear understanding of

life's true origins and mankind's greater abilities.

If you are confused about life's meaning and why you are here, you will not be able to live as effectively as you might otherwise do. If you truly believe that life has no extrinsic meaning, it will then have very little inherent, individual value and may be needlessly squandered in the process.

All is not hopeless, however. Something is in the wind, as the saying goes, and it is a start. A minor start perhaps, but a necessary one, a reflective step away from the majority conjecture of current science, taken by author/physicist, Paul Davies.

Regarding the mystery of life's origin, Davies stated that in his opinion there was a huge gulf in our understanding. "To be sure," he said, "we have a good idea of the where and the when of life's origin, but we are a very long way from comprehending the how. The gulf in understanding is not merely ignorance about certain technical details, it is a major conceptual lacune. I am not suggesting that life's origin was a supernatural event, only that we are missing something very fundamental about the whole business. If this is the case, as so many experts and commentators suggest, then something truly amazing is happening in the universe, something with profound philosophical implications. My personal belief, for what it is worth, is that a fully satisfactory theory of the origin of life demands some radically new ideas. Many investigators feel uneasy about stating in public that the origin of life is a mystery, even though behind closed doors they admit that they are baffled. There seem to be two reasons for their unease. First, they feel it opens the door to religious fundamentalists and their god-of-the-gaps-pseudo-explanations. Second, they worry that a frank admission of their ignorance will undermine funding, ..."

Taking Davies' thought provoking ideas into account

leaves us with an interim objective to first examine that which is, "very fundamental about the whole business" and leave any further discussion and conclusions until afterward. Until then, this brings up a point made by Winston Churchill more than half a century ago. "There are no experts," he said. "Only varying degrees of ignorance." No doubt about that, because, while some claim to have solved the mysteries of life's origins, it is a hollow declaration that explains little and only reflects a true ignorance. Regardless, there are always choices that can be made. Consider the following quote from the book, *Honoring The Self,* by Nathaniel Branden.

"To use our consciousness appropriately in any given situation is, as I have said, neither 'instinctive' nor automatic. We are not wired so as to always choose awareness over blindness, knowledge over ignorance, fact over delusion, truth over falsehood. The design of our nature contains an extraordinary option - that of seeking awareness or avoiding it, seeking truth or avoiding it, focusing our mind or unfocusing it. In other words, *we have the option of subverting our own means of survival and well being.*"

Not only do we have the option of subverting our means of survival and well being, as Branden states, that is exactly what we seem to be doing at the present time in a very impressive and most dangerous way. But still, if one went back in time and queried the then living of previous generations, perhaps they all would have felt the same way at their point in history so maybe that aspect of it is nothing new. What is different from any other time in history, however, is the scale. Technology is both a blessing and a horror. Used wisely, it can bring comfort and well being. Wrongly used, it can bring us to the edge of extinction, more so now than ever before. Now we have "the bomb." And chemical and biological weapons. We have also allowed the by products of technology to badly pollute the environment and create global warming, the adverse effects of which we are just beginning to experience in the form of glacial melting, sea level rise and extreme changes in weather patterns. We have also allowed ourselves to grossly over populate the planet which only serves to exaggerate and exacerbate all the previous problems. Serious, yes. But not the most serious of all.

By far in terms of potential threat, misinformation, lack of a sensible morality, greed, fear, hatred and ego top the list. These are the things which drive civilization to the brink. Only mutual respect, kindness, caring and cooperation will keep it from going over the edge. **Realizing that life is not just some cosmic accident and therefore without any higher meaning would go a long way in helping the human race return to the real truth of existence.** But that is not where the majority opinion lies, at least not with any real clarity, conviction or common perspective. Why? Perhaps it is because, as physicist David Bohm stated, "Thinking within a fixed circle of ideas tends to restrict the questions to a limited field. And if one's questions stay in a limited field, so do the answers."

Understanding that and looking closer, it seems fairly clear that much of the thinking of today's professional world is, in its own separate way, just as tunnel visioned, restricted and self limiting as the words that come down from the pulpit. So, where do we go from here? If we do not want to continually end up having to invent artificial ways to give life meaning (as even such notables as Albert Einstein and Viktor Frankl believed was necessary) we will have to expand the range of questions we ask and be willing to look at a wider range of evidence than has thus far been allowed into the the mainstream of critical thought.

THE PHILOSOPHICAL VOID

Every life has its own truth. On the daily level that truth is determined by the particular uniqueness of individual surroundings, the interactions one has with and within those surroundings and the personalized interpretation and conclusions they give to those experiences in explanation as to what life and the world is all about. For some that environment ends at the edges of the remote village they were born in while for others it may extend as far out into the universe as their telescopes and minds can reach. Regardless of that extent and depth, mentally, physically and emotionally, each individual forms a world view that is unique to them. Fortunately for most, their lives also have many aspects that are shared by others such that living then has some level of predictability and cohesiveness and becomes the accepted everyday reality they know, sane or insane, as the definitions of still others may apply. But is that really all there is to it?

Religion is mankind's creation, pure and simple, with its origins hidden somewhere in the race's murky history. Whatever purpose it may have served or now serves, it is not there because of some fundamental, immutable quality of the universe. Other than the fact that religion exists, in and of itself, it has no built in, intrinsic truth to it. If religion were truth, there would be but one religion, not a multitude of different religions all in conflict with each other. If there were but one true religion it would have already prevailed and would stand alone. That is the logic that religious devotees overlook. The very fact that life is full of conflict and turmoil and ranges from something bordering on divinity down to abject depravity should make it clear that something else is going on here. That there is a different kind of meaning to it all and a different set of reasons for why things happen the way they do, extreme tragedy and suffering included. And, until those reasons are clearly explained, nothing can be truly brought into full perspective.

Exploring life's purpose and attempting to define it in a logical manner becomes a particularly difficult challenge under present circumstances, however. It is made difficult by the formidable collection of debilitating negativity that has thus far been put forth by some well recognized individuals in the field of science. Their message, if taken seriously, could easily get an honest inquirer trapped into thinking that things are so hopeless there is not even any point in raising questions. On the other hand, once these experts opinions have been sidestepped, a larger perspective will lead us to a point where we can only wonder how their imaginations could have been so severely limited to begin with. Regardless, here is their desolate message.

On that negative side of things Stephen Hawking stated that the human race is a chemical <u>scum</u> on a moderate sized planet orbiting a very average star in the outer suburb of one among a hundred million galaxies. Then, if that isn't dismal enough, add to it the statements of others like David Deutch who said, "Life, far from being central, geometrically, theoretical or practically, is of almost inconceivable insignificance." Sartre claimed that man exists as an individual in a purposeless universe. "Existence is absurd," he said. "There is no reason for it. No outside purpose to give it meaning. It is obscene and superfluous." Adding to this mind set, Stephen Jay Gould claims that, "We are all glorious accidents of an unpredictable process with no drive to complexity, not the expected results of evolutionary principals that yearn to produce a creature capable understanding the mode of its own necessary construction."

Biologist George Simpson further made the claim that humans are the product of countless special historical accidents. The list goes on and on, coming across as some grizzly oath. The dues one must pay to gain acceptance

into the scientific fraternity. State in writing and sign in blood that, life on earth is accidental and therefore meaningless. And finally a quote from Bertrand Russell ....
"That man is the product of causes which had no prevision of the end they were achieving; that his origin, his growth, his hopes and fears, his love and his beliefs, are but the outcome of accidental collocations of atoms; that no fire, no heroism, no intensity of thought and feeling, can preserve an individual life beyond the grave; that all the labours of the ages, all the devotion, all the inspirations, all the noonday brightness of human genius, are destined to extinction in the vast death of the solar system, and that the whole temple of Man's achievement must inevitably be buried beneath the debris of a universe in ruins - all these things, if not quite beyond dispute, are yet so nearly certain, that no philosophy which rejects them can hope to stand..... Brief and powerless is Man's life, on him and all his race the slow, sure doom falls pitiless and dark...."

As stated, the list of other scientists who echo this conclusion is a long one with much of science seeing life as some peculiar, meaningless anomaly, making scientists the largest group of doomsayers alive in the world of today. There are dissenters in the crowd, however, but their numbers are few and they have no clear, well defined statement to make as yet, either. Just an idea that the big story is flawed and incomplete which has created a growing controversy by asking, is there a trend towards increasing complexity in life forms? Is there some, as yet undefined, inherent natural drive towards creative function and evolvement? Do the laws of nature lean towards the generation of life and is "mind" included? If this were provable it would give evidence of some larger purpose in the universe, some ultimate, grander meaning to it all. Unfortunately, thus far such questions have, for the most part, been pushed aside. That and every other dissenting idea, large or small and is of little real interest to the mob of Darwinians who thus far rule the day, the later day saints of a strict, completely accidental explanation for life in all its many forms. (Please note that for the purposes of this book no attempt will be made to distinguish between the earlier advocates of the theory and the later day, so called Neo-Darwinians. Those geneticists, molecular biologists and the rest because, bottom line they all espouse the same basic explanatory tenets which ends with, a Darwinian is a Darwinian.)

Ordinarily, one might just leave them alone with their demoralizing summations and dead ended thinking. But since a person's beliefs are the driving force behind their actions and since the scientific viewpoint is the only one allowed into the classroom, it still spreads out into all levels of the surrounding world where, even if it is rejected, it still helps create a climate of debilitating confusion and distrust. As a result we are compelled to live in a suicidal, homicidal, drug and alcohol oriented society full of violence and inhumanity that a goodly portion of people are driven to try and escape from, one way or another. Any clear sense of unified morality does not exist.

For the young it can also become an overly self indulgent and self destructive expression of rebellion. An attempt to hurt their proginators for bringing them into a world full of chaos and not providing them with a working philosophy and set of meaningful standards with which to live their lives by. Harming oneself because it brings pain to others is somewhat perverse, but often effective. If nothing else, it brings attention to the perpetrator where negative attention is better than no attention at all and serves to validate existence one way or another. And in a world without meaning, what else is left?

As for religion, with all of its limitations, it can still make a difference in those lives where it has a presence. Fear of hell and promise of heaven can motivate people to treat their fellow beings more kindly but as long as someone has the devil to blame for misbehavior and can be "saved" no matter how many times they stray or how horribly they act, it is still absurd nonsense that comes at the expense of intellectual compromise. Additionally, if one also accepts the idea that they don't even have an innocent beginning but are born flawed and sinful and cannot escape, it becomes a dark cloud that hangs over their life and weighs them down. Regardless of any and all discussion on the point, however, it would be hard to dispute the fact that if people knew that they were born into a state of innocence and grace instead, where life had an inherent positive meaning and a higher, deeper purpose, their behavior would be far different than it is at present. So then, where is the truth?

Do we merely come into this world not having asked to be born, with life forced upon us, condemned to cope and live it out in suffering? Where we are also alone in dying with no one ever completely able to comprehend our separate joy or pain along the way? Where it is ours to deal with (or not) as we go along, secretly hoping it has some meaning we can neither seem to see or grasp while living fearfully that it may not. Out of nothing, back into nothing? Is it, after all is said and done, really that simple? Is that all there is? Given a chance, the answer would most certainly seem to be no, and to the contrary. The more steps one takes back and tries to gain an objective view of the situation, the more it appears that religion has stalled out in its search for higher meaning and that science has overlooked a most significant amount of evidence that would tell a different story?

Unfortunately for so many of those who find it impossible to accept either the dark, depressing, very limited and premature views of many theorists or the overly simplistic incantations which religion has put forth in this matter, there is little else to turn to that is objectively satisfying on an epistemological level. Cultish craziness is certainly not the answer. Nor is trendy new age nonsense or other forms of diverting, circular non-explanation. As a result these intellectually independent hold-outs often find themselves living in what might best be described as an uncommitted <u>philosophical void.</u> They are there because, on a deeper level, they sense that there is a lot more going on than seems to meet the eye. They are also not willing to compromise the integrity of their own minds by settling for simplistic, placating answers that do nothing to clarify the issue of whether life really has a higher meaning or not and what that greater meaning may be, if it has one. This philosophical void also exists for many of the less intellectually demanding who would simply like things to be a little less confusing in general so they had a clearer idea as to how they might best live their lives on the everyday level in terms of morality and accountability. Maybe, if nothing else, they would just like to understand why life sometimes seems so unbearably cruel and impossible.

Regardless of the personal situation one might find themselves in, maintaining intellectual independence is not always an easy thing to do. This is especially true in a world where far too many are willing to abdicate the sanctity of their own minds and turn their thinking over to others who rarely ever have anything but self interest in mind. <u>Regardless of one's conclusions in the matter, however, there is still some final truth. Life has a separate and higher meaning and purpose that extends beyond the physical world or, it does not. One or the other. It is that simple.</u> But, which ever it is, no one can make either point of view the truth through declaration alone, nor, as previously stated, can it be decided by polling the religious priesthood or those segments of the scientific community which have declared themselves to be the final voice of authority in the matter.

Religion gives lip service to a spiritual side of life but that aspect of it is so poorly defined and so badly misunderstood that it is of little real value emotionally, psychologically or intellectually. Additionally, as it exists in the world today, religion is not capable of "proving" anything. Because of the way it is so rigidly structured it does not have the depth, the understanding or the tools to do so and probably never will. As for science, if it can't be empirically verified, it doesn't exist. Worse, how could anything be empirically verified if it has already been decided that it does not exist to begin with? It cannot. And that, as we see, is exactly what mainstream science has decided. The universe, even though it gets a quite fuzzy on the quantum level, is still mechanistic and mathematically tangible (material realism), so that is the end of the story. Questions about life having any higher meaning beyond the fact of its existence are therefore a frivolous waste of time. There is nothing left to investigate except for filling in more of the details as to how life was able to originate in pond scum and evolve into fully functional human beings, passing through ape-hood along the way. Pond scum, random sequences, mutation and selectivity of the fittest, from single cell organisms to multi billion celled organisms, the Darwinians. A new form of cultism no matter how it is viewed.

On one level we find that exploring the sub atomic world and ending up using that information to build weapons of mass destruction is a kind of ultimate, undeniable confirmation that science works when it comes to the physical world. Difficulties arise, however, when individuals in the scientific community rush to judgment and begin making statements about the rest of it before all the facts are in. This is what has happened with both evolutionary theory and the big bang theory. Together they have destroyed any idea of life after death and literally deprived much of mankind from having a preeminent side to existence. As a result and in that regard, they have done more to harm mankind's future than religion, making religion, with all its faults and limitations closer to some bigger truth than science. In the end, however, that bigger truth should be and could be more within the grasp of science than religion could ever hope to find but will only be arrived at when scientists open the door to what an ideal practice of science should be. One where EVERYTHING is open to study and examination.

As for evolution, as previously agreed upon, there is no doubt that certain living things undergo change. Some things change and then change back again. Or change and keep changing without any improvement in ability to survive but don't become extinct either while still other things change and evolve into something more complex or devolve and disappear. Nowhere in any of that is there anything that makes evolution theory universally true in any sense of the word. To the contrary. Where evolutionists have failed most annoyingly, is in terms of limited imagination. Other than divine creation, they do not seem to be able to come up with explanations that could account for the entire process in all of its details. As for those who haven't had the opportunity to explore the evolutionary subject very far as yet, a few basic examples of how the theory is flawed will be given in passing without making a serious attempt to refute the entire "theory" in this document. This has already been done in great detail with great success by other authors who will be pointed out as we proceed.

First of all, for Darwinian evolution to be universally true would require that every living species show relatively smooth, observable changes over long periods of time without significant perturbation. For the biologist (until humans discovered how to do gene splicing in the laboratory) the only mechanism that could bring forth change was mutation. Mutation created changes in the genetic code and produced variations in species. Evolutionary theory in turn states that these mutations were completely random in nature and become significant over extremely long periods of time which then caused the least

29

fitted offspring to be sorted out due to inherent weaknesses in their makeup. As for these random mutations, what was the mechanism? What caused them to occur in the first place? Background radiation in the environment is cited as the major possibility. Other than that, perhaps some kind of genetic injury to the parent. Maybe a forced, radical change in diet, a disease, cellular malfunction, it doesn't really matter. Something, to be sure with one exceptional, but. That "but" is that the mechanism of mutation on its own, mathematically, in a period of four billion years, or forty, could never have produced a single gene, let alone an entire living single celled organism in that short of a time period by purely accidental means alone. It is but one fact continuously sidestepped by the theory's proponents who start in the middle of things and go on from there.

Regardless, if we still want to believe that that was possible and living things somehow came into being through chance alone, then very definitely and without variance, over millions of years <u>every</u> living species should have undergone change. If the theory is valid, that becomes mandatory because all living things are exposed to the same basic environment and most certainly to the same background radiation and environmental stress. Therefore mutation should occur in all species at every level. But that is clearly not the case. Somewhere along the unfolding eons long story of evolution someone forgot to tell cockroaches and crocodiles and other species about this scientific law of the universe? How did that happen? If the theory is valid as claimed, there has to be a logical explanation for this radical departure from the norm. But none seems to exist. Nor is this the only place where the theory runs up against a wall of inexplicable facts that cannot be reasoned around. The list goes on. So much so that it is no surprise to find opponents of the theory invoking God as an explanation for how it came about instead, a position no more dogmatic than that of their opponents.

Fortunately, there are others out there who are beginning to also raise their voice. As stated by renowned molecular biologist, Masatoshi Nei, who rejects Darwinian evolution's natural selection hypothesis states, "any time a scientific theory is treated like dogma, you have to question it..... You have to question dogma. Use common sense. You have to think for yourself, without preconceptions. That is what is important in science."

THE BATTLE

The modern day battle for control over people's minds regarding mankind's origins and ultimate purpose might be said to have begun in 1859 when Darwin's "Origin of the Species" was published. The historical chain of events is already well documented in the literature so there is little point in attempting to reiterate how widely his ideas were embraced at the time and how blindly they have been accepted and built upon since. "Blindly" is the key word here since many objections to the theory have been put forth over the years as previously stated, most of which are logically more compelling than the theory itself. Unfortunately, like their predecessors, later day promoters of the theory still seem to have gained little scientific objectivity in the matter. Instead they have not only allowed their thinking to slip over into emotionally defensive tirades against anyone who would dare point out any logical deficiencies in evolution theory but have also declared the theory to have elevated itself out of the scientific realm into something akin to divine truth, never to be questioned. What seems to be forgotten in the process though, is that if this was indeed the case, that if what they say is true, then the theory would stand every test it was ever subjected to and would not need an emotional defense to back it up.

Equally astounding is what so many of the intolerant proponents of the theory don't seem to realize, or don't want to admit. Some of the major aspects of the theory were not Darwin's creation at all. They were "borrowed" from the work of one Alfred Russell Wallace, a contemporary of Darwin's in an act of outrageous plagiarism. One of those borrowed ideas was the concept of, survival of the fittest, the most singular thing that gave the theory its doubtful plausibility. A historical review of the time clearly shows that Wallace and not Darwin was the original author of this tenet of the theory and may well have had an even larger unrecognized, no credit given, hand in the matter. The other completely overlooked fact is that Wallace, after he had first proposed the survival idea, loudly recanted it and went on to list several reasons why he felt it was not valid. Regardless, it seems that no one wanted to hear those, then or now.

One of the most significant objections Wallace raised was the brain size argument. Why, he asked, do humans in particular have brains that are hugely over sized in comparison to what they would need to be if survival alone was the driving factor. Why did they so grossly over-evolve and how can the present theory account for such anomalies? It cannot. To Wallace, the breadth and power of human intellectual and moral nature suggested some other influence, law or agency to account for them and that man's mathematical, musical and artistic faculties, among others, could not have been developed through natural selection. Instead he suggested that a superior intelligence had guided the development of man as opposed to other life forms, just as man guided the development of many animal and vegetable forms. Truthfully, however, at the time, scientific research was not something an average person could make a living at.

As stated by Jeffrey Goodman in his book, *The Genesis Mystery*, science at that time was the domain of eccentric aristocrats and moneyed gentlemen and Darwin was a member of that privileged fraternity and a man of great independent wealth. Wallace, on the other hand, not only lacked wealth but the influence that came with it. The limited recognition that he eventually gained only came much later, after Darwin received major credit for evolutionary theory. A theory, not a fact.

At any rate, honestly arrived at or not, the Theory of Evolution became a far reaching conceptual contagion that afflicted the minds of the proclaimed-to-be-scientists of the times. It also spilled over into other areas of the culture because Darwin and many of his admirers also used the theory to support Darwin's own personal views regarding other races of humans. For one thing, dark skinned individuals were declared to be considerably inferior, mentally and otherwise, compared to members of his own race, something Wallace also clearly disagreed with. Unfortunately, in the end Darwin's views led to racism, more imperialism and colonialism. The only really positive thing about the new theory was that, if nothing more, it gave its acceptors an argument against and reason for rejecting the restrictive religious atmosphere of that era, something perhaps long overdue. Needless to say, however, the theory had a profound affect on the many branches of science, on religion, philosophy, psychology and eventually the child in the public school classroom of today who is forced to listen to a teacher who is not allowed to present any opposing points of view.

Along the way, over zealous individuals even faked evidence to promote their academic standing and occasionally still do. Not only did the proponents of the theory try to use the theory to prove that white men were more evolved than blacks, the implications of the theory have been used to imply that individuals who accept the theory are therefore somehow smarter than people who don't agree with it. So much so that people like one seemingly near rabid British physicist, end up calling dissenters stupid and insane or, like Martin Gardener, made rash comments which state that only an ignorant creationist would refuse to call the theory of evolution a fact. For the most part though, these people came along much later in the game and some of them are still alive today.

Regardless of the fact that proponents of the theory have found it necessary to call other people names, there is only one logical extension of the theory that can be made. To say that life was nothing more than an accidental happening leaves no alternate but to conclude that life therefore has no meaning above and beyond itself in the bigger sense of the word and is thus without any higher purpose. It is a mechanistic universe created out of chaos, period. Once said, it didn't matter if any of this was provable or not. Simply posing the question had its effect. It didn't matter either if anyone living in the western world had ever directly heard of Darwin or not, or even understood what the claims of the theory of evolution actually were. The broader implications of the theory still created an atmosphere of background thought people had to live in.

Not only had organized religion been forced into a defensive position by the rise of Darwinism, but thanks to something equally insidious called Social Darwinism, every devious minded individual could then easily justify any extreme of behavior by quoting the theory because that made life a game of pure survival of the fittest alone, with no ultimate accountability where the only gauge of success was money and/or power. It was a philosophy which spilled over into the business, financial and professional worlds of the day and still seems to dominate. From small time shop keeper to Wall Street trader to banker to corporate policy maker to medical doctor defrauding the social security system. Not that it ever happened before. It did, but not on such a grand scale as in the late nineteenth century and on through the twentieth and into the twenty first, leaving the great depression of the 1930s in its wake and culminating in the great recession of the early twenty first century.

And then there is the fact of war which also comes back to the same idea. Those with the most power have the right to prevail. War is the most barbaric example of human behavior possible, whether it is world encompassing or just a bloody skirmish between local tribesmen. War, sadly enough, never resolved any human issue that could not have been settled by peaceful means instead. Part of the problem is, of course, that some parts of the world are not run by sane individuals. Too often the psychotic masters of deceit rise to the top of the pile, swept along and supported by gangsters, thieves and killers seeking outlets for their own sick perversions. And for what? Regarding life on earth, irrespective of where we think we are at, it would seem we still have a tremendously long ways to go in our evolution as human beings. Not physically, the brain capacity is certainly there, but socially, psychologically and morally. Except for technology, which is not a measure of human progress, the last several thousand years might be said to have yielded little in the way of over all social progress, only more efficient ways to kill each other. Again, why?

An alien visitor to earth with an interest in sociology would most certainly be shocked by the extremes of human behavior and some might say that this propensity for war is a serious example of defective gene structure in humans. But, if this were the case, then, because of our common ancestry, we would all be infected with the same biologically based problem and would not be able to rise above it without some earnest genetic re-engineering. Taken as a whole, that would seem to be an unfair assessment. If we look beyond the statistics of war, we see that the majority of humans are, for the most part, living in some kind of basic harmony where most people seemed to have some sense of morality and fairness. They would for the most part, be interested in doing the right thing. Once again, however, we come back to the same old underlying problem. The lack of a common guiding philosophy regarding life's basic issues and deeper meaning.

If only the idea of what the right thing to do were more clearly defined, life would be more harmonious overall. Yes, knowing the difference between right and wrong is a test for sanity in most established justice systems. But, and this is where trouble begins. The definitions of right and wrong varies to the extreme from system to system. One system allows the judged to be stoned to death for an unfaithful act while infidelity in another system has little or no penalty attached to it. Something, it would seem, is clearly lacking over all. A more enduring and endearing philosophy perhaps, to fill up the void that leads people to do some of wayward things they do in the first place. In the meantime there is one certainty that seems almost universally true.

When it comes to understanding what life is all about, what its meaning and purpose really are, in that regard most people are terribly confused and at great disagreement with themselves and with each other and continually struggle to find out who and what they are.

Although large numbers of ordinary people have to some extent rejected the idea that they had their origins in pond scum, they still have to deal with the unhealthy effects that Darwinism has imposed on society. Faith and religious pronouncement alone are not enough. Nor are gut level intuitive feelings without anything more substantial to back them up, and that is the way things have been. Then finally, as far as philosophy is concerned, Creation Science, which was anything but scientific, appeared on the scene in the 1960s. Unfortunately, in a failed attempt to force all of earth's history into a 10,000 year period, Henry Morris's bizarre ideas were, for the most part, laughed off the stage as a serious ideological, explanatory contender and proved that religious expository was no match for the pseudo-scientific pronouncements of Darwinists who still won all the battles, both in court and the classroom.

Then, in 1991, a voice of reason appeared on the scene when Phillip E. Johnson's substantive book, *DARWIN ON TRIAL,* was published and the real battle began. Now those who disagreed with the Darwinians had the force of clear logic to back them up and didn't have to resort to name calling to defend themselves. Johnson and his supporters have received a lot of un-scientific bashing in return, however, which would seem to indicate that the later day Darwinians are feeling severely threatened. They also attempt to discredit this landmark work by saying that it is religion based, which it is not. Although the author freely admits his own religious affiliation, his writing fully reflects his mental ability to step back and apply the full force of reason to his far reaching analysis of the intolerant and disintegrating position the Darwinians have gotten themselves into. What it clearly says and repeats is that there are a huge amount of things which evolutionary theory alone cannot clearly explain and that there is room for an argument of "Intelligent Design" in the discussion. Why that should be so appalling to someone with an open mind is quite astounding nevertheless. Especially since Johnson does not bring God or divinity into the discussion.

At the other end of the scale, however, the religionists have their own, purely faith driven agenda and have the same extreme determination to prevail as the Darwinians, both in the courtroom and on the street corner. For them, Johnson's work is, as they might describe, a timely God-send. Something they can use to promote the idea that it is their personal God who is the intelligent designer. Understandable, of course, in a behind-the-scenes way, but the concept of intelligent design, in and of itself, still stands alone and the promoter's personal religious views become irrelevant in terms of the main argument. The concept of intelligent design is thus every bit as valid as the opposing mechanistic view of things and deserves to be treated as such. Darwinians, however, refuse to acknowledge any possibilities other than their own, especially the thought that the theory of evolution is just that. A theory and not a fact.

Refusing to openly acknowledge this is exactly how these scientists have dug the hole they are now attempting to climb out of. Instead of allowing the entire issue to remain in the theoretical domain where ongoing discussion and evaluation would be welcome, extremists in the group keep telling the rest of the world that they are stupid and insane because they don't agree with them. Not only is such an attitude immature and dictatorial, it is coercive and guaranteed to make some strong enemies. The whole issue might well have gone away, however, if other members of that same community had come forward and admitted in a clear voice that this was not a unanimous position and back tracked on their colleagues defensive attitudes. But they have not and as a result the issue has become a "Battle for America's Soul" according to some members of the scientific community such as Kenneth R. Miller, author of, *Only a Theory*.

Miller sees the idea of intelligent design as a most appalling prospect with little merit because it has no theoretical, predictive basis and no testable hypothesis associated with it, which may not necessarily be true at all. In spite of this weakness he still seems to view the idea of intelligent design as a serious threat, not only to Darwinism but to the future of science as a whole. The threat appears because, to him, what else could be the source of intelligent design other than "God?" Therefore, letting a teacher discuss the possibility of intelligent design is letting religion into the classroom in violation of the constitution. Once that happens that opens the door to other religious intrusions which will lead to an ultimate downgrading and displacement of science in the American educational system and that, according to Miller, has serious nationalistic overtones. Evolutionary theory must prevail or America will fall back into the dark ages of closed minded religious zealotry. America will cease to be a world leader in the areas of science and technology and will suffer unduly because of it. After all, he asks, what's the alternative? "Unintelligent design? Random design? Or no design at all? A universe of molecules weaving through space and time without meaning?"

These are odd questions indeed when, by definition, his version of evolution is random, unintelligent and without intrinsic meaning. Regardless, Miller also tells us that "we must find the strength to embrace what evolution tells us about the nature of reality. Faith will ultimately redeem our souls." And in the words of other scientists,"We must accept such theories because we have nothing better to take their place."

The only conclusion one can draw from this is that Miller obviously believes that the search for genuine truth is already over when it comes to mankind's origins. The Darwinians have the end of the story, take their word for it, we need not question it any longer. Just do what the religionists, the people he seems to fear the most, tell their followers to do. Take evolution <u>on faith</u> because he is saying it. He says that, even though taking things "on faith" is exactly the thing he criticizes the religious community for.

Good science, however, doesn't take anything on faith. At least it is not supposed to because that doesn't meet the criteria of good science. Fortunately, however, just because its proponents see no alternates to their theory does not mean they do not exist. Additionally, the concept of Intelligent Design is still a plausible one if it is viewed in a non-religious way, impossible as that might seem at first. Intelligent design, in and of itself, does not unequivocally mean that there is a singular designer involved or that that designer is the Christian God of the major challengers to Darwinian theory even though these religionists have chosen to use this as an argument to promote their own agenda. Choosing to interpret the concept of intelligent design as proof of God only further clouds the issue and further serves to limit the intelligent design discussion, scientific or otherwise. And with rigid, righteous extremists on both sides of the issue, what else could there be but a battle for America's soul, scientific or otherwise? But why the phobic need to convert everyone to some specific acceptance of what has now become "dogma" on the part of both sides? Regardless, even if every person on earth could be convinced to accept one point of view or the other, that would not in any way make that one true and the other false. Truth does not arise from majority opinions any more than it does from self righteous proclamation. Truth derives from truth and when individuals strive so hard to sway people's minds, we can only wonder at the reasons why? Who will be the real benefactor?

And now, a small addendum. Evolutionists have recently come upon a phenomenon they labeled, rapid evolution or, a quick drive towards adaptation which they insist supports Darwinian conjecture, not realizing what happened instead. Inherent physical change in living things requires gene mutation. Gene mutation is a result of an outside agent or agents. Cause and effect. Mutation first, change second. Only then can there be "survival-of-the-fittest," selective adaptation. A biologist experimented with guppies by changing their environments and came up with a, not so profound, conclusion. "The risk of death alters the ways organisms allocate resources for survival," because within a few short generations, male guppies changed their reproductive patterns. Instead of being supportive evidence of Darwinian evolution, it is the opposite. In the least it infers intelligence driven purposeful change on the part of a species to adapt to environmental differences. One form of intelligent design. Humans do the same thing. People living in third world countries with higher infant mortality rates and poor living conditions have significantly higher birth rates than in developed nations with higher standards of living.

THE CHALLENGE

Disregarding the workplace where the majority of people appear reasonably competent doing what they need to do to earn a living, it still seems fair to say (once again) that aside from that, MOST ADULTS ARE CONFUSED ABOUT BASIC ISSUES. All too often the workplace becomes the main source and sustenance of their identity. Away from the job or apart from their social circle, however, they do not have a clear sense of themselves or a guiding philosophy. Their sense of justice and right and wrong is ambiguous and prejudiced, their concept of who or what God is, is fuzzy and ill defined, as is their idea of what we are all doing here on the planet in the first place. This being the case, how could anyone expect the world to be anything other than what it is. Not only does it reflect itself, it compounds itself in the process.

Because of this compounding action, the reason why we are seeing so much unusual and unacceptable behavior in today's world is not so much because people are abnormal but because the world has produced a psychological and emotional atmosphere that is conducive to abnormal behavior. Under the circumstances, it is not unusual at all. It is possible that people are behaving in a quite normal manner considering the intellectual and philosophical climactic void they find themselves living in. Unfortunately, that does not make it right. Nor do they fail anyone but themselves by not trying to change it. And, in that regard.....

If there is indeed some other, greater, hidden truth behind the physical facade of apparent existence, then the only way it will ever be discovered is for both scientists and religionists to realize that there is no such thing as scientific truth and another that is religious truth and that they are separate and different. There can only be one, all inclusive, fully encompassing truth. The challenge is to

42

look beyond the ordinary. If there is a greater reality that exists behind the physical reality we know best, that is the way to find it. It begins by flatly rejecting the dark and hopeless philosophy of Bertrand Russell and all the rest of those who echo him, along with the overly simplistic and demeaning religious concepts of heaven and hell. It then continues by realizing that behind the fabric of apparent reality and interwoven through it all there has to be a more universal, more fundamental truth that ties all things together on a deeper level and gives them meaning. A meaning above and beyond the ongoing confusion and complications of everyday involvement, even when and where it seems there is none to be had.

Scientifically or philosophically acceptable or not, the evidence to prove that there is a greater reality hidden within the physical reality we consciously experience, already exists. Not in some, yet to be discovered archeological bone pile, or in some far away galaxy in outer space, or in some seventeen mile long underground tunnel in Switzerland. No, it is much more immediate than that. The evidence we need to look at already exists in the vast range of everyday human experience that surrounds us, day in and day out. That something that sometimes nags at us but is all too often seen as psychic anomaly, random coincidence or pure oddity and routinely dismissed with a shrug or even simply denied because there is no really acceptable framework to acknowledge or examine it in.

Stupid as it may sound to some, however, this is exactly where the real clues to a much greater reality lie and it is here where our focus must come to bear. Read between the lines, look in the shadows, peek thru the keyhole to see what else is going on. Examine everyday life from a deeper perspective, turn it inside out if necessary and explain that which is too easily dismissed as unexplainable because that too, like it or not, is also an integral part of the real world and needs to be included in our theorizing. Then, perhaps, we will not have to give up on life or invent fictitious ways to lull us into believing it is important but instead have something specific to confirm that which we often subconsciously suspect and hope for. Life already has a built in meaning and purpose.

With that in mind let us first take a look at what might appear to be a considerable amount of otherwise unrelated, poorly explained and grossly overlooked phenomenon that are just as real as any other aspect of life on the planet. Then perhaps we will be able to see that nothing happened by chance and that all change, or even the apparent lack of it, is driven by other factors instead. In doing this it is not necessary to first discuss quantum physics as some later day authors have done and then make disjointed leaps into Buddhism, Eastern philosophy or meditational practices, or become mystical in an attempt to link science and spirituality together without really explaining anything. Nor is it necessary to revert back to faith based conclusions to explain things that are not capable of being explained in such a manner.

ASPECTS OF REALITY

Not all living things have a brain and central nervous system but still function marvelously well in their separate environments. Certainly the argument can be made that these life forms, like all the rest, have only become able to do that through selective, survival-of-the-fittest adaptation and they evolved into what they are by pure chance alone. Still, if one chooses not to dismiss the issue so quickly and look closely at the behavior of these so-called lower forms of life, it seems that in addition to a blind, reflexive response to stay alive, there is also some form of intelligence associated with their actions. One quite remarkable, in fact. A point we will return to later.

Humans, of course, do have brains. They do not have the largest brains in the animal kingdom, however. Nor do they have the largest brains in the history of humans. Cro Magnon man had a brain that was physically much larger in size than that of modern humans but became extinct anyway so the question becomes, is brain size a direct indicator of intelligence and does it increase a species chances of survival? Obviously not because some living things are brainless and have been around almost from the beginning. Additionally, if true, the range of human intelligence would not extend from almost zero to off the chart in terms of being able to measure it. Instead IQ's would be closely grouped around the average value where those with the largest brains would have the higher scores. Not only is the brain size claim wrong, there is well documented evidence to prove it. The brain of the average adult male weighs about 3.1 pounds. Albert Einstein's brain, however, only weighed 2.7 pounds. About thirteen percent less than normal. And while that is perhaps not all that physically significant, it still verifies the point made by Thomas Harvey, the pathologist who made the measurements. A large brain is not a necessary condition for exceptional intelligence, the real proof of which comes from yet another source.

Back in the last century a British neurologist, John Lorber was introduced to a college student who had an IQ of 126, had an honors degree in mathematics and functioned normally in all aspects of his life. A CAT scan of his head, however, revealed that he literally had almost no brain. The brain cells that he did have were in the form of a thin lining about a millimeter thick around the inside of his skull and the rest of the space was taken up with fluid. Further studies by Lorber and others showed that this was not an isolated case. Other people were found who had brains that were only 3 to 5 percent of normal size. Not all of these individuals were normal in function, however, but some had IQ's over 100 so the point is clear nevertheless. Brain size has little or nothing to do with intelligence and brings up all those additional, same old questions. If you don't have a complete brain, or no brain at all, how can you have a sense of identity and awareness? Much more important, if memories are stored in the brain cells and a person literally has almost no brains cells, then where are their memories stored because how could such a person have an IQ of 126 and gotten through college without a physical memory bank to draw on? That does not mean that the author is implying that most people could do without their brain cells, however. Studies do show that the brains of Alzheimer's victims shrink as the malady progresses and these people become very limited in function. Regardless, studies also show that people who have had severe brain injury or have had extensive brain surgery, where sizable portions of tissue have been removed, often make astounding recoveries. It is also not true that aging by itself, necessarily means brain loss and deterioration in terms of mental function.

The autopsy of a Dutch woman who died at the age of 115 clearly showed that her brain was healthy and displayed no signs of Alzheimers, dementia or deterioration, causing the doctors to conclude that in contrast to general belief, the limits of human cognitive function may extend far beyond the range that is currently enjoyed by most individuals. But why some and not others? Modern medicine considers Alzheimers to be a disease and has been looking for a specific cause for decades. It is also still looking. At one point it was considered to have been caused by cooking in aluminum pans, then it was zinc and a few other things. More recently many consider it to be genetic susceptibility and there is a growing trend to blame almost everything on the genes. A good try, perhaps, but as long as researchers stay locked into such narrow concepts about life, the real answers will remain hidden from view because, as will be discussed later, Alzheimers may serve a different purpose entirely.

Leaving that for whatever it might be and getting back to those odd cases of fully functioning but essentially brainless people, it should be noted that this kind of evidence also points to some additional serious flaws in evolutionary theory. Unless something beyond the purely physical, mechanistic view point is involved, there is no way to explain such anomalies in development and ability to function. All these individuals should have died at birth. Yet they did not and all the unanswered questions remain. One thing seems reasonably certain, however. There are far more dimensions to physical reality than we ordinarily choose to acknowledge and almost none of them have been explored in any serious manner. One rule that seems to be applied most often in such cases, however, is, if it can't be explained in a way that can be supported by the theories one insists on evoking, ignore it. Maybe no one will notice. Maybe the enigma will even go away. Take the world of plants, for example. Can a plant, which doesn't have a brain at all, have both a sense of self and have awareness of what is happening around it? Obviously, it can.

Cleve Backster, ex CIA interrogation expert, hooked

47

a polygraph up to a rubber plant and made some surprising discoveries. The plant not only responded electrically to the killing of shrimp dropped in boiling water nearby, it even reacted to the mental threat of doing so, along with the threat of having its leaves burned. Another plant that had purposely been beaten by a friend of his continued to react every time that person walked into the room. This plant also seemed to be able to pick up on his own emotional state when he was miles away, things which have been fully verified by other experimenters. Additionally it has been shown that trees also communicate with each other over long distances in response to animal threats. Knowing that, what else could these demonstrations by plants be but an exhibition of some level of consciousness coupled with some level of memory? But where does plant consciousness come from and where are its memories stored when it very definitely has no brain or selective set of specialized cell structure to accomplish that? And with this being an ability of plants, what else has been overlooked with respect to other things, perhaps living in terms of the biologists definition, or not?

Hopefully, most people understand that animals respond to the care and treatment they receive from humans. They can become warm and loving or learn to become defensive, wary and sometimes vicious. But plants? Plants, of course do not have the physical ability to respond equally but they can and do reflect their treatment by humans in other ways. In a controlled experiment conducted at the University of Arizona, not only was thought and treatment able to affect the evaporation rates of water from plants, it also affected their viability and growth rates. Plants in the control group were left alone. Plants in one other group were soothed with classical music while plants in a third group were sent "good" thoughts or prayers. The results showed that good thoughts doubled the sprouting and growth rates of that group and classical music increased the sprouting rate by 50 percent and growth rates by 25 percent. Variations of this experiment have been repeated over the years with similar results, in the laboratory and elsewhere. Not only does positive thought improve growth rate and give plants greater resistance to insects, negative thought reduces it, so where in the theory of evolution is there any explanation for facts such as these? One could argue that the actual sound vibrations of music could have a beneficial effect on plant life in some as yet undefined way, but thoughts alone, coming from outside the organism? That would seem to be good evidence for extra sensory perceptiveness on a psychic level for plants. And if so for plants, why not for the animal kingdom as well? Who would disagree with the fact that the internalization of our own thoughts does have very specific effects on our own bodies and state of health. But, projected outward?

And what about plain old yogurt. A layer of yogurt is laid out in the bottom of a petrie dish, electrodes are attached and connected to a sensitive voltmeter and the dish covered. A nearby individual is given a series of suggestions that are emotion evoking in nature. Each time one is made, the yogurt responds electrically. So what do we have here? One aspect of this experiment is the ability of the material to produce an electrical output which, in itself, is not abnormal for a biological substance. The other, however, is the ability of the substance to pick up on the thought process of a nearby person and respond to it. Clearly, the brain of the human is sending out some sort of energy, electromagnetic or otherwise as yet undiscovered, but real nonetheless and certainly worthy of investigation. What it means is that, as shown by such experiments, thoughts have an express reality all their own and are able to interact with and affect physical matter. Thoughts are not simply confined to the brain tissue, they are also emitted and penetrate space. Thoughts exude energy and have substance, thoughts are things, as some will say. But how to deal with such odd characteristics of life forms as a hard core evolutionist must do, sooner or later? Well, one can do what the Egyptologists have done.

Several years ago a group of scientists went to Egypt to demonstrate how the Giza pyramids were most probably built. They quarried a number of stones in the one to two ton range, showed that they could be moved on rollers or sleds with ropes and raw manpower and piled them into place, constructing a very minimal, mini pyramid. The conclusion... that explains it all. The humungous Giza pyramids were built the same way. Other scientists have also gone to Easter Island to show how the giant statues, the moaii, might have been transported across the island. This culminated in placing a 10 ton replica on a wooden sled where 40 volunteers were able to drag it a distance of 230 feet. So what is the problem with that?

First of all the Giza pyramids were not made entirely of stones that weighed only one or two tons, even though the large pyramid contained over two million of them. There were also 115 thousand casing blocks that weighed about sixteen tons each and these originally covered the entire outside of the structures. Additionally, the great pyramid was built on a site twelve acres in size that required thousands of blocks whose average weight was 100 tons each to make it level before building the main structure. Difficult enough, but the big pyramid is also 481 feet high and half way up inside it at the King's Chamber there are several 70 ton stones precisely set in place. Most of the regular stones in the structure came from across the Nile twenty miles away but the King's Chamber stones came from the Aswan quarry 500 miles away. As for the Easter Island statues, some were 33 feet tall and weighed 80 tons and were moved up to eleven miles from the quarry site. So what could any of this possibly have to do with Darwinism? Stones, according to any present, scientifically acceptable theory, are not living things. But....

Moving one or two, or ten ton stones is not the same

as moving an eighty or one hundred ton stone. Carving, transporting and moving thousands of one hundred ton stones into place is nearly impossible even in our so-called, hi tech modern world. Demonstrating how small stones can be moved explains absolutely nothing in terms of the bigger issue, even though moving stones of this size was a somewhat more common occurrence back in days long gone in human history because these feats were not just restricted to Egypt.

In Ollantaytambo, Peru, stone blocks weighing from 150 to 200 tons were moved to the top of a cliff and fitted into place. In Baalbek, Lebanon there are three huge cut stones in a wall weighing approximately 750 tons each. Not only that but such unexplained feats have happened all over the world, from South America to the middle east and beyond, which brings up the enigma of the Coral Castle in Homestead, Florida.

At first look there is nothing awesome about the "Coral Castle" at all. Nothing astounding in its design or its proportions or it's reasons for having been built in the first place. What is awesome, however, is how it came into being. First, it was built entirely out of coral rock (limestone), that was quarried from the ground with hand tools by just one man working alone. This man, Ed Leedskalnin, was five feet tall and weighed about a hundred pounds. During the course of several years he not only quarried over two million pounds of rock, he also shaped it into a wide range of configurations and moved it into place. This might not have been such an astounding feat if all the blocks he dug out were the size of bricks or concrete blocks but they were not. Instead, they ranged in size from several hundred pounds each up to one rock in the wall that weighs twenty nine tons or nearly 60,000 pounds. Another rock weighing almost as much is over forty feet long and stands upright. The castle, or tower as it is called, is made of stones weighing from four to nine tons and the amazing statistics go on from there.

One of these is the fact that this project began in 1918. There was no electrical power available at that time. Neither did Leedskalnin have a tractor, truck, crane or any other piece of motorized equipment so the big question is, how does a one hundred pound man carve out, lift, move and set in place a twenty nine ton stone by himself plus at least one hundred others, some almost as big? He often told those who asked that it was simply a matter of weights and levers. Is that possible? Technically, yes. But! What would it take for a one hundred pound man to lift just one end of a twenty nine ton stone using nothing but a lever? Even if one could find something sturdy enough to use as a fulcrum and something else strong enough to make a lever out of, with the fulcrum located one foot from the lifting end of the lever, the lever itself would have to be three hundred feet long. Could a one hundred pound man even lift a three hundred foot long lever, let alone manipulate it? Suppose that you only wanted to lift the end of the big stone one inch with such a device. One inch down on the short end of the lever places the other end twenty five feet up in the air. Now you need a tall ladder to reach the lever. And something to lean it against. And so forth, and so forth, making the whole approach preposterously unfeasible. Which leaves the real big question. How did he do it? Some people explained it simply by saying he was a genius, which of course explains less than nothing.

Approached logically, since many thousands of people have personally seen the stone structures created by Leedskalnin, in addition to the fact that they have been photographed, measured and studied in detail, it would seem that it can be said with a high degree of certainty that they are a part of the physical world, dumb and unnecessary as it may seem to point that out. So, they do exist. Secondly it is well documented that Mr. Leedskalnin did not receive help from the surrounding community. To the best of everyone's knowledge he worked alone and mostly at night and, very importantly, without the help of heavy machinery or equipment. So, what does that leave? Again, how did he do it? Logically, there are only two possibilities. First, he could have had visitors from outer space who aided him with an anti gravity device or, second, he actually did it entirely by himself as the evidence certainly indicates. What else is there to say? The place came into being somehow. So did the Giza pyramids, the great walls and structures around the world, the huge statues of Easter Island and much more along with all the remaining questions left behind. Obviously one has to think far, far outside the box to get the needed answers.

With that it may appear that the subject matter has strayed a bit from evolutionary theory and the origins of life. The point is, however, that in trying to explain life's origins the evolutionists do the same thing as the Egyptologists. They move small stones around and hope no one notices that they have totally avoided explaining how the big ones got there. They, like the later day, would-be pyramid builders, cannot. In truth, however, there is an explanation for how all the stones ended up where they are, and probably a very interesting one, as of course there is for the presence of life, which, hopefully, will become more apparent.

Irrespective of how that goal might be approached, it is not necessary to make long lists of the fine points of evolutionary theory to pick apart when some of them actually appear to be true. As previously stated, there have been and are evolutionary processes at work in the world. Living things change and adapt to variations in their environment. (thankfully, of course, or they wouldn't be here) But the important question is, are they nothing more than blind, survival-of-the-fittest changes or is there something else happening which we have failed to take into account?

Regardless, trying to extrapolate the very limited,

pro-Darwinian evidence into an all-inclusive theory to explain how life went from nothing to its present state of complexity simply does not work. It does not work because it cannot explain some of the most fundamental aspects of the complete process. Creating amino acids in the laboratory as Miller and Urey did back in 1952 is one thing. Creating even the most simple of life forms is another. Even if sunlight and scum could have brought about that still unproven but necessary first step in the process and created a single celled organism in spite of the mathematically impossible odds against its happening, what about all the rest of the multi trillion mandatory steps in between then and now?

Of course the same thing can be said for intelligent design but that does not mean that the argument for intelligent design is not just as valid as that for evolution at this point in history. Carefully note, however, that there is a very big difference between intelligent design and creationism. Intelligent design, as used here, does not mean that a specific "designer" is involved in the process and blindly injecting God into the equation does not answer any questions at all. It only serves to further cloud the issue and add to the conflict between religion and science.

Giving "God" the credit is one thing. Saying that there appears to be intelligence involved in an evolutionary process is something else. Unfortunately the concept has metaphysical connotations, another place where mainstream science refuses to go. They search for reasons to dismiss intelligent design instead. They point to human limitations as cases in point. One scientist claims that the human heart is very poorly designed, therefore it did not have an intelligent designer. He knows this because he had some serious heart related problems of his own. But, is it? Or did this individual have heart problems because of lack of exercise, poor diet, smoking, emotional stress and other damaging abuses to same? Or maybe evolutionary blind fate just dealt him a bad set of genes instead. Or, is there some other process at work here instead? Perhaps.

Look at it from a different perspective. Pick an individual who has lived to be one hundred, as more and more people seem to be doing. Assuming an average heart rate of about seventy beats per minute, that person's heart will have beat at least four billion times and pumped multi millions of gallons of blood through their system. Given the proper resources, could science design an equivalent mechanical devise that weighed no more than a few pounds and consumed no more energy but still pumped an equal amount of fluid and had such extreme reliability? And also come up with something that has the ability to self maintain and repair itself when given a chance?

Another, if there was an intelligent designer criticism, is about the back, the skelature of the spine and its associated cartilage, ligaments, muscles and tendons. Something else, which if it had a specific designer, was contrived by some source with very limited mental ability because a large portion of the human population has "back problems" at some time or other during their life. Okay. So instead of questioning that, let's assume it's true and go from there. The question is not that some humans have back problems but instead, specifically who has back problems, and why?

Who would buy a passenger car built primarily to be used on the highway, fail to maintain it properly, over load it and attempt to use it as a four wheel drive off-road muscle-truck and then blame the designer because it kept breaking down? Well, what about the body? A lot of people are grossly over "design weight," if you will, Americans in particular. This not only burdens the back but the hip joints, knee joints, feet, heart and other organs. Additionally, many of these people also do not do proper maintenance. Proper maintenance means proper exercise, decent posture, reasonable diet and more. Poor performance is not necessarily the designer's fault at all. It is more likely that of the irresponsible user instead. Additionally, it may simply be a case of the mental side of one's nature directly affecting the physical as is becoming more and more clear to those who are willing to accept the idea. See the books of John E. Sarno. The Mind Body Prescription, Healing Back Pain and The Divided Mind.

Getting back to the story line, however, the one major objection to intelligent design by evolutionists is that neither they nor its proponents can think of a way to verify any of it experimentally. At first glance it seems to be a legitimate argument, even though there are also a large number of things about evolutionary theory that have the same problem. They can't be experimentally verified either. Regardless, that alone does not negate the concept of an involved intelligence and should not bring about an all inclusive dismissal. To the contrary. If an imaginative experimenter had a clearer idea of what is meant by intelligent design in terms of the context used here, they would realize that it then becomes a testable hypothesis. Meantime, remember that many aspects of the theory of relativity were not verifiable at the time it was proposed either and it was a good many years before some of the more important ones were. The same was true of quantum mechanics. There are also some features of quantum theory which are not provable at all but are simply taken on faith because others aspects of it hold true. And then there is the Big-Bang creation of the universe theory, also stated as fact but now falling into dispute. Some scientists accept the idea that it too, may be in trouble.

Ideally, however, as has been said before, science should be an ongoing quest for knowledge. Regardless, not too many generations ago it was the opinion of some that science would quickly become a dead ended pursuit because almost everything that was of any scientific significance had already been discovered. Then the field exploded along a multitude of other avenues, verifying instead that the more we seem to discover, the more apparent it becomes as to how little we knew to begin with. In spite of that, the prevailing view of many scientists today is still as follows. Material reality is a set of fields which obey the principles of special relativity and quantum theory. The intensity of a field at any point gives the probability of finding the fundamental particle associated with that field at that location. Fields interact as do their associated quanta which mediate the interactions. That is all there is, end of story.

So, there you have it. We are back to that. What else is there to learn on a fundamental level? Again, nothing according to the some authorities in the field of physics. Except for the fact that relativity and quantum mechanics have yet to be combined in a larger, all inclusive theoretical manner, it is just a matter of filling in the details.

Well, no problem with that. Hopefully, however, it might be better to allow room for surprises as we go along. How do we really know what the limits of our abilities to learn and know are unless we keep pushing? For those who invoke God, God gave most humans an intelligent and inquiring mind. Where in the rule book does it say we are not supposed to use it? If evolutionary changes occur but cannot account for the beginning of life, nor for everything that has occurred since, and one wishes to probe a little further into the mystery of life and its meanings, what else is there to look at? Is it possible, for example, that the changes seen only as successful accidents along the way have instead been brought about with intent? <u>Not by some higher, removed omniscience but by an inherent intelligence built into all things, capable of assessment and action, brain or no brain?</u> And, beyond that, what? And where in all that is there some inherent meaning greater than a self generated one that must be separately invented by each individual to keep them from giving up along the way? Somehow **it would seem that if living things did not know on some deeper, spiritual**

and biological level that life had a more profound meaning than that which science has assigned to it, there would be no life at all.

Unquestionably, the vast majority of people on earth accept the validity of their own feelings and emotion, even though there is nothing tangible about any of them. True, one can do a series of MRI's and watch somewhat specific parts of the brain light up when various feelings are evoked during a study or wire up the body and brain and look at nerve impulses on a monitor but that does not in any way capture the essence of what is really going on. Unlike bodily organs such as the heart and liver, emotions and feeling cannot be isolated from the living creature. An investigator cannot carve out even one milligram of love or hate or desire or agony or contentment, place it on a tray in a laboratory, weight it, measure its density and opacity, its acidity or alkalinity or define any other verifiable characteristic of it that would prove its existence, either in space or in time.

One cannot directly see the wind either, if it comes to that. Nor an electric, magnetic or gravitational field. They can only be measured in a secondary manner by the effect they have on other things but are still accepted as a defined part of reality. So, too, are feelings and emotions whose peripheral effects on such things as heart rate and body chemistry can be measured, as well as the resulting exterior action they can produce (one person punching another on the nose). But what about all the rest of it? What about all those other things which also occur that presently fall outside of our ability to somehow reproduce them at will and measure them, directly or indirectly? Is it fair to state that such things do not exist because we cannot take them into the laboratory and objectively analyze them? Or is it just that technologically we are not advanced enough to do so?

When scientists dismiss the possibility of certain

things that fall within the paranormal sphere, should we believe them and stop searching? Of course not. As history shows, no self respecting scientist of the mid nineteenth century would have ever believed any of the high tech accomplishments of the twentieth century were possible either. Back then no one even believed it was possible for man to fly in a heavier-than-air, aircraft. And, most certainly they would have scoffed at the idea of an electric power grid, an atomic bomb, a manned flight to the moon, television, cell phones or any of the rest. Today's skeptics often make the same mistake in a premature rush to judgment as to what is, or is not, possible in the future.

Regardless, when veering off into the realm of the *paranormal*, it is always necessary to proceed with a highly critical mind and a great deal of skepticism because the field is full of predators, liars, cheats and other forms of despicable individuals who take advantage of the weaknesses and gullibility of others. It is also contaminated with the badly informed, the grossly un informed, the misinformed, the genuinely misguided and the downright delusional. Many of these people promote themselves as psychics, healers, life coaches, spiritual guides and more who consult with everyone from the Archangels to the ascended masters to the holy spirit Shekina, to Ashtar, to the Pleidians and the Arcturians who give them the wisdom and power to deal with every aspect of human concern. Scrambled and disconcerting as that may be, the field of metaphysics still deserves a more in-depth look than it has received thus far because it is still full of clues that can lead to a greater understanding of the whole of existence. So can a few things that don't seem to fit into any formalized category, like psychic ability.

Edgar Cayce 1877 - 1945
A relatively uneducated man, Edgar Cayce was able to go into a trance and tap into prodigious amounts of in-

formation, ranging from very specific details regarding the present conditions of health and well being of individuals to events that were global in nature. He predicted the stock market crash of 1929, the start of both world wars, the deaths of President Roosevelt and Kennedy, the end of communism in Russia, rising ocean levels, severe weather changes and much, much more. Additionally, and far more significant, when in trance he was able to give over 14,000 diagnostic readings for more than 6000 people who had health problems that ranged from indigestion, to cancer, to other, otherwise terminal illnesses and could do it remotely from his location for anyone, anywhere on the planet. Having never learned any language but English he was also able to give fluent readings in over two dozen languages. Not only did he do the diagnosis, he gave the necessary treatment required for healing, often stating the exact doctor or person to be found to give the treatment. Extremely unorthodox as some of his prescriptions were, his "patients" often had difficulty in getting conventional medical doctors to provide the required remedies and therapy. All in all, however, in the thousands of documented case histories, Cayce never lost a patient when his instructions were properly followed. Some people still did die, however, but only in cases where the doctor involved remained skeptical and refused to follow his instructions. Understandably, many members of the medical profession bitterly opposed and attacked him during his lifetime but his accomplishments are still a matter of record. More than fifty thousand pages in all, housed in the library at the Association for Research and Enlightenment in Virginia Beach, Virginia.

Not only was Cayce able to tune into the body of the remote individual seeking help, he was also able to describe what they wore, their immediate surroundings, the exact name and address of the doctor or therapist who could help as well as what pharmacy to go to for a specific medication and sometimes tell the pharmacist exactly where on the backroom shelf to find the required item needed for treatment clear across the continent in a place he had never been to. Cayce was also capable of making accurate business and stock market predictions but was strongly opposed to doing so and regretted the few times he did even though there were many times during his own life when he was near destitute. Regardless, even during the worst of times he never turned anyone away because they were poor.

Jane Roberts   1929-1984
Jane Roberts was often described as a psychic and a channeler even though channeler is a word she strongly objected to because it was too narrow to describe the full range of her experience. Regardless, she was extremely psychic by any definition of the word and her accomplishments are well documented for those who choose to examine her work. And that is the point.

Edgar Cayce, in spite of having been the subject of dispute in medical and scientific circles, is still widely accepted for his comprehensive achievements and ability to help others. But even though what he did is still unexplainable scientifically, it was straight forward and simple. He went into a trance, connected with a "patient" or other individual and gave a reading. He was what he was and there seems to be little stigma attached to his name, should one decide to mention it.

Jane Roberts also went into a "trance," and allowed someone else to use her voice to pass on information. Okay, nothing new about that. The world is full of people who claim to be doing just that which is part of the reason why Jane Roberts' work is brought into question and all too often dismissed without review. Worse, she was also somewhat hijacked by many in the New Age community as it evolved from good intention into a complexity of psycho-babble and circumlocution and be that as it may. In all fairness, however, there is absolutely no comparison between the reach, depth and profoundness of her work when compared to the rest of everything else that is out there. It is complex and extensive, thousands of pages long and more than twenty five books in all and there is nothing simplistic about it. And for those who understand that there is nothing simplistic about life, creation and the universe, it is by far one of the most valuable sources of information presently available to the world.

Additionally, of further significant difference between Jane Roberts' other voice, who goes by the name of "Seth," and other so called channelers is that the others simply regurgitate the words of "their" source in a fixed, one sided monologue as though in recorded dictation. The Jane Roberts' personality, however, was actively present during the sessions and fully capable of having a "real time" conversation or discussion with questions and answers, something with its own profound implications. Additionally, the range and depth of information given goes far beyond anything that could have come from the limited life experiences of Roberts alone. And not only is that information factual, it is also verifiable except in those cases where it goes beyond the present limitations of science, philosophy, psychology and religion. There are also many filmed and documented sessions which verify this "live" presence of the Seth personality, with exchanges between Seth and others present at the time. Unanimously, for those psychologists and other researchers who interviewed him, they all came away with the admission that they had been in the presence of a "massive intellect." One of these, Eugene Barnard of North Carolina State University wrote that, "The best summary I can give you of that evening is that for me it was a delightful conversation with a personality or intelligence or what have you, whose wit, intellect and reservoir of knowledge far exceeded my own," and for those who take the time to read some of her thousands of pages of information, most will end up saying the same thing.

Want to know about the origin of the universe, what really drives evolution, the history of religion, the psychology of mankind, mental illness, what the fundamental physical particle of matter is? It's all in there somewhere and there is nothing simplistic or dogmatic about any of it and all of it far exceeds anything Jane Roberts had access to on a personal level from her own educational background. As the Seth character stated, this was one of the main reasons she was chosen as the conduit for the material to begin with. She was not an over educated individual with an acquired set of scientific, religious or emotional biases that would distort or dilute the information she passed on.

John Edward

John Edward is a man with his own unusual ability. Professionally, he is a medium and an author, now one with international fame. He can communicate with the deceased and as such verifies the fact that dead is not dead after all, a statement guaranteed to provoke some strong disagreements from many. Whether or not mainstream science would outwardly accept this claim is not important, it still meets the test as thousands of individuals would agree. The exact number is unimportant. If he was able to contact someone otherwise known to be dead just once, it would still prove a point. The fact that this has occurred thousands of times simply adds weight to the argument. And, as anyone who has seen him work can attest, it is not some contrived encounter. Things are revealed by the dead that no amount of coincidence could ever account for, deeply personal things that have very specific meaning only to those living individuals seeking information about deceased relatives or friends.

As would be expected, John Edward is not the only person alive with this ability. There are many, and with wide variations in talent. It is impossible to give them all the recognition they deserve here. Along these lines, however, scientifically viable experiments were conducted at the University of Arizona by Gary Schwartz, PhD. where they were, "trying to allow survival of consciousness to prove itself." Unknown deceased subjects were "read" by five different persons or mediums under controlled conditions wherein the mediums had no advance information about the subjects. The verifiable information received by the mediums was an amazing 83 percent, with the separate accuracies of the readers varying from 77 to 93 percent. The idea that this could be attributed to nothing more than coincidence is simply ludicrous.

Later, one of these readers, Suzane Northrop, in one twelve minute session with a subject unknown to her, generated 136 pieces of information with an accuracy rate of more than 80 percent. At this point what else was there for the experimenter, Gary Schwartz to say except, "These experiments provide quantitative data that are consistent with the hypothesis that some form of anomalous information retrieval was occurring in these skilled mediums." A superlative understatement, to be sure. And while the experiments do not explain the how as to why this was possible, the kind of data obtained not only speaks for itself but also most certainly shows something else is at work here. One thing that seems evident from this is that when we die our energies do not merge with some universal force and we, as individuals, do not cease to exist. An idea thus far unacceptable to mainline science which, to some extent, is as it should be.

As stated, with a world full of charlatans, frauds and predators, a healthy skepticism is mandatory. A blanket dismissal of any and all evidence of certain phenomenon, however, denies the individual of ever witnessing or experiencing it themselves. At least on the conscious level. It does not mean that it does not happen. It only means that a rigid belief system can block it from view and create denial. That should be self evident. Argue for your limits and they are yours, as the saying goes. Your beliefs are the limit of your existence, is another. Beliefs are beliefs. Sometimes they are also the truth, sometimes not. It doesn't matter. Insist that they are true and start defending them and they become the individual's personal truth, right or wrong. Scientist, layman, beach bum or criminal. On the other hand, if a person is on middle ground and undecided, there is nothing like personal experience to help them decide where the truth is.

OTHER ODD EVENTS

On October 5, 1930 the 777 foot long British dirigible R-101 crashed and burned in France on a trip to India, killing all of the passengers and most of the crew. Two days afterward a psychic medium from London, Eileen Garrett, began speaking while in a trance, saying that the messages received were from Lt. H.C. Irwin, a crew member killed in the crash. Irwin, through Garrett, then proceeded to lay out a long list of problems associated with the dirigible that caused the catastrophe. First of all the engines were too heavy and too limited in power for the size of the craft. The propellers were also too small, the fuel injection was faulty and an air pump failed. The cooling system was bad. The weather was wrong for the flight. The fabric covering of the craft had severe tension on it and became chaffed and waterlogged. The superstructure was far too heavy and stiff and the airship was unable to gain enough altitude and maintain proper trim for flight. Lastly, the dirigible built up a static electricity charge on its skin from air friction which then caused the fuel oil and hydrogen gas that made it a lighter than air vehicle, to explode and burn.

The first session Garrett engaged in was conducted by a psychic researcher named Harry Price. The following ones involved a Major Oliver Villars who had been a friend of Lt. H.C. Irwin, the man who had spoken through Eileen Garrett. Other deceased members of the crew also came through in the following sessions and in addition to reasons as to why the airship crashed, they also related other aspects of the design, recollections of other test flights, political pressures, unrealistic deadlines and more. Refer to the book written by John G. Fuller, *The Airmen Who Would Not Die,* for additional details. In the end Garrett's statements about the airship and the crash were specific enough to engender the suspicions of the British government and she was investigated but adjudged innocent of any complicity with people involved in the actual dirigible program.

Twenty years later, at 7:27 in the evening of March 1st, 1950 the West Side Baptist Church in Beatrice, Nebraska blew apart due to a gas leak in the basement. There is nothing unusual about that, gas leaks often cause explosions. What was exceptionally unusual, however, was this. It was the night of the week when the members of the choir always met for practice. Almost without fail, they were all always very prompt and ready to start by 7:25. Over the years a member or two might be a little late but there was never a time when every member failed to get there promptly. Until the day of the explosion. On that evening all 15 members of the choir, plus the pastor, were late in arriving and not a single individual was caught in the blast.

Two people were late because the person who was giving them a ride was late. The pastor, his wife and daughter were late because the mother needed to iron the daughter's dress.

One member was working on a letter and lost track of the time. Two more were late because something happened at their mother's house that needed last minute attention.

Another had been taking care of his young sons and didn't realize until the last minute that he was late. The dedicated pianist had planned to come half an hour early but had fallen asleep after dinner and caused both her and her mother to be late.

Two high school students were late because one of them insisted on listening to the end of a radio program while the final member of the choir had waited until the last minute because of the cold weather and left her house just as the church blew up. With this in mind, was this just more examples of coincidence or was there something else working away behind the scenes that created such a diverse and individualized set of circumstances that kept the entire choir out of harms way? Perhaps if one, two or three people escaped the tragedy. But all fifteen? Some people can only describe such an incident as a God given, personalized miracle, not realizing that it isn't god who is looking after them, it is another side of self that has the ability to do that when we still have unfinished business in the world and allow ourselves to listen. In that regard consider the following regarding 9/11/2001.

There is some variation in the numbers depending on which information source is quoted but it is essentially irrelevant in terms of the complete picture. At the time American Airlines flight 11 hit the North Tower of the World Trade Center there should have been somewhere between 45,000 to 50,000 people in the Center complex. Instead, according to the best estimates possible, there were only 17,400. That is a difference of more than 27,000 people which is why the final death toll of two thousand nine hundred and ninety six was far, far lower than expected and first predicted. The big question is, where were all these people at the time instead of where they normally would have been, and why? Why were 54 to 60 percent of the people who normally would have been there either late in arriving or elsewhere when tragedy struck? The difference is so extreme that any logical individual would have to realize that it is statistically very significant and has to be far beyond coincidence. There had to have been some other phenomenon at work.

As for individual specifics, there is no detailed documentation available to support this extreme anomaly but there are innumerable individual stories. One person, contrary to habit, stopped for coffee and a muffin. Someone else missed the commuter train by half a second. Another dallied on the phone while others were delayed because the bus was later than normal or the taxi driver took a wrong turn. Others got sick at the last minute while many more simply decided to take the day off for no good reason. The accounts go on and on, undocumented, of course, as such things usually are. But seriously, how can anyone argue over the truth of these anecdotes when the facts show that regardless of what all these people were, or weren't doing that caused them to be late or absent, 27,000 is a large number of people and it is more than half of those who would normally have been there, undoubtedly far more than ever happened before in the history of the Trade Center.

With regard to the Pentagon, however, there do not seem to be any publicly available statistics to show how many people were either late or didn't come to work on that day but for the airline flights that were hijacked, the smaller number of passengers on board that day is also quite significant. The normal passenger load for the four flights involved would have been 299 on a typical Tuesday. On Tuesday, 9-11 the total was only 213. The 19 hijackers are not included in these numbers because having hijackers as passengers would hardly be routine, making the regular passenger load on that day 30% less then normal, another very notable difference that is difficult to account for.

And what about you? Have you ever personally had the experience or met a person who for some reason refused to get on an airplane at the very last minute and later learned that the flight had crashed? Or a person who went to work a different way than usual, only to later learn they had avoided a major accident on their regular route. And why wasn't the death toll at Oklahoma City far worse than it was? There are a lot of stories out there from a whole range of different individuals who for one odd reason or another either didn't go somewhere they normally would on some fateful day because of some, not normal for them, change in routine. Why? There has to be a reason why such things happen, something to which should become more apparent as we go along.

In a somewhat different vein on May 25th, 1979, American Airlines flight 191 crashed on takeoff at O Hare airport in Chicago when one of the planes engines came loose and fell off, killing 258 passengers and 13 crew members. Prior to that a man named David Booth kept having a vivid, re occurring dream that foretold of this event. Not the flight number, exact time, date and location but certainly the scope and horror of it. It bothered him so much that he even called the FAA but without more specific information there was nothing that could have been done that would have been preventative. The case is otherwise well documented and was predictive in a way that far exceeded chance.

In the same manner several years ago I also started having a re-occurring dream. It was a very dark night somewhere along a country road, an accident scene. Police cars with red lights flashing and something tragic off at the side, all very ominous. At the time I worried about my son, a young man with a very large motorcycle who would ride down west coast canyon roads late at night at high rates of speed with some of his daredevil friends. The thing that didn't make sense, however, was that a good friend of mine from work was also always in the dream, standing there in silence, looking on. Always the same and very disturbing, it repeated itself night after night until one day I went into work and found that my friend was not there. Later, finding out why, I learned that her young son, one I didn't know she had but the same age as mine, the first day home on leave from the navy, was traveling down a country road at high speed late at night with his girlfriend. Going far too fast, the car went off the road and wrapped itself around a big tree, killing them both. Definitely precognitive, a dream like that is hardly coincidence no matter what the skeptics claim. And then, a few years later, I had another difficult to explain personal experience.

Boating off the California coast as we had done many times before, my then wife and I had spent the day fishing on the far side of Anacapa Island. It was early evening when we came in and we were tired and ready to go home. Outside the harbor at Oxnard there is a long, high breakwater made from stones. I was at the controls, just coming around the southern end so we could head up the channel to the docks when for some unknown reason I felt compelled to ask my wife if she wanted to go down to Port Hueneme which was about a mile south. Why, I had no idea. Remembering the one previous time we had been there years before, there was no reason to repeat the experience. It was just a very small harbor that belonged to the Navy and all it contained was a few old rusting ships. Regardless, she shrugged her approval and off we went as I seemed to feel some sense of unknown urgency. Again, coming in past the breakwater there, the same old scene. A few rusty hulks of ships. Different, however, was the fact that now there was a crowd of people standing on the inner breakwater all shouting and waving frantically, pointing to a place somewhere out in our direction. Obviously serious, we began trying to see what they wanted and where they wanted us to go. Unfortunately the wind was up and the water was very choppy so we could neither make out what they were shouting or see whatever it was they might be pointing at. Who knew, maybe it was shark. Then finally, and luckily, we saw the problem. A man in the water floating on his back, not moving. At first I was sure he was dead.

Between the wind and the waves it was nearly impossible to get very close without the risk of getting him tangled up in the propeller. Finally, however, we got the boat properly oriented with the wind and were able to lift the poor man aboard. Cold and unconscious, definitely hypothermic, he seemed dead. But then we found a pulse. Back at the helm I got on the radio to the Oxnard harbormaster while my wife covered the man with a blanket and massaged him vigorously as we roared back up the coast and down the five mile per hour channel at full speed to where an ambulance was waiting. Still unconscious but still alive, the man left the scene in the emergency vehicle, sirens wailing.

Months later someone knocked on our front door. It was the survivor. He had been fishing from the breakwater and had been swept off the rocks by a large wave. Between the wind, waves and heavy clothes he was wearing, he was unable to swim back to safety. He said for sure he knew he was going to die and at that point had given up. Tragically, he had taken his two small daughters along with him and they were trapped there on shore, watching the entire event unfold. I don't remember the exact number but he told us what his body core temperature had dropped to and it was one of those situation where another five minutes would have given the story and entirely different ending. So again, the question becomes, was this just another coincidence? Wait until something similar happens to you and then decide for yourself.

Also on the personal side there is a category of psychic experience that I call the "Turn in here," phenomenon which, for lack of better words, I would consider to be bursts of useful intuition. For example, a few years ago I was driving around the country in my old truck seeing family members and an old friend or two. My ultimate goal, though, was Florida, where I wanted to do what so many people have done. Swim with the dolphins. Not in an aquarium, however, but in open water. Not having researched exactly how I was going to do that I started driving down the highway on the way to Key West. Cruising along on a four lane section of the road passing through Key Largo I came upon a side road that disappeared into the trees and something literally told me to, turn in there. Going too fast, however, I had to go on by, do a turn around and come back and found an old house down at the end of this side road. But, getting out of my vehicle, it soon became clear that there was no one around. Then I noticed an elevated wooden walkway that wandered off through the reeds and tall grass. Following the urge to proceed, I came to an immense wire meshed enclosure where several people were working. Once there one of the women said, "you're just in time, get busy." Doing what, I wondered but didn't ask because it quickly became apparent.

It was a rescue station for injured pelicans. There was a hurricane on the way, I was told. Every bird had to be captured and put in the basement of the house I had seen. If left in the cage the wind would blow them around and seriously injure or kill them. A few hours later the job was done so I thanked the woman who was in charge for the experience whereupon she asked me if I had heard about the baby whale. No I hadn't. What whale?

Back in my vehicle again, unconcerned about the impending hurricane which I was not previously aware of, I headed back north. A few miles away was a Hilton Hotel and there was a wide channel that flowed across the island from east to west. In that channel was another group of people trying to save the life of a baby sperm whale. It had been found beached on the shore farther up the coast and brought there for this rescue group to manage. Just an infant about ten feet long, it had to be feed, burped, exercised and kept afloat. There were five or six swimmers in the water around the clock to help do that and their intent was to ride out the storm wearing football helmets to protect them while they did. Feeding was done through a large plastic hose stuck in its mouth through which gallons of human baby formula were poured on a regular basis. Burping was accomplished by rolling it over in the water a few times after feeding. Exercise was forced by manually moving its flippers and tail back and forth and I took turns with some of the rescuers in the water.

By morning the hurricane had skipped on past, however, and the baby whale had made some progress so I told the group leader I was leaving. He asked where I was going.

"Key West," I said. "I want to swim with the dolphins in open water," and with that he found a scrap of paper and wrote down the name and phone number of a woman in Key West who had a boat. A few hours later I was out in the open water being dragged by a rope, surrounded by a pod of eight or nine dolphins. Not only had I achieved my original goal but because I had listened to that inner voice I had two additional very compelling adventures to go with it. Was this all just coincidence? Perhaps, but not to me.

Although nowhere as dramatic, such things happen all the time and most are very convenient and helpful. Take the old tractor/backhoe I had acquired. A stroke of luck, I had gone to a used equipment yard and bought it very cheaply the day after it arrived there. Using it on the property I owned I got several hundred hours of use from it digging ditches and building a long driveway. Based on the hourly rate it would have cost if I had hired the work done, the tractor had more than paid for itself before anything serious happened. Then worn out bearings in the differential gave way, all the teeth on the ring and pinion gears were destroyed and the only solution was to replace the entire unit. New parts were no longer available and a used differential sold on the internet cost more than a thousand dollars, plus shipping and handling.

Now what, I asked. Even if I paid the price it would take at least a week to get it and I couldn't wait that long. Backtracking, checking the metal tag on the unit I saw it was made by Rockwell. Rockwell, as I knew, made rear axle assemblies for large trucks. Calling the only truck wrecking yard within driving distance I was told they had no such thing. Then, that little voice. There was an auto wrecking yard down the road about ten miles. My logical mind said, don't bother. All he has is cars and small trucks like pickups. I knew that, but without calling ahead, I went there anyway.

Knowing the owner, I told him my problem. He looked at me oddly for a second then pointed out the window of his office. There, right in the parking area blocking one side was what was obviously a truck rear axle, two old rusty wheels with flat tires still attached.

"Some dumb ass dumped it there in the middle of the night, last night," he said. "I have no idea what it is off of but if you can use the damned thing you can have it for getting it out of my way."

I went outside and looked at it. Old and beat up as it was, it still had a tag on it that said it was a Rockwell unit, although not the same number as on mine. But still, I pondered, went home, got my trailer and hauled it off. As I soon found out after taking it apart, the differential gear box was the same as that in my tractor, the only difference being that the axle shafts on the truck unit were longer than those on the tractor which accounted for the different tag number. But, they were the same diameter, however, and had the same number of splines on the shaft. Thus, with the exception of having to drill two of the twelve mounting bolt holes in a slightly different place, this new differential fit perfectly into the rear end of the tractor and was actually in very good condition internally in spite of how bad it looked on the outside. So, somehow, by some quirk of fate, a very expensive and hard to resolve problem was fixed without cost, all in one day's time. Again, it was about not letting logic rule the moment but learning to listen to that inner voice instead. Once you learn to do that, similar things happen all the time. Perhaps not always as significant but there never-the-less.

Proceeding, the literature is full of strange accounts of other incidents that routinely occur, things which the skeptics all too easily dismiss as coincidences. But are they really? The reader may already be aware of some of these accounts but they are still worth repeating because, all taken together, they are more than suggestive of other underlying phenomenon that are ultimately, also explainable. Here are some of them.

In 1972 a graduate student named Jeffrey Goodman from the University of Arizona contacted a psychic named Aron Abrahamsen for archeological help. Abrahamsen then did a reading for Goodman from his home in Oregon which led Goodman directly to an archeological dig site near Flagstaff, Arizona where human artifacts more than 100,000 years old were found in the exact location given by Abrahamsen. Equally interesting is what led Goodman to contact this psychic in the first place. He, himself, had previously had a very detailed precognitive dream about the particular aspects of the site itself, but not its geographical location, which is where Abrahamsen came in. Not only was Abrahamsen able to tell Goodman exactly where to dig but what he would find at various depths as he did the excavation and how deep to go to find the most important artifacts. So, what is the moral of that story? Perhaps if more archeologists would learn to trust their intuition and turn to psychics for help, we would know a lot more than we do about human history.

In 1898 novella writer, Morgan Robertson produced a work entitled, Futility, or the Wreck of the Titan, a story of a shipwreck. Fourteen years later in real life the Titanic sank. So what, one might state. But, first look at all the parallels between the fictional story and the real life event.

The Titan was fictitiously described as being the largest craft afloat with four smokestacks, three propellers, practically unsinkable and without enough lifeboats that hit an iceberg on its starboard side 400 miles from Newfoundland on an April night in the North Atlantic and sank, losing more than half the passengers on board.

In 1912, the Titanic, the world's largest luxury liner at the time also had four smokestacks and three propellers, was described as being virtually unsinkable and also did not have enough lifeboats on board. Additionally, going at almost the same speed as the Titan, it struck an iceberg on its starboard side 400 hundred miles from Newfoundland on an April night and sank, losing more than half of its passengers. Say what one wants, that is one large amount of coincidence by any standard.

Moving on, in 1927 a Russian writer named V. Nikolsky accurately predicted in his novel, the date of the first atomic explosion 18 years later in 1945.

In a similar manner, Science fiction writer, Robert Heinlein described a Uranium-235 atomic bomb being dropped on an enemy city and was accused by the FBI of disclosing military secrets until it was pointed out that the book he had written was published back in 1941, four years before the actual event, back when such a possibility was pure speculation. More coincidence, or what?

Previously, back in 1934 a Brit named Henry Richards unknowingly slept in a hotel room that had previously been used by terrorist conspirators. In the middle of the night he had a vivid, detailed dream. A strange street in a strange town where two men were shot and killed, one who he recognized as French Foreign Minister, Jean Louis Barthou, and the other, King Alexander of Yugoslavia, as identified by his picture in the morning paper. Very disturbed, he told his dream to one of the police chiefs of the Surete National. Impressed with the dream account, the Chief recognized the area Richards described as being a particular section in Marseilles where the Foreign Minister and the King were known to be so he telephoned a colleague who lived there, only to be laughed at. At least until that afternoon when both the King and the Foreign Minister were gunned down.

Why are so many so-called coincidences, not coincidences at all? As for others, what else is there? This particular item of interest had been floating around for years but it is still worth another look. It concerns our two presidents, Lincoln and Kennedy and goes as follows.

Lincoln was elected to congress in 1846, Kennedy in 1946.

Lincoln was elected president in 1860, Kennedy in 1960.

Both were concerned with civil rights issues and both wives lost children while living in the White House.

Lincoln's secretary was named Kennedy and Kennedy's secretary was named Lincoln.

Both presidents were shot on a Friday and both in the head.

Lincoln was shot in a theater named Ford and Kennedy was shot in a car made by Ford.

A week before Lincoln was shot he was in Monroe, Maryland while the week before Kennedy was shot he was with Marilyn Monroe.

Lincoln was shot in a theater and his killer ran and hid in a warehouse. Kennedy was shot from a warehouse and his killer ran and hid in a theater and both killers were assassinated before they could be brought to trial. Additionally, both presidents were assassinated by southerners and both were succeeded in office by southerners. Lincoln by Andrew Jackson, and Kennedy by Lyndon Johnson. Any attempt to try and make sense of these historical events would seem to be a waste of time even though it is interesting to be aware of something so beyond explanation.

And then there is the "Hundredth Monkey Phenomenon," a phrase apparently coined by Lyall Watson in his book, *Lifetide.* A very brief description of the phenomenon goes like this. The Japanese had been studying monkey colonies on isolated, remote islands for years. At one point on the island of Koshima the animal colony was given a new food item, raw sweet potatoes. Unfortunately, they were covered with sand and grit and the monkeys refused to eat them because of the dirt. Then one bright young juvenile learned to wash the potatoes in a stream. She then taught her own mother and her playmates how to do it also and these playmates in turn passed the knowledge on to their mothers. Next the young monkey discovered that if the potatoes were washed in the ocean instead of in the stream, the salt water added to the taste. In summary, the point of the story is this. At first the knowledge gained, a dirty potato can be made edible by washing the dirt off of it, plus be made even tastier if washed in salt water, was spread from monkey to monkey by direct observation. But then it seemed, somehow in the course of events, when some critical mass number of monkeys had learned the trick, a threshold was reached wherein, almost immediately, this knowledge was somehow psychically passed on to all the rest of the members of the monkey community. Not only did it spread across the island of Koshima, it jumped to other surrounding islands as well and even on to monkey colonies on the mainland many miles away.

Critics, doing what critics do, however, rise up in debunktive ire and say such things couldn't happen. The first monkey learned what she did by pure accident. Coincidence. Then other monkeys learned through observation, one by one, until all the monkeys in the colony gained this knowledge. And then of course, how else could it have been, monkeys began swimming impossible distances from island to island and back to the mainland, passing on the skill. What better way to side step the greater implications of phenomenon that defy conventional explanation. But, leaving that alone for now, let's talk about crystals.

As Watson also mentions, what about crystals? The crystal phenomenon has some important similarities. Crystals have also uncannily jumped some natural barriers in their development. Again, extracting from Watson's book, *Lifetide,* we find the following. For more than 200 years glycerin had been extracted from natural fats in the form of a liquid. Despite every imaginable way possible in attempts to do so, it was decided that glycerin could not be crystallized and had no solid form as opposed to most all liquified substances. Then, in spite of all this, early in the 1900s something very unexpected happened. A barrel of glycerin was shipped from Vienna to London in a sealed container. When it was opened, however, it was not in the liquid form as expected. It had crystallized, something deemed impossible until then.

At this point it was also found that, just as one might expect, samples from this unusual barrel could be used to "seed" other samples of glycerin and get them to crystallize too. What was impossible to explain, though, was that all the other glycerin samples in the laboratory also began to crystallize at the same time. Not by seeding, but spontaneously and independently, all by themselves. Even those that were in sealed, airtight containers. Not only in that particular laboratory but, once the barrier had been broken, the process continued itself in other locations around the world in what might be described as a 100th monkey effect. Suddenly something previously deemed impossible became routine. But how? As yet there seems to be no scientifically acceptable answer. Nature does not oblige science, however, and does what it does anyway. In spite of human opinion as to what is, and what is not possible, nature continues to express itself in unusual ways in spite of the fictitious limitations humans sometimes try to impose upon it. Thinking something to be impossible and rejecting it in advance, however, does not invalidate the truth, it only blinds the disbeliever to it.

The most important leaps in scientific progress have not been achieved by those who tried to build on the prevailing consensus of the day but by those who stepped away from it and acknowledged something more fundamental. Then they came up with such things as mathematical theory, electromagnetic theory, quantum theory and the theory of relativity, cosmology and all the other cornerstones of modern physics and our present understanding of the universe. The physical universe. That which is, there is no more universe, reminding the reader once again that that is still the prevailing attitude among many of the eminent in the field of contemporary science. But again, there is choice. We can leave that alone and quit there. Or, we can ask, is there some reason to continue? What evidence is there that would justify further inquiry? The answer is, a lot. While some of it has just been presented and while more will come later, there are still some conclusions which can already be drawn.

First of all, coincidences do occur but coincidence alone certainly does not explain everything that is otherwise unexplainable. It cannot. If someone still stubbornly insists that that is the case, however, knowing what we know at this point, then we have to leave them behind.

More than 27,000 people were not in the Trade Center buildings on 9/11 that normally should have been and 100 people did not get on the hi jacked airline flights involved in the attack that normally would have. In a similar manner, left to their own resources, animals head for higher ground in advance of an on coming tsunami. A psychic can make contact with the deceased crew members of a dirigible that crashed and obtain important evidence relating to the cause of the disaster. On and on. Regardless of personal opinion, this well of information is far too vast to simply brush aside and ignore. Even though science is as yet unable to put an antenna up in the air and find and measure the signals, it is almost impossible to deny that from plant to plant, insect to insect, crystal to crystal, monkey to monkey, human to human, human to plant, human to honey bee and beyond, none of these things can be explained without recognizing that there is some clear form of information transfer that occurs, regardless of our present ability to measure within our present technological limitations. Being unable to measure something does not in any way mean that it does not exist, however. It only points out the limitations of our technology in its present level of development.

If there were a more open acknowledgment of this, it could be explored in greater detail than presently possible and mankind could benefit tremendously. Obviously, if humans, along with animals, have the ability to sense impending tragedies in advance, such as a church blowing up, a terrorist attack, an earth quake or any other upcoming disaster, recognition and improvement of such skills would be of great benefit. So would a better developed ability to communicate on other levels besides just the verbal.

Regardless, whatever it is and however it is explained, <u>the ability to psychically access and transfer information is a fundamental aspect of reality and is as much a part of it as the atoms of the physical world.</u> Besides those cited, there are two additional ways of accessing information in a psychic manner. They are dowsing and remote viewing which are also hard to dispute. Before we get to those, however, what about the birds, bees and animals?

Princeton ethologist, James Gould disproved the idea that most animal intelligence is the result of prewired behavior patterns by observing the way bees locate new sources of food. Setting food at various locations, he then systematically moved these sources and let the bees re find them. Surprisingly, after a few such moves, instead of having to wait until the bees discovered where the food had been relocated, he found the bees already there waiting for him, having somehow deduced where he would place them ahead of time. How did he explain what happened? He couldn't. The experience was so disturbing that he was quoted as saying, he wished it hadn't happened.

As for other kinds of creatures, what about cats and dogs? As a personal experience we once had a mother cat and several of her kittens whose food dish was in the garage and the garage door was often left open so they could come and go. All was fine until a big stray Tom cat started coming around, raiding the food and threatening the kittens so one day in desperation, I let him in the garage and shut the door. Capturing him, I drove six miles across town to the animal shelter where I tried to get him through a trapdoor into an enclosure. But, by then he was so angry for having been caught and given a forced car ride that he clawed and snarled his way back out, climbed up on the roof of the building and disappeared. Well, at least he was gone, I told myself and that was that. At least until four days later when, there he was, strutting down the sidewalk big as ever, heading for our open garage door. Six miles is not very far for a cat to travel, as we shall soon see, and that is not the question. The question is, how did he find the way back? Maybe he just lucked out. But then, how do you explain this documented case?

An Australian family left their pet indoor cat with relatives on the other side of the country so they could take an extended overseas vacation. While they were gone, the cat ran away and was given up on. Then, one year later, there he was back at his own home, mangy, beat up and starving but alive, waiting for the daughter to get home from school. All in all, it had taken the poor cat more than a year to make a trip that was over a thousand miles long. Just surviving the extremely hazardous and nearly endless desert of the Australian outback is one thing. But traveling cross country without a road map, homing device or other help makes it something else entirely and would seem to be impossible. How would he even know what direction to start off in to begin with, let alone stay on course over such a great distance? There is no scent trail to follow and no road signs in cat language to use for guidance. Furthermore, all the coincidences in the universe would not be enough to pull that one off, not in one year's time anyway, especially if you were just a short legged little cat. Anecdotal as it may be, this cat is not alone. Many cats and dogs have a way of finding their way home. A Florida cat took two months to do just that after a two hundred mile trek and a Minnesota cat traveled for 140 days and covered 350 miles. Another cat made a 1600 mile journey from Dunkirk, New York to Denver, Colorado in four months. According to Makana Yarbough, ex director of the Lynchburg Humane Society, if let alone about 66 percent of all displaced cats will find their way home. So will many dogs.

A dog was given away when his owners moved from Illinois to Michigan. Apparently, not liking his new owners, the dog set out on a six week journey and found his original owners new home 260 miles away. Another widely published dog story took place in the Vietnam war. The dog and his handler were dropped into the thick jungle by helicopter. The dog's handler was wounded and air-vacted out while the dog was then left behind. Three weeks later, however, the dog walked back into camp looking for his handler without GPS, trail markers or scent trail. Again, the accounts are innumerable but even if they were not, it wouldn't matter. One valid case of a cat finding its way clear across a continent is enough and cannot be arbitrarily dismissed. Nor can it be accounted for as one professor of animal behavior stated by claiming that the wild relatives of animals, in running all over the place to find food and being able to return, had survival value and those with the greatest talent would have had their genes passed on. An explanation which misses the point because it does not address the phenomenon in play. That innate ability which provides the animal with the directional information required to accomplish such feats in the first place.

Do dogs and cats have little magnets in their brains

like some birds and insects are supposed to have which allow them to migrate accurately year after year? It doesn't appear so. Still, suppose that they did. Again, what does that explain? A lost or abandoned pet does not need a compass. A compass would be useless unless that critter first knew what direction to travel in to begin with. Even if they did, how does one explain the pinpoint accuracy required to end up precisely on their owners doorstep, rather than five miles away? Without an address or a specific set of coordinates, even a human is incapable of such an accomplishment. Clearly there is some other bona fide source of information available that animals can access in times of need. In this regard Duke University's Parapsychology Lab did an investigation and found legitimate cases where 28 lost dogs, 22 cats and four birds did the unthinkable and found their way home by themselves.

And, speaking of birds, there once was a pigeon which had a band on its leg with the number 167. Number 167 showed up in someone's home in Summersville, Virginia, tired and hungry. It was adopted and cared for by a twelve year old boy. A few months later the boy was taken to a hospital about seventy miles away for surgery. It was now winter. In his bed recovering after his operation on a stormy night, he noticed something at the window. He called a nurse who came and opened the window. In flew the bird and went to the boy. If it had been any other pigeon the case would have been open to dispute but with a band on its leg.....? Not a look alike pigeon which might have been mistaken for his pet, but pigeon 167. How does a pigeon travel seventy miles in a snowstorm, not only to the right town but to the right part of town, the right building and find the right window to peck at without a map and an address or a GPS system and a set of destination coordinates? And, speaking of animals, this brings up other claimed abilities that animals are reported to possess.

Besides all these remarkable accomplishments, there

seems to be some consensus that sudden changes in animal behavior might be used as an early warning system to predict earthquakes, even from people in the scientific community. There are many well known but subtle earth changes which occur before an earthquake actually happens, most of which are far too benign for humans to sense unaided. Some of these are minor ground vibrations, tilting, groundwater changes, electrical or magnetic field variations, radon gas emissions and thermal changes. Postulating such a theory is one thing. Proving it is something else. Creating a laboratory generated, bona fide earthquake is literally impossible. Underground nuclear explosions can be used to generate mechanical shock waves of locally high magnitude but they are devoid of all the other naturally produced side effects that occur in nature prior to an actual earthquake event. Setting up observation posts to monitor animal behavior is also a losing situation simply because, as is already very evident, earthquakes are thus far extremely unpredictable, both as to when and where they will occur.

To verify any such thesis would require that animals be placed in observable situations where they could be continuously monitored around the clock, not for minutes or hours or even days, but quite possibly for years until something of large enough magnitude occurred that would produce meaningful data. That something would be a quake of sufficient size to do harm to animals and humans because it seems that animals do not react to the background of non threatening minor tremblings which occur constantly but only to those with more serious consequences. While there are about half a million earthquakes occurring every year around the planet, only twenty percent of these can actually be felt by humans and of those only about one hundred cause reportable damage. Even if someone picked one of the most earthquake prone places on earth to set up and monitor animal behavior, it could still be a very long wait. Regardless of this, the Chinese and Japanese both regard animals as having some natural ability to sense earthquakes in advance and Chinese experts believe there are at least fifty eight species of animals which exhibit this ability and snakes, bats and rodents are high on the list.

In 1975 droves of hibernating snakes woke up and left their hideouts in the Chinese city of Haicheng. It was enough to cause the city to be evacuated and avoid the 7.3 earthquake that then occurred, saving thousands of lives. Unfortunately the following year a very large quake also hit the city of Tangshan in China and killed at least 650,000 people. It seems that there were warning reports of unusual animal behavior but they were largely ignored because of all the political turmoil at the time due to the Communistic culture revolution.

Elsewhere in the world prior to quakes, frogs were seen migrating, mice were running wildly in the open and farm animals were restless prior to a large quake while workers at the Smithsonian Zoological Park in Virginia noticed clear changes in captive animal behavior prior to a 5.8 magnitude quake which hit the area. The stories go on and on as the interested ask their questions, with many prejudgments limiting the scope of possibilities. The pragmatically minded insist that it has to be some purely physical phenomenon related to animals much greater ability to sense and react to the extremely small chemical, thermal, electromagnetic or vibrational changes which occur prior to a quake. If that is so, however, how do we account for this?

On December 26th, 2004 there was a major 9.1 earthquake deep under the ocean centered off the north west coast of Sumatra. Among other things, this quake created a major tsunami which caused damage as far away as the east coast of Africa, thousands of miles to the west. Closer, but still hundreds to more than a thousand miles from the hypo center, waves were generated that were more than 90 feet tall and devastated coast lines all around the Indian Ocean, killing almost a quarter of a million people. Prior to the huge wall of water onslaught many observant people reported animals running from the coastline seeking higher ground. Later in the damage assessments it was found that there was an exceptionally low number of animal bodies found in these areas. As a result it seems evident that they somehow knew of the impending threat early enough to know to leave the lower lying sites. The fact that the quake center was deep under water and for many, thousands of miles away, would seem to show that none of the regular precursor, purely sensory cues were there and were responsible for the animals behavior.

To say that this behavior was purely instinctive also answers nothing. Clearly, they responded to something. This something was information. And, it was information received far enough in advance to be effectively acted upon. Because of the under sea origin of the quake, the only possible physical clue that could be picked up on would be earth vibrations. Even if this were possible at some of the great distances involved, how does earth vibration alone translate into an incoming Tsunami in an animal's brain and cause them to retreat from the coast instead of running around in circles or along the beach in the wrong direction? It does not. The other aspect of this event is the human toll.

230,000 is a lot of people by most any standard. At the same time, however, the earthquake and tsunami happened in a very densely populated, equatorial region of the world that is also   full of tourist and vacationer destination stops at that time of year because of the beautiful beaches and balmy weather so one can only speculate as to how many millions of people actually had their toes in the water or were sunning themselves at the time the tsunami hit the shorelines. Regardless, considering the fact that some 27,000 people were not where they would normally have been at the moment tragedy struck on 9/11,

2001, it seems quite sound to expect the same kind of thing happening in December of 2004 around the Indian Ocean and beyond. Not just for humans but for animals as well. And, most importantly, consider the fact there was absolutely nothing chemical, electrical, thermal or vibrational coming out of the ground prior to 9/11. Likewise, except for the possibility of minute earth vibrations, the same was true for the Indian Ocean Tsunami. While it may be true, or not, that human death tolls from such occurrences may be proportionately higher than that for animals, it is also true that humans are under considerably more mental and emotional stress, are far less spontaneous in their actions and thus less able to respond to the subtle clues intended to get them out of harms way.

As for the information itself, it just seems to be "out there" somewhere, not like the information cloud associated with the internet but much more all inclusive with information from both the future and the past. Information that both animals and humans are receptive to. There is no other way to explain it. Without trying to categorize and label everything, this ability falls within the same realm as telepathy although, generally speaking, telepathy is considered to be a human, person to person ability. As defined by Lyall Watson in his book, Supernature, telepathy is, "access to information held by another without use of the normal sensory channels," something which he states has been proved beyond a reasonable doubt.   But, even though it is one sided, isn't it still the same phenomenon that occurs when a plant or a dish of yogurt picks up the thoughts of a human and responds accordingly, living thing to living thing?

Beyond that there is also a category which might be called, mind over mind. To prove a point, the before discussed psychic, Edgar Cayce, showed that he could get someone to come to his office by summoning them through a thought process. As claimed, the individuals showed up, confused and upset as to what they were doing there. Once done, it was also upsetting to Cayce who was shocked to think he had that kind of power over others and he therefore refused to ever use it again.

AND IN ADDITION TO THAT

Regardless of how else it may be viewed, all of the foregoing examples are evidence of "something." Unfortunately, until that something can be isolated and demonstrated under closely controlled conditions, it will probably continue to be dismissed as irrelevant or fictitious by many and thus never receive the attention it truly deserves, which, as promised, now brings us to remote viewing and dowsing. Here, as the reader should be able to see as we proceed, there are many parallels between the abilities demonstrated by Edgar Cayce and those involved with dowsing and remote viewing.

Referring to the book, *The Seventh Sense* by Lyn Buchanan, a very informative work about Remote Viewing, the author talks about a point where the funding agency, the CIA, wanted to justify shutting down a remote viewing project. To that end the CIA hired a statistician and a "psychic debunker." The statistician did a review and determined that the data obtained during the project was of statistical significance. The debunker, however, in what often seems to be true of debunkers, did as follows. Quoting directly from the book, "The debunker declared that there was, indeed, statistical significance and reported that the science of statistics was therefore as flawed as the science of parapsychology. He suggested that the unit be disbanded until the science of statistics could become accurate enough to prove how useless and false parapsychology was."

Ludicrous, extreme and horribly limiting as this kind of thinking obviously is, it is exactly what happens when results bump into prejudice and pre formed opinion. It is akin to the scientist who, when presented with experimental data that contradicted his personal views on the matter, stated that he wouldn't believe the results even if they were true. And, so much for open minded, unbiased objectivity. The mistake is not in pursuing new avenues of thought, the mistake is in listening to close minded people and letting their opinions become a deterrent to the further pursuit of knowledge. So, keeping that in view, let's move on and consider the field of remote viewing, which has its own group of detractors. Regardless of that, the practice of remote viewing further demonstrates the ability of humans to remotely access additional amounts of significant information in paranormal ways. Remote viewing is a practice that is also closely associated with the field of "Dowsing" and we will begin with a remote viewing experience of a "dowser."

A water dowser and well driller named Peter Harmon from Maine called a new client he had yet to meet in person who lived in Oklahoma, a place where he had never been. While talking on the phone to this client, the dowser saw the other man's property in his mind and told the man that out in his back field there was a big dog house and that not far from the northwest corner of the dog house there was a Coca-Cola bottle on the ground and that the best spot to drill for water would be right by the bottle. Then he asked the client to go and see if he was right about the description he had given. He was and the, probably astounded, client asked how he knew that. Very aptly put by Christopher Bird in his book, The Divining Hand, Bird stated - "Unhampered by any scientific constraint, Harmon offhandedly replied, 'Well, I can see it because *I'm* there.' "

Unhampered is a key word here. Remote viewing is not quite the same as sending a camera equipped drone out to fly over an area and send back pictures. It is also not something that could be labeled an exact science. It is instead an art, an ability, a facility, a special craft, an aptitude perhaps which, surprisingly enough, can be learned with the proper training. And, as has been statistically shown, it does work. It works best, however, as stated, when "unhampered." Since it is a paranormal ability which derives from the para sensory attributes of the mind, it is also sensitive to the mental environment in which it is expected to work. As a consequence, if the ability to remote view or to dowse or to influence the operation of some electrical or mechanical device was not susceptible to the negative attitude of skeptical critics looking over the viewer's shoulder, it would not work to begin with. That is the point demanding scientists continue to over look.

When dealing with such extrasensory aspects of the mind, however, a person does not have to be an ardent believer. As it turns out, it is best that they are not. The overly enthusiastic can side track the results just as easily as the scowling skeptic by only seeing what they want to see and either end up not allowing the full story to unfold or reading far more into the results than is actually there. The best results, the ones that have statistical or real life value are obtained by those who are able to maintain a certain level of open mindedness and neutrality. For themselves if directly involved, or, for any subjects under their control that they may be trying to observe. If they cannot separate themselves intellectually and emotionally from the process, their biases come through and all they end up proving is that which they originally believed to be true. Not universally, but only for themselves on a strictly personal level, nothing gained. It is a case where logic should not be allowed to override intuition.

For an in-depth view on the subject of remote viewing, there are at least two well written books available. These are, *The Seventh Sense* by Lyn Buchanan as already listed and, *Remote Viewing Secrets* by Joseph McMoneagle. McMoneagle's book will also provide a well detailed account of remote viewing history, naming key individuals who contributed to its present level of development as was (and still may be) used by the military and by private individuals or companies who provide it as a service to others. What must be understood, however, is that none of these people or organizations "invented" remote viewing. They did, however, coin the title and find ways to expand on this natural ability and turn it into a semi formal discipline. Quoting McMoneagle, remote viewing is defined as, "The ability to access and provide accurate information through psychic means, about a person, place, object, or event, that is inaccessible through any normally accepted means, regardless of distance, shielding, or time." With that as a working definition, the formalized investigation of remote viewing began with Harold Puthoff and Russel Targ of Stanford Research Institute and Ingo Swann, an artist, author and psychic; the primary researcher and central figure who gave structure to the procedures and methodology of formally directed remote viewing.

Irrespective of that, remote viewing is still a natural psychic ability, however, and as such is probably as old as the human race and reflects some still heavily disputed but very fundamental quality of life. It may just be one aspect of whatever it is that makes life possible to begin with. Aside from that, the important thing to be pointed out at this time is that it works. Remote viewing is indeed possible but as with most everything, it has it's limitations. One cannot just flip a switch and get a full color presentation of a targeted location or an individual on a big screen monitor with hi fidelity audio but, for those with the talent and/or proper training, the results are unequivocal.

In the movie, The Emerald Forest, a young boy takes a hallucinogenic substance which makes him able to project his consciousness into an eagle and go in search of his father, remotely viewing what the bird saw. While such a method may have made the concept of remote viewing more palatable to the theater audience, it certainly is not something that is necessary to accomplish the feat. Purportedly, an Australian Aborigine can do such a thing completely unaided, psychically exploring the landscape for food or water and an early Native American could send his consciousness down the river with the water to see if danger was ahead. But then, so can some present day individual with either the natural talent or the training. And, they can, more or less, do it just as effectively. The major difference between the native and the modern viewer is that the native can undoubtedly accomplish the feat, not only much more spontaneously, but also under far more adverse conditions outside of a controlled environment. As a modern day discipline, however, remote viewing is predominately done under precisely regulated conditions and is labeled, Controlled Remote Viewing.

Remote viewing begins, of course, with some individual or agency looking for specific bits of information. This could be anything from, where is someone's lost puppy to, what is going on out in some remote area in Iran, to where in building X is the vault with all the secrets in it to, what does it say on those documents to, what is going on inside the head of terrorist XYZ. Once defined, the task is then handed off to a "Viewer" and a "Monitor." The viewer then accesses the site or "target" as best they can under the, as required, guidance and assistance of the monitor. This is done in such a way that neither of these two individuals is given explicit details in advance regarding the task initiator's presumptions that may bias the findings or allow the viewer or monitor to imaginatively contaminate the results.

What would also seem to be of major significance regarding remote viewing is that when the task initiator wants to know what is out in some far off secluded place it is not necessary to describe the location verbally as in, go seventy five miles east of ___ in northern Siberia and tell us what you see. Instead, it is only necessary to tell the viewer to go to north latitude xxx and longitude yyyy, even if the viewer has no idea or concept of where on the planet that might be. Then the instruction is given in an open-ended way such as, tell us what you see or, describe what you see and not, tell us what buildings or structures are there or any other description that would subconsciously slant the viewer's output by him/her trying to please the tasker.

As one can understand, a verbal output alone would be entirely adequate in some situations but if it were something akin to a military situation the viewer would not only be asked to verbally describe what they saw but to also sketch and diagram their findings. With all that said, and regardless of the particular situation where remote viewing is used, the final question still becomes, how was that accomplished? How was someone able to do that? What specifically went on? And here is where the controversy begins.

Many adamantly state that it is all a massive hoax. Who's kidding who, they don't believe it no matter what. But, as Ingo Swann himself said, <u>"True skepticism does not begin by being anti-anything. The processes of open consideration and examination will ultimately establish whether something exists or not."</u> With that as a starting point, it seems almost indisputable that remote viewing is a valid form of information gathering. The mistake made is to slam it because it is not one hundred percent perfect. But, so what? Scientific research is far from perfect either and the journals are full of invalid and embarrassing claims. As for remote viewing, what's wrong with seventy or eight or ninety percent? The results are far beyond those that would be realized by chance alone, so why get sidetracked there.

Nearly all accounts of remote viewing also only report the end results and do not attempt to explain the actual how. Reviewing sketches made by viewers, however, the perspective and point of observation often seems to be from above as if the viewer was hovering nearby during the observation. One possibility for the how of that would be for the viewer to go to the location in an out-of-body state, another highly disputed phenomenon. Regardless, remote viewing in these cases is essentially identical to those so called, out-of-body states experienced in near death situations where clinically dead individuals come back to life and report what occurred. A typical example is the declared dead person who witnesses the operating room scene as viewed from above during that period before they "came back to life." Later, after resuscitation, when they are able to, they can describe everything that happened during that interval in great detail, right down to the actual conversations between the doctors, nurses and staff, along with their actions. As a phenomenon, out of body travel comes naturally for some who can, regardless of the state of their health, do it on demand. Others can be taught how.

If the identity consciousness can leave the body under near-death duress or after a person has been declared clinically dead, then there is also mobility of consciousness as a willful act as displayed by the dowser or remote viewer. Indeed, as previously stated, if you can locate the right Australian Aborigine you might also find that he can sit down under a tree, put his body at rest and depart to explore the landscape ahead, allowing him to find both the waterhole in the desert and his next meal.

Nor is this faculty restricted to the untarnished native. Many reliable contemporary authors have acknowledged and written about their own experiences in this field. Most notable of these accounts are those by Mathew Fox and Robert A. Monroe. The writer Jane Roberts, her husband and many of her students were also extremely adept at this. In addition to flying in a plane, author Richard Bach of Jonathan Livingston Seagull fame wrote that he also used to spend time traveling in the out-of-body state.

Meanwhile, even though some people loudly deny it, as sleep studies show, everyone dreams whether they remember or not. Likewise, everyone has out-of-body states where the consciousness leaves the body for short periods of time during sleep and sometimes for brief moments when they are awake. The sometimes remembered feeling of flying during sleep is one indication of out-of body travel. Therefore, for those who can accept the possibility, out-of-body travel would be one way of getting to some remote site to retrieve information. Not to deterred, however, let's move on to "Dowsing."

Quoting Christopher Bird in his exceptional book, The Divining Hand, *"to dowse* is to search with the aid of a hand-held instrument such as a forked stick or a pendulum bob on the end of a string -- for *anything;* subterranean water flowing in a narrow underground fissure, a pool of oil or a vein of mineral ore, a buried sewer pipe or electrical cable, an airplane downed in a mountain wilderness, a disabled ship helplessly adrift in a gale, a lost wallet or dog, a missing person, perhaps a buried treasure."

Dowsing, as such, is another seemingly mysterious human ability that has also been vigorously attacked by other professionals, namely geologists, geophysicists and engineers in the oil, mineral and water resources business. It is also blindly dismissed by many in the scientific community at large, at least until they try it for themselves and succeed. Then they become some of dowsing's biggest advocates. Unfortunately for dowsing, along with remote viewing, psychic contacts with the deceased and all the rest, there is as yet no acceptable theory in existence that accounts for these phenomenon and lends itself to the rigors of the laboratory. Regardless, dowsing in particular works extremely well and there is a preponderance of evidence to support that claim if one would make the effort to seek it out. It won't be found in this book, however. The intent here is not to prove anything. It is only to assemble information and introduce the reader to what may end up being provocative questions that will expand the individual's concept of life and the meaning thereof.

As for the hand held instrument, it serves as an important aid to the dowser and each individual seems to have a preference but, as it turns out, most anything will work, from fresh cut willow branches to metal or plastic rods to pendulums made from a polished crystal, an acorn or an old rusty washer tied on a string. A few of the more experienced can also do very well with nothing more than an imaginary device during a time of need. This too, gives results simply because the answer already exists and is retrievable independently of the specific tool the individual dowser prefers. As for the actual practice of dowsing, itself, there have been some very notable successes. One of these was at Lake Elsinore in California.

Prior to 1927, the six mile long lake was fed by the San Jacinto River. In 1927 the river was dammed, the major portion of water diverted elsewhere and the lake slowly dried up. By 1951 it was essentially bone dry. For specific details of what followed, the reader is referred to the book, The Divining Hand, but in very brief form, this is what happened.

A dowser named Verne Cameron made the claim that an abundant supply of water existed below the dry lake bed sufficient to refill and maintain the lake. His claims were strongly ridiculed by a host of California's geologists and state engineers and for a variety of reasons the project proposed by Cameron was side tracked. Then in an attempt to solve the problem, a 250 mile long pipeline was built in 1957 and water was imported to fill the lake. Not only was this water extremely expensive, it also had a highly corrosive, concentrated salt content that destroyed metal pipes and fixtures. Additionally, once filled, the lake did not stay full due to evaporation. At last, however, after years of in fighting and frustration and the loss of several million dollars, Cameron finally prevailed and wells were drilled in 1965 which produced more than an adequate amount of water to re fill the lake. Right on cue after the first well came in the old guard group of experts, however, the geologists and engineers, loudly stated that what had been found was only trapped water and that it would pump dry in a few days. Except that it didn't and, like it or not, a dowser had solved the problem, the same dowser who, had he been listened to, could have saved the city of Elsinore about fourteen years of time and several millions of dollars. Additionally, the citizenry could have had access to the lake for recreational purposes and visitors' dollars.

On the other side of things, claiming to be a dowser does not make a person a dowser, or a person a psychic, just as an apprenticeship does not make a competent tradesman or the appropriate degree make a capable doctor, lawyer, engineer, psychologist or anything else. Every field, professional or otherwise, has its share of fraudulent practitioners and the world is full of scam artists and con men without conscience. The fields that are most open to pretenders and predators, of course, are the ones that are unlicensed and un regulated, aided by an uninformed or misinformed public. It is in these areas where track record and reputation are everything. If a skeptic wishes to deride and debunk dowsing, remote viewing or any other such practice, all they need do is find a few, claimed-to-be practitioners, and point out their poor rates of success. More fraud and nothing proved.

As opposed to that, pick a well known dowser. Choose one like Paul Clement Brown and look at his track record in the search for oil. Not only was he able to tell someone exactly where to drill the well, but also how deep to go and what kind of a yield to expect when it came in. He was also very good at telling people where not to drill, as often proved by other experts who felt he was wrong, drilled there anyway and did not succeed. Brown did not dowse a modest ten or twenty wells during his career but more like a thousand, all of which had reserves that made them financially successful and many of these were drilled in places where geologists and geophysicists insisted there was nothing there to be found. In summary, his success rate was essentially one hundred percent, not only for location, but also the exact depth at which the oil would be located, the amount that would be found and what kind of pump rates or barrels per day that could be extracted. Additionally the man was able to find platinum and uranium deposits through his skill as a dowser. Regardless of how opposed to such "witchcraft" as one might be, once they can get past the emotional barrier, the evidence is again literally undeniable.

As quoted from Christopher Bird at the beginning of this section; "to *dowse*...... is to search for *anything*," and that would seem to be a very broad claim. Regardless, the worst thing a competent dowser could do would be to let the skepticism of others limit what they would be willing to try. After World War I a Frenchman, Abbe' Alexis Bouly, a well known water dowser was solicited by a General from the military to located unexploded shells buried in the ground and to state if they were of German, Austrian or French manufacturer before they were dug up so the excavators would best know how to handle them. Bouly's performance was said to have been faultless. Moving on after founding an organization to help make dowsing more scientifically acceptable, he began studying microbes and through use of nothing but his pendulum was able to identify cultures of microbes in test tubes as accurately as one could with the use of a microscope.

Skipping ahead, another Frenchman and fellow dowser, Father Alexis Mermet, came to the conclusion that if hidden objects in the earth could be found by using a pendulum, then why couldn't a pendulum also be used to detect otherwise hidden conditions in animals and humans?

The answer to his question, as he found out once he

started checking, was that this method worked very well and Mermet, as he himself said, invented the method of pendular diagnosis, the use of dowsing to diagnose disease. Without any attempt to accurately describe how the progressive use of dowsing for medical purposes evolved, we now come to Father Jean Jurion, a French Catholic priest who was inspired by Bouly, Mermet and a Father Jean-Louis Bourdoux who spent sixteen years in a Brazilian jungle and gathered and studied medicinal plants. In addition to studying homeopathy, Father Jurion began investigating the practice of dowsing in great detail. Eventually, after shedding the misleading collection of limiting fallacies and false beliefs that had built up over the years surrounding the practice, Jurion found that he could, "dowse anywhere, any time, under any conditions," and be successful and with this he began experimenting with medical diagnosis. As confirmed by medical doctors, this too proved worthy and he found that his most startling results were obtained with patients that doctors had given up on.

Keeping medical records over the course of twenty five years, Jurion had successfully worked with over 30,000 patients, undergoing many clashes along the way with the Order of Physicians, the French equivalent of the American Medical Association. Regardless, he inspired and supported other dowsers who followed and eventually, medical dowsers were recognized as a professional group by the French Ministry of Labor and allowed to practice freely in the country just as was the case in Germany, Great Britain and Holland.

Over the years there were many individuals who were important to the medical dowsing movement who will not be mentioned here because that history has already been laid out in detail by Mr. Bird in his previously named book. One who will be, however, is Aubrey Westlake, an English physician, primarily for some of the conclusions he arrived at through his personal use of

102

dowsing for medical purposes which, at that time had been given the name, radiesthetic dowsing. In general, he stated that in order to become successful as a medical dowser one had to abandon many of the misconceptions forwarded by formal medical training and approach the subject from a totally different viewpoint.

"The central weakness of ordinary medicine, he concluded, was that because it stressed pathology above all else, it dealt mainly with the gross final results of disease rather than their underlying cause. True diagnosis, he felt, was to be sought in a radioesthetic analysis, not of pathological tissue, but of a harmonious balance of energy patterns constituting health. So many medical men, when first introduced to dowsing, seemed to profit little from it because they thought in terms of pathology instead of function, disease instead of health, and matter instead of energy."

This line of thought quickly leads to some of the many misconceptions of modern medicine, the major one being why people get sick to begin with. Unquestionably it is quite evident that many people become ill simply because they do not take care of themselves. They over indulge and under exercise, creating a multitude of health issues. But why? Why are some people so reluctant to take care of themselves? Could it be a question of self worth? It takes more than a prescription to remedy that and it would seem that a nation where more than fifty percent of its people are morbidly obese has something else wrong with it besides too many fast food restaurants. Other than that, disease is usually seen as a consequence of pure chance and bad luck. Being in the wrong place at the wrong time such that some malicious germ mysteriously makes its way into the body and the individual becomes infected. And, as the story goes, the only reason why people get cancer and a lot of other debilitating diseases is because of faulty genes or bad luck, pure and simple.

On the other hand it seems quite clear that there are

direct connections between the state of one's mind and the state of one's health. Analyzing studies that correlate state of mind with physical health, Howard Freidman, professor from the University of California, found that certain states of mind are "absolutely toxic." Chronic irritability, pessimism, cynicism, depression and anxiety all double the risk of getting a major disease, be it cardiovascular, cancer or something else life threatening. Unfortunately, many doctors still end up treating the symptoms rather than the cause. But what else is there to be done? That is the way the system is structured. It is simply not possible for society to re engineer itself so that people's lives do not get backed up, stalled out or dead ended and their energy short circuited to the point where it is forced into negative expression within the individual's own body. Likewise, it is highly unlikely that the medical profession will be able to revise its own thinking regarding germ theory and how the importance of an individuals internal harmonious balance has more to do with good health than cholesterol levels in the relatively near future because of its own inertia and bias. Meanwhile, balance comes from a reasonable amount of self esteem, a certain level of emotional well being, some degree of meaningful satisfaction with one's own life and gets us back to the idea of mind over matter and the fact that the state of a person's mind has a lot more to do with their state of health than regular visits to the doctor.

If a person has a hard time accepting that, let them ask why, if the tenets of modern medicine are so vital to health, how did the human race survive all those thousands and thousands of years without it? Furthermore, why do nations which have the most highly developed medical technology and widespread health care facilities have life expectancies that are lower than in some remote countries of the world where medical care is essentially non existent? Also absent are prescription drugs, vitamins and other dietary supplements and balanced diets. Not only do these people live longer, they also remain healthy and fully functional to the end without slipping into the middle age deterioration process so common in the US. A place where the statistics are further distorted by artificially extending people's lives with technology without adding to its quality.

This is not meant to say that there aren't many dedicated, caring and concerned people in the medical field. There are, and some of them are extraordinary in terms of devoting their lives to helping others. Additionally, medicine has become very surgically adept and has done remarkable things when it comes to carving out the effects of disease and repairing and rebuilding bodily structures damaged by trauma. That is all for the better. Where medicine errs, however, is in its viewpoint that falsely perpetuates the idea that humans are inherently weak and susceptible to begin with. That disease and deterioration are the norm and not the exception. It is why doctors as a group have more health problems than the population in general. Surrounded by illness and disease, their perception becomes negatively prejudiced in favor of sickness and eventually influences their own state of health, along with that of the rest of the population which picks up on it and accepts it. In this regard the medical profession has created a self fulfilling paradigm because <u>thoughts are far more contagious than germs</u>. It is why people who do not trust their bodies and take their health too seriously, end up being unhealthy despite all the organic vegetables and dietary supplements they ingest. Poor judgment can also get in the way. In that respect, ask yourself what sensible person would take something to prevent heartburn in advance that puts them at risk of a heart attack?

Meanwhile, not only do we live in a vast surrounding sea of germs, they also inhabit the human body in prodigious amounts. Both bacteria and viruses alike. Most are technically harmless and beneficial while others are potentially very dangerous and life destroying. These could maim or kill us very quickly if they decided to do so. But, generally speaking, they do not and that comes back to our mental state and attitude towards life. If this weren't true, how else could such things as the workplace health phenomenon be explained, for example?

Pick a company, almost any company that has several tiers of responsibility in it and ask why it is that the ratio of sickness to well being varies radically from top to bottom. Typically, top executives work far longer hours and are subject to much greater demand and stress than those on the factory floor or out in the back. Regardless, the members of this upper management group not only rarely ever come down with colds, flu and all the more mundane illness but also very few of the major ones. The greater the job responsibility and the more individual control that can be exercised in the performance of the job, the less illness and down time. Busy people spend their time thinking about their achievements and most are too involved to get ill. They also are better rewarded for their services, feel more valued and needed and have a better sense of their own self worth. They also have better reasons to want to stay involved, don't want illness to interfere and as a result, don't become ill. Those on the bottom, meanwhile, often use all their paid sick time and more. Additionally, they actually become ill, not realizing that they are indirectly doing it to themselves because their jobs are often boring, unsatisfying and demand little respect.

Regardless, the other message here is that when it comes to diagnosis, dowsing has also been proven to work very well, often times better than blood and serum tests, X-rays, MRIs and many of the other overly expensive but limited tools available to the medical practitioner. Unfortunately, should any medical practitioner attempt to diagnose patients this way in the United States, he or she would most assuredly be deprived of their license and so much for that, so, let's return to the subject of out-of-body

106

experiences and travel.

As suggested earlier, being able to separate ones self from ones body is one way to accomplish a remote viewing task. It could also be claimed that any out-of-body experience is a remote viewing experience because whatever an individual is experiencing while in that state, he or she is removed from their body and "remote" from it, whether the actual separation is near by, or half way around the globe. Once more, however, as with remote viewing and dowsing, there is nothing hypothetical about this phenomenon. What is significant about it is that, of all the uncommon displays of the psychic and/or the paranormal, the idea of being able to separate oneself from their physical body, maintain awareness and be able to travel about at will and return to describe what they experienced still seems to be one of the most abhorrent of ideas ever imagined and most definitely totally unworthy of any formal recognition by contemporary science. As such, OOB travel has been labeled everything from hysteria to psychosis to delusion to hallucinatory fantasy to functional disintegration to cognitive-perceptual schizoidism and beyond.

The idea that there is more to a human being than just blood, bone and brain cells seems to be a very threatening concept to most objectively minded, scientifically disciplined individuals because no one has yet been able to design an experiment capable of sensing or imaging the out-of-body condition of another in the laboratory. This occurs primarily because the ability to project consciousness, to be able to dowse to find almost anything, the idea of out-of-body travel; these are all transcendent to the existing laws of physics. As such, it has become a situation where it is much easier to ignore and dismiss than to try and deal with. **It must be recognized, however, that if these "paranormal" happenings are "real" then there is an, as yet officially unacknowledged, additional di-**

mension to existence. Furthermore, if all this paranormal ability is true, then it is not paranormal at all. It is instead a part of nature regardless of opinion, and therefore just as "natural" as being able to see, hear and speak. Furthermore, to say something does not exist simply because it is thus far unmeasurable is as farcical as an early 19th century scientist stating that it would never be possible to communicate wirelessly. Whether or not one privately accepts such an idea or not, the possibility must be approached more open mindedly before any valid assertions can be made. Even then, approach is critical, as preconceived ideas can bias the best laid experimental plans.

Sometimes, however, the most adamant of skeptics become the most ardent of supporters. Doctors, MDs and PhDs, engineers and scientists give dowsing a try and become serious practitioners and outspoken proponents both. Other skeptical individuals are sometimes blindsided in ways that cause them to alter their opinions. It may be a stress related event, the loss of a loved one, a forced revision of life perspective, or seemingly, nothing at all. It just happened. They have a full blown "psychic" life changing experience. A recently deceased old friend shows up at the foot of their bed in the middle of the night, they find themselves floating over the operating table in the hospital listening to the conversations of the medical staff, they have a serious precognitive dream or any number of other possibilities that are other wise inexplicable to the normal individual. In some respects such an experience is akin to that had by someone who has seen a UFO, something else it is usually best not to talk about overly much. But, once someone has seen such a thing, not at a distance as a fuzzy light in the sky, but up close and personal, it no longer matters what the experts and disavowers say. The final point is, a person does not need the endorsements of contemporary science to have a predictive dream, to engage in remote viewing, to dowse for water or oil or minerals, to diagnose disease or to indulge in out-of-body flights around the universe, alone, or with a companion.

On the personal side, dowsing itself has been an interesting experience. For years I have watched people who have started out well but lost their perspective in the process. Obsessed, they ritualistically dig out their pendulums and ask for answers to personal life questions, some important but most of them not. It is as if they have come to a point where they no longer trust their own judgment on basic matters and have appointed the pendulum to the rank of all-knowing. It is an unnecessary, tedious mistake. If the answer is already out there somewhere and accessible through dowsing, then the answers (if not already known by the questioner on a subconscious level) are still readily available. For those who have progressed beyond such a dependence, they have learned to simply shut down the often over riding, logical portion of the brain, ask the question and just let the answer come through. For the most part this approach is much more expedient and seems to provide an accuracy that is better than that of the pendulum for this kind of work.

When it comes to other questions, however, the pendulum can be amazing. For example my automobile suddenly began operating very poorly. The diagnostics were run but no computer codes came up. Neither did the repair manual provide any clues so I tried reasoning it through. These are the symptoms, what could be the cause? Had some electro-mechanical part like the distributor worn out and was failing. Had one of the many sensors failed, had some computer component died, was there a faulty electrical connection somewhere? What else could be wrong? Modern engines rely on the outputs of several sensors to function properly, the out of tolerance or failure of which can affect performance and yet not show in a diagnostic scan. As a result I removed parts, examined and tested them individually, replaced a few that could have been responsible and still no success. Then, in desperation, I found a pendulum, went back under the hood and started holding it over various engine components. To my pleasant surprise it suddenly started spinning wildly, something I had never experienced to this degree before. Looking closely, it was over a pair of small insulated wires that ran to one of the engine sensors but I could not see the problem. Then I disconnected them and used an ohm meter to check continuity. As it turned out, one of the wires had broken inside the insulation in a way that did not show externally but when soldered back together, solved the problem. And so, what is the probability of such a pendulum experience happening by pure chance alone?

MIND OVER MATTER

The idea of "mind over matter" conveys different meanings to different people. One of these is exemplified by the fact that: <u>The world situation we live in today is the way it is because that is exactly where human thinking has carried it.</u>

Houses do not simply appear out of nowhere, skyscrapers do not automatically rise from the ground, bridges do not jump across rivers unaided and airplanes do not build themselves. Except for that which nature has done for herself, everything else in the world of man first appeared as a concept in the mind of man. Everything from his shoes to the automobile, to television, to landing on the moon. Without that beginning, none of it would exist. Nor would there be social, political or religious organizations, chocolate bars or instant coffee.

By the same token, poverty, illness, misery, suffering, mayhem, murder and war are not the arbitrary consequences of pure chance, either. Or impulsive quirks or impositions of nature, or inevitable laws of the universe. Lastly, and most certainly, they are not the manifestations of a disappointed, disquieted, irascible God or a despicable, conniving devil determined to side track the human race. Very simply, they are also products of the human mind. So, too, are the abstract constructions of mathematical theory which are used to explain physical reality. As representations of reality, they can be useful for making predictions about reality, but they are still very limited, especially in the subatomic world. Descriptive concepts but never the complete story, the best that can be done under the circumstances and good enough for the laboratory. Except, sometimes under critical scrutiny, they don't always make the grade. Here, on more than one occasion, the clever theorists have then "invented" new particles, simply to make the mathematics rigorous and binding. Then, because that is the only way the formulations will

111

hold together, the problem is turned over to the experimentalists who set out to look for and verify the existence of particles which had to be first imagined before they could then be discovered. And there have been several.

One such particle was the neutrino whose verification only cost a few mega millions of dollars, and lastly, making the headlines in a big way, the Higgs boson which took a ten billion dollar research facility to authenticate, plus operating expenses. At least it seems to have been verified to the satisfaction of some members of the scientific community even though that acknowledgment is based purely upon supposition after supposition and extrapolation on top of extrapolation, along with a mountain sized amount of faith that every last bit of the giga sized ultra-complex operating and sensing equipment worked properly from end to end. Ultimately, the extreme number of things that had to have happened correctly is somewhat akin to the number of steps required to turn a mushroom into a mountain. Most interesting is that these individuals, the discoverers and their supporters, seem to be able to fully accept the indirect data they come by as proof of an invisible and nearly impossible to find particle but are at the same time adamantly opposed to any ideas of psychic phenomenon, something which is orders of magnitude more directly obvious and far easier to verify when the interest exists. But, back to the topic.

Absurd as it may sound at first, one could still ask the question. Have neutrinos, Higgs bosons and their like always existed? Were they always a fundamental part of the universe or was their lack due to otherwise purposeful little gaps in nature as yet not understood which the present state of mathematical theory was unable to describe? If that was the case then were they brought into existence through intent in a "mind creating matter" way like the "observer effect" that gained a certain popularity a few decades ago? The idea that there is nothing there physically until a qualified observer "collapses the wave function" and brings things out of the probability field into the material realm. A question of mind directly creating matter, something which is otherwise laughed out of the ballpark. Originally it was applied only to the quantum world and had something to do with the "uncertainty principle" of Heisenberg but in the end the macro world is built up from the micro world so if the observer effect applies to one, it must apply to the other also.

The entire question of who or what a qualified observer really is, however, becomes a bit nonsensical if carried to the extreme. At the far end of the intellectual spectrum one university professor was even able to use quantum theory to re-instate mankind back into the pre-Copernican center of the universe where the universe was created solely to serve mankind's needs. Other individuals, scientists and academics, were bold enough to state that only humans were "qualified" observers. All right! But then what about the fact that there are still dinosaurs in the fossil record, along with millions of other species which existed long before humans supposedly came on the scene. Who brought them into existence? And then there is the debate about atomic particles. Do they really exist all the time or are they nothing more than pure probability until a scientist comes on the scene? If so, how did the desk I'm at and the chair I'm sitting on get here? Regardless, way down deep there is still some fundamental truth related to mind, or consciousness being able to convert what might be labeled psychic energy into physical matter. Not through simple observation but mental volition instead. So, do desire, intent and volition alone have the power to bring things up out of the vacuum of empty space into the subatomic world and then give them form in the material world? Perhaps. Certainly, as will be seen later, mind alone can affect matter. And, since it has the power to do that, can it also, in some sense of the word, create matter, not by collapsing wave functions en masse but due to some other connection between mind and the energy matter is created from? Can it even go so far as to pick a material object, cause it to dematerialize through the power of mind alone and then cause it to be rematerialized somewhere else? Bizarre as it may sound, it would certainly be an easy way to build a Giza pyramid or put together a Coral Castle if we could bring ourselves to take such a giant mental leap. Meanwhile, there is still all that business about Schroedinger's cat.

For the unfamiliar, Schroedinger's cat is a purely fictitious feline used to show one interpretation of quantum mechanics. This particular cat is placed in a box with apparatus which may, or may not, kill it within one theoretical minute. The cat who, poor thing, doesn't realize that once the box is closed and the experiment set in motion, he is, according to the cruel experimenter, both fifty percent dead and fifty percent alive at the same time and stays that way until a qualified observer is able to determine the truth by opening the box after a minute has gone by. That qualified observer of course, has to be a human, at least for most theorists. But how would it feel if you were in the box instead and the experiment was stretched out to an hour instead of a minute? What would it be like to be 50% dead and 50% alive at the same time? Makes the whole thing sound a little silly we considered that way. And, is it really all that simple? Not if one takes into account some of the other abilities cats seem to have which most experimenters don't appear to be aware of, part of a larger reality which somehow has to be factored in to get a more complete concept of overall reality.

It seems that cats, for example, can very good at picking up on the thoughts of humans. Cats were put through a maze at Duke University as humans sat behind one way mirrors and tried to mentally influence them as to when and where to turn in order to navigate the maze. Some cats produced exceptionally high success rates far beyond chance. One other cat also demonstrated a different kind of ability in another unusual situation.

In the 1970s, physicist Helmut Schmidt, who was at Duke University at the time, hooked a random number generator up to the switch of a heat lamp in a shed behind his home during cold weather. The system was designed to statistically turn the lamp on and off for equal amounts of time, and upon verification, this was found that to be true. Then he placed a cat in the shed during the winter and again recorded the on/off cycles. Surprisingly, they did not stay the same. The presence of the cat in the shed changed the results, with the heat lamp staying on far longer than chance alone would allow. Schmidt's cat, in other words, was fully capable of changing its environment by some means other than physical. Understanding that, the right cat in Schroedinger's box would be able to alter the decay rate of the fictitious isotope also, just as some humans can do (as we will see later) and extend its life indefinitely. Furthermore, what makes the entire issue bogus to begin with is the fact the the experiment is incompletely rigged.

Pick a criteria for declaring the cat dead. Say the end of brain activity. Put a sensor on the cat's head that will register brain waves and have it transmit that information to the experimenter and the ambiguity goes away because the only place it ever existed was in the theorist's mind to begin with. In reality, nothing is half alive and half dead, nor does a sub atomic particle half exist and half not. Only a lack of information makes it seem so. Nor is the human observer the final authority on such matters. The rest of the universe doesn't need a human stamp of authenticity to do what it does.

This, in turn, brings us back the issue of "observation" in general. Is observation a purely passive event or does it have an active component to it? If active, then what is that component, theoretically or otherwise? If entirely passive, however, then how could the act of observing dark energy back in 1998 by astronomers potentially reduce the life expectancy of that dark energy and contribute to bringing the universe to an early end, as postulated by physicists Chown and Krauss? If this is the case, then should humans stop looking at the sun or at the stars in the night sky because they may be shortening the lifetimes of all these heavenly bodies, ludicrous as that may sound? Do humans really have that kind of power?

Meanwhile, as speculation about the cat's real life or death state continues, the cat is fully aware of his own state of existence, as would his mate be, or a close cat friend, probably without even having to rip open the box to find out. But indeed, if everything revolved solely around the human, would a cave man have been considered to be a qualified observer? What about a squirrel or a tree? Do all the other life forms on the planet know of their existence without, and in spite of, human validation? Unfortunately, the idea that other life forms have an importance all their own, independent of humans, is an offensive concept to those individuals committed to the, life is an accident, you only go around once and, dead is dead, thesis. What if instead, there is yet another dimension to this entirely? What if there is a level of awareness on the part of everything in the universe and that, instead of there being an "observer effect," everything brings itself into existence in some grand, cooperative venture, one way or another. <u>Why couldn't the material universe be the physical expression of something beyond physicality?</u> It is a very fundamental question. One difficult to give plausibility to, however, without further evidence, so we move on to the next category of mind over matter. The one where the minds of both humans and animals can produce changes in physical things through their presence or thoughts alone.

In this regard the same Helmut Schmidt also used radioactive substances to produce random event generators that ran light displays and video game occurrences. Then he brought subjects into the scenario who knew nothing about the internal workings of the mechanism and asked them to mentally and remotely try to influence the outcomes and found outcomes that were better than chance alone would allow. Even more significantly, he did the following. Instead of continuing the study in real time, he disconnected the random event generators from the system and then played back recorded displays of the previous day's happenings to his subjects. These subjects were unaware of this change and thought it was another live, ongoing event and were again asked to try and influence the outcomes as before. In other words, unknown to the subjects, they were asked to reach back into the past and change something that had already happened. And they did. Numbers of separate tests showed just that, through test scores that were significantly higher than what chance alone would allow. Scientifically speaking, this should not be possible but happened anyway.

Enrico Fermi, atomic scientist, had a reputation for being rather destructive. Not intentionally, however. It was said that he functioned at such a high energy level that his presence in a laboratory would cause motors and other electrical apparatus to short out and burn up or simply to fail and stop operating when he put in an appearance.

In experiments conducted at City College in New York, psychic Ingo Swan of remote viewing fame, was able to raise the temperature of graphite blocks inside a thermos container at the far end of a room, simply by thinking about it.

Other past experiments have shown that simply by concentrating on the task, individuals can speed up or slow down the decay rates of radioactive materials by amounts that become statistically significant. Professor Chauvin of Strasbourg University scientifically demonstrated this ability of mind or thought using uranium isotopes over thirty years ago. The same is true for changing the ph of water.

And then there is the human body. Two Innuit friends had gone hunting on snowmobiles. Returning home, one decided to drive down the frozen over river while the other stayed on the bank. The man on the river hit a patch of thin ice and went through into the freezing water. Unable to help get him out, his friend left to go into town several miles away for assistance. Along the way his vehicle broke down and he was forced to walk most of the way in the cold and wind and barely made it to town. Getting help, however, he was able to return the several miles back to the river location, many hours later, fully expecting his friend to be dead.

The fact was that no matter what kind of clothing a person might be wearing other than something like a waterproof, heated space suit, the cold would eventually seep through the fabric and bring death through hypothermia and the man in the freezing water should have died within minutes of falling in. But he did not. Not only did he survive the impossible, he was no worse off for the experience than before and required no treatment whatsoever, while his friend ended up in the hospital for frostbite. As to what made it possible, the man could only say that mentally he kept wondering what it would be like to be a polar bear and imagined himself to be one.

This mind over body phenomenon also shows itself through hypnosis. Exactly what hypnosis really is, is still a matter of discussion but a universally agreed upon definition doesn't really matter. It is nevertheless, a state of high suggestibility and concentrated focus on the part of the hypnotized individual, whether self induced or otherwise, and it is the results that are important. In the last century there was a period where hypnosis was used by dentists and surgeons in situations where it was advantageous to have the patient both awake and pain free during the procedure and for those who were good subjects, it worked extremely well, even in situations such as tooth extraction where the pain would otherwise be excruciating.

Not only can hypnosis effectively suppress pain, it can directly affect, or prevent the effect of injury to the body. A lit cigarette can be held against the skin of a subject under hypnosis and the person will not only, feel no pain, but the skin will not burn nor will there be a blister from the heat. In other cases the skin can be skewered with a metal rod and removed. Not only does the wound not bleed, there is no evidence of the skin having been pierced. Elsewhere in native societies, and still being done in motivational seminars, some people can mentally get themselves into a place where they can walk barefooted over hot, glowing coals without burning their feet. Not a good idea for some westerners, however, because they, or their motivators, cannot get them into the proper mental state before attempting the feat with the resultant severe burns.

One of the most significant things hypnosis can accomplish is to cure someone of a congenital disease. A congenital disease occurs as a result of a defective gene or genes. Curing the inherited disease means that hypnosis was not some superficial, temporary masking of symptoms but actually changed the victims DNA in a permanent way. It also works well with warts, psoriasis, shingles and a wide variety of other conditions which resist normal treatment.

The list goes on, and it is a long list of what becomes possible. Hypnosis can be used to help people stop smoking or drinking and break bad habits. It has also been used to cure other bodily disorders through the use of proper suggestion. Suggestion is the key word and the subject does not always have to be in an induced state to be susceptible to suggestion. Through repeated suggestion, we can and do brainwash ourselves, or let family, friends and acquaintances do it for us as we in turn do to them. The internal dialogue with self, the positive or negative. The comments, innuendos and judgments from without. It is the things that we allow ourselves to accept that have a major effect on our lives, true or false. Whether coming from others or because we infer and invent them for ourselves, doesn't matter. If allowed to persist like a broken record, endlessly repeating themselves on a conscious and/or subconscious level over long periods of time, they can have a serious affect on our lives, good or bad, creating limits to one's abilities and personality that would otherwise not exist. It can even affect our health and aging, for example, for they too can become the result of outside repetitive commercial innuendo and/or suggestive self hypnosis, those constant, almost subconscious messages we pick up on and keep telling ourselves about ourselves regarding our own well being.

Either way, the state of one's mind has a strong influence on the state of one's health and is another example of mind affecting matter. Our mind affecting our physical body. And with that as a starting point, let's take this idea another step further. Let's move on to people being able to create a separate independent invisible entity with both a distinctive personality and the ability to move heavy physical objects through the "power of mind" alone.

His name was Phillip and he was conjured. In 1972, A.R.G. Owen and eight friends decided to try and create their own ghost. They gave the ghost to be the name Phillip, decided what century he was from and where he lived, along with some historical details, gave him a distinct personality, an uncaring wife and a girlfriend. It took a year and a change in approach before Phillip came alive, however, but then one day Phillip began tapping on the table to let them know he was there and at that point they established a code for the raps so they could communicate. Not only did the ghost relay back the history and characteristics he had been assigned but he added to them in great detail, expanding his life story and rounding out his personality. Ordinarily the episode might have been easy to dismiss at this point but then, along came the Canadian Broadcasting Corporation and filmed an episode where Phillip put in a startling appearance. Caught on film, the invisible Phillip unaidedly moved a table from a place below the stage to a place on the stage without help in a complicated situation, having to maneuver it up some overhanging steps where he then answered questions from the show's moderator, all the while remaining body-less.

This is not the only documented example regarding the movement of tables without direct outside help, however. A British psychologist, Kenneth Batcheldor, has not only shown that the hands-off levitation of heavy tables is possible by groups of people but that smaller ones can be made to be so heavy they become impossible to lift at the time. All these phenomenon have been reproduced by another Englishman named Colin Brooks-Smith who went even further and outfitted objects with strain and height gauges and recording instrumentation.

As for Phillip himself, what was he exactly? Certainly to a large extent he was dependent upon those who created him. When certain members of the group were absent at his conjurings, he was unable to provide answers to questions the absentees would have known but at other times he was fully capable of providing original answers which were completely independent of his creators' knowledge and background. In every respect, however, he clearly had some level of substance about him if he was able to move a heavy table around unaided. Additionally, the fact that he developed a distinct personality made him much more than just a simple poltergeist. But, unfortunately, he was never visible to either his creators or anyone else. Not so in the case of Alexadra David-Neel.

Ms. David-Neel spent fourteen years in Tibet studying mysticism, including how to create a phantom, which she later tried to do. She decided to see if she could produce a short, fat, innocent, happy little monk. It took a few months of concentrated effort but slowly he came into being, looking very life like and would appear whenever she gave him the proper thought. As a result he became a guest of sorts that lived with her and all was just fine until she started traveling about. Then the monk began appearing spontaneously without being summoned and took on individualized characteristics she hadn't asked for. Finally, and quite surprisingly, she lost control of her creation. The monk went from fat to lean and turned into sometime rather obnoxious, troublesome and bold. Additionally, not only was he visible to her, he became visible to other people who would see him and ask about him, whereupon she decided to put an end to it, and him, but that took six months of struggle.

All in all, this is a very intriguing story and evokes some extremely interesting questions. What would happen if this ability to create were turned into a full blown experiment? What if, for example, once the apparition became visible and began to develop along independent lines as did happen, that that process was monitored and allowed to continue. And, since the ghost was visible and wore clothing, it had sufficient substance or density to reflect light such that other people could see actually see it. This means that one person's mind did indeed create physical matter. From what? Beyond that this physical apparition, which started coming and going spontaneously, had thusly developed a mind of its own and could materialize and de materialize through its own volition, obviously without a physical brain. At least in the beginning. But then, what if? What if a snippet of the cloth were sent to the laboratory for analysis. Or a skin sample? What would that show?

Additionally, if it could have been manipulated into

standing on a scale, did it have weight? Or bodily temperature? Beyond that, since it was capable of independently projecting itself into the physical realm and developing a personality of its own creation, what else might have happened if allowed? Would it have continued to become less ghostly and more human? Would it eventually turn into blood and bone and brain cells? And would it eventually get to the point that it became so "real" and "physical" that it would lose the ability to dismantle itself and become trapped in human form? Then what? Still more questions, even though we have already gone far beyond anything that modern science or the laws of quantum physics can explain.

More ordinary poltergeists appear to be almost everywhere, however. Big city, small town and tiny village. Any where there are young people who are <u>usually</u> conflicted and undergoing psychological stress or have unresolved emotional states. When they appear, poltergeists make scratching and rapping sounds, slam doors, open windows, pull things out of cupboards, break things, set fires, cut off people's hair, injure them, move heavy items of furniture around, make gravel fall on the roof of their houses and on other people's and on some occasions actually put in an appearance as visible apparitions which speak. And the list goes on. Not only are the antics of poltergeists rampant and widespread, they have also been examined in great detail. So much so that there seems little reason to question this well documented phenomenon.

Such subjects have also been studied in detail at various places such as Oxford University and it seems that there is a group of people who possess naturally occurring, uncontrollable energy that systematically keeps destroying their electrical household appliances in great number. In like manner, but at the other end of the spectrum, there are also certain individuals who have the opposite talent and seem to be able to get things to run properly simply by looking at them or touching them.

On a different note, not only can humans and animals psychically influence the world around them but humans can also create ghosts through imagination and visualization. It begins by creating mental images or patterns, a psychic blueprint, if you will. Once that exists, concentration and repeated re visualization bring energy to the situation which is them transformed into a focused energy field capable of actively interacting with matter, or, going even further, it can become composed of visible matter and capable of volition. There is no other way to explain such phenomenon. Psychic energy can be converted into an atomic form that has its own sense of identity, limited as that may be. But if we accept such a possibility, how do we incorporate such an idea into our definition of what or what does not constitute life? Certainly the ghost Phillip and the monk created by Ms. David-Neel displayed many of the characteristics we attribute to life. And beyond that, what else is possible?

The author and psychic, Jane Roberts and her husband had been having a bad year. Among other things there were financial difficulties and personal loss. Additionally, as an author, she also felt psychologically blocked while her husband had ongoing severe back problems which the doctor wanted to put him in the hospital for. She, however, decided that his problem was due to extreme stress so they took a short vacation to a resort town where they sought out a nightclub to cheer them up. Once there, with her husband clearly in constant pain, she began looking around the room. Then she noticed an older couple sitting across the room from them who really frightened her because of the uncanny resemblance the two people had to themselves. "Did we look like that," she asked herself, unable to stop staring at the couple who seemed very aloof and bitter. Then she pointed them out to her husband.

At first he looked at them and groaned with a painful back spasm. Then, to the complete surprise of them both, he stood up suddenly, grabbed her arm and insisted that they dance, something they hadn't done in their eight years of marriage, and to music they were unfamiliar with. Not only did they dance but they did so for the entire evening and from that point on her husband's physical condition made a remarkable improvement and his whole outlook on life turned brighter. What was that all about, they later asked Seth, after he began coming through to her in trance. Until then Jane Roberts thought that the entire episode had been a case of classic psychological projection and transference where people project their private fears outward onto other people and then react to them.

But no, they were fragment personalities, he told them, created by themselves from the culmination of all the destructive negative energy they had turned inward which was of such an intensity that it finally became materialized in physical form and presented itself.

"Your dancing represented the first move away from what those images meant and strong action was the best thing under the circumstances.... If you had subconsciously accepted the images as to where you were headed, it would have marked the beginning of a very severe deterioration for you both, personally and creatively and a subtle transformation would have taken place within yourselves if you hadn't so forcefully rejected them."

As for things which are openly acknowledged as living, it seems that each already has such an existing blueprint somewhere behind the physical. Biologists would like to attribute the growth process entirely to chemistry and genetic codes but such a proposition is critically incomplete. So too, is the actuality seen in the healing process, which, when examined in detail, is extremely complex. In the case of injury, how does the body know it has been damaged unless it has the ability to compare what has been broken or torn away with what it used to be and is supposed to be? That requires some higher level of information to work towards before healing can even begin. A blueprint. Then it becomes a question of logistics. Exactly the right atoms and molecules must be transported to the wound site in exactly the right sequence to be inserted into the right location in the right amounts in the correct order, one by one, molecule by molecule. There must be an advance knowledge of where the bone ends and a particular type of tissue begins also. And where the blood vessels go and how they all connect, along with nerve fibers, lymph ducting, cartilage, muscle and more. Healing even a relatively minor bodily wound is every bit as complicated as repairing the hole blown in the Pentagon by terrorists. Before it could begin, blueprints had to be reviewed. Then it was concrete, rebar, electrical wiring, water pipes and plumbing, air ducting, plaster, paint, tile and all the rest, all in the right order and amount.

What else would allow some creatures to grow new legs or tails? And, cut an earth worm in two and one part grows a new tail while the other grows a new head, to give two fully functioning worms as perfect as the original. Something impossible unless the blueprints to do that already exist, along with some intelligence capable of assessing the damage and surmising what needs to be done to correct the situation. No doubt DNA has a definite role in the entire process but it alone cannot provide for everything that needs to happen, either in the growth process or the healing process. In the end it all comes back to the blueprint. That such a blueprint does exist for all creatures large and small would seem to be evident, even when considering something as simple as a sponge.

A sponge is a porous marine animal without bones, distinct bodily organs, brain or nervous system which lives attached to underwater surfaces. Knowing that, take two live sponges. Using harmless vegetable dye, dye one yellow and the other one blue. Then force both of them through a mesh so as to separate their individual cells from each other and stir them together to make a uniform greenish looking mush. Next pour this gooey mess into a tank of salt water and wait. Quite interesting is the fact that slowly but surely the two separate sponges will put themselves back together such that we once again end up with both a yellow sponge and a blue sponge, separate from each other. Then the question becomes, how is this possible? Without a brain or nerves, where do the blueprints reside for doing this? Healing injury is one thing. A living organism putting itself back together after having all its cells completely scrambled is another. It takes some higher level informational set to do that.

The same is true in the construction of a bee hive, a birds nest or a termite mound. What is the information source that such creatures are able to tap into during construction. To dismiss such abilities as being instinctive explains nothing. It is like trying to explain all of human behavior by saying, well, it's just human nature. A non-explanation. So let's look more closely at termites.

Remove a large section of an African termite mound, then place a metal plate down the middle of the missing section and watch the termites repair the damage. One grain of sand at a time, the termites will rebuild the structure exactly as it was before, such that when the metal plate is removed, all the sides of all the individual chambers match up exactly with each other. It is not even that all termite mounds have the same identical master plan built into their little heads that is being followed. They all vary individually in shape, size and internal construction. So, about all that can be said at this time is that the correct information exists somewhere in the form equivalent to an individualized "blueprint" that guides and oversees the detailed construction. It is also in a form such that even though the termites on one side of the mound are completely isolated from those on the other and cannot directly compare notes, the mound gets rebuilt correctly to the same pre-existing pattern.

And, before moving on, there is one other aspect of the termite world that should be looked at. It concerns the so-called compass termite colonies in northern Australia. In terms of their individual size these little creatures are proportionately building something equivalent to the world trade center for humans and almost as relatively complex, completing structures from billions of separate grains of sand all precisely cemented in place. The finished edifice is nine, ten, twelve, fifteen and in rare cases over twenty feet tall, looking like a huge wedge or monster tombstone pointed on top and oriented along a north-south axis. Internally it is honeycombed with thousands of ventilation shafts and passageways. As the sun rises in the morning and sets in the evening, the area exposed to sunlight is large and warms the structure and its interior but as the sun moves up, the exposed cross section becomes less and less, with minimal area at noon to keep the mound from getting too hot. Also internally, the ventilation shafts are capable of being opened or closed by those termites in charge of temperature control so that regardless of how intense the sun or how hard the wind blows, the internal temperature of the entire superstructure is as closely controlled and stable as that of any modern air conditioned, humanly constructed skyscraper.

Say what one wants but none of this would be possible, even in a very simple form, unless every termite involved worked cooperatively along side all the rest and was able to tap into or receive detailed guidance every step of the way. Relatively speaking, coordinating the combined efforts of thousands of termites is every bit as complicated for them as it would be for humans to build a World Trade Center tower. Furthermore, they can complete their task without a visible master plan, several layers of supervision and a paycheck. But seriously, can all of this be simply be brushed aside and dismissed under the heading of "instinct" as some would so conveniently try to do? It is easy to close one's mind to the implications, however, and they are significant. In the end it all comes back to the concept of a "blueprint" and some form of intelligence.

That such blueprints exist is almost impossible to dispute and some have suggested that something like a termite mound, an ant colony or a beehive are each in a way equivalent to a larger complex organism where the individual insects correspond to the individual singular cells of the larger life form, all with their separate functions and purpose. Perhaps so, but that still doesn't answer anything because we are still left without a clear explanation as to where the controlling brain/mind is that makes it all possible. Clearly, something must be in control because, in the final analysis, every last insect in the colony must be in communication with that brain/mind or no individual worker would know when to start, specifically what to do and when to stop and do something else. Each individual has to somehow be in touch, either with the overall plan and the detailed information that determines the final outcome, or, some source that is continually providing them with those details on an ongoing basis as the work proceeds. Then, once the structure is done, something beyond the individual coordinates the overall ongoing activities necessary to keep the structures internal temperature stable so the population as a whole can survive and reproduce. None of this is possible through blind chance alone.

Evolution, however, as presented by its advocates, is purely random and blind. Not that it has to be. But as presently formulated, that is the substance of the theory. That and the survival of the fittest perpetuating force that keeps it going. It is also essentially "mechanical." There is no room in the theory anywhere for such a thing as a "psychic blueprint," or for anything else that lies outside or beyond that which is purely physical. But since this "thing" or phenomenon can be demonstrated to exist and influence the physical world, we have even more proof that the Darwinians are wrong and we must move on and not let them inhibit our thinking. At the same time, since mind can and does influence matter, it only adds to the fact that your thoughts have a definite affect on your own body and its state of being so why not try to take advantage of it on a personal level. And while we are at it, let's see what else can be made of all these other odd, unusual happenings and bits of information which continue to present themselves.

In experiments with the handicapped, totally blind people were given various denominations of paper money, one at a time and asked to state the value. A one dollar bill, a ten, twenty, fifty or one hundred. If the money was new or relatively new, the success rate was no better than pure chance. But, when they were given old bills that had obviously been in service a long time, they had an almost one hundred percent accuracy rate for getting it right. So, if they cannot see, what else could they picking up on except some mental field left behind by those who handled the bills before. Something physically indiscernible but real nonetheless or such things would not be possible.

And then there is something similar to a transfer of energy to physical objects. Eastern Airlines flight 310 crashed in the Everglades in December of 1972 killing the captain and second officer along with 97 others on board. Afterward, a number of assemblies from the wrecked plane were salvaged such as seats, radios, fans, panels, ovens and other components which were then used as replacement parts and reinstalled in three other aircraft of the same type. Shortly after this happened both passengers and crews of these three planes began seeing what were to them, solid apparitions of the captain and second officer who had died in the crashed airplane. Even the passengers who had never met the deceased pair still identified them from photographs. These odd happenings continued until the airline removed all the previously salvaged, crashed plane parts from the aircraft in service and only then did the ghostly visitations end.

Automobile parts, it seems, can also acquire and manifest some dark energy of their own. James Dean, a rising Hollywood star at the time bought a Porsche in 1955, much to the chagrin of a then famous star, Alec Guinness. Guiness was adamant and wanted Dean to get rid of the car before it killed him. A few months later it did. The wreckage was then bought for salvage by Mr. George Barris, who failed to heed the premonition he had gotten when he first looked at the car. Too bad. The first thing the wrecked car did was to slip off the truck it had been loaded on and break his mechanics leg. Secondly the salvaged engine was put into a race car which killed the purchaser the first time on the track. The transmission went into another car which crashed and seriously injured its purchaser in the same race. The body of the car was sold and was to be placed in an exhibit on road safety but the truck hauling it away crashed and killed its driver. Transferred to another truck, the body of the devilish vehicle continued on until some part fell off onto the road and caused another accident and then went on until the brakes failed on the carrier which smashed into a store. Eventually the body of the fatal automobile disappeared off the train in route to Miami, never to be seen again.

Even more noteworthy is the story of the car that Archduke Ferdinand was assassinated in, in 1914. Two weeks after that incident the same car ran over two men and killed the driver when he swerved into a tree. The next owner had four accidents in the car and lost an arm in one of them. It was then sold to a doctor who was crushed to death when it rolled over him. The next owner ended up as a suicide victim in the car and the following purchaser was killed the first time he drove when it ran into a wall. Next the car overturned on a corner and killed its new owner and finally the mechanic who repaired it, along with four friends, were all killed in a collision on the way to a wedding. However one chooses to try and explain such chains of events, if they are just blandly dismissed as coincidence, these are examples of a series of dire events which of course, "could happen," probability wise. Even so, the nature of these events is still so extreme and bizarre they seem to extend far beyond the possibility of chance alone.

Other autos also appear to have minds of their own, too, somewhat similar to those in a Disney cartoon movie. All except for the talking. They start by themselves with no key in the ignition and move down the road or across the parking lot, usually without serious harm to humans. One such auto however, was owned by a Florida woman which was given to her by her husband as a gift. In spite of his good intentions, she still hated the vehicle with a passion. Then one day in a supermarket parking lot the spiteful car, perhaps antagonized by her hatred, started up after she was out of the vehicle, dropped itself into reverse and ran over her, not once or twice but kept circling round and round several times for fifteen full minutes, making sure she was dead.

Besides such accounts of which there are many, it seems train engines often have minds of their own, too. They start by themselves and roll off down the tracks unmanned, sometimes smashing into other trains killing people, sometimes just out for a harmless cruise until boarded and brought to a stop. Vehicles having a mind of their own is one thing but beyond that, returning ghostly experiences for a moment, how is one supposed to account for phone calls from deceased individuals?

In 1987 an Air Force jet crashed into an Indianapolis motel at 9:15 in the morning, instantly killing the ten people in the lobby at the time, one of whom was the switchboard operator, a young man. Later, at 9:40, the phone rang at the man's mother's house just as she was leaving to go to the site after learning about the crash. Answering, she heard her son's voice and asked him if he had been hurt. He told her, no, he was okay, so she told him she and his father would be right there. Later at the site she learned that he had been killed immediately when the plane hit, twenty five minutes before she had received the phone call from him.

Other people claim to have had phone conversations with the dead also and that is one thing. But there are also several cases on record where more than one person has talked to the same deceased individual, minutes or hours after the death.

A NEW BEGINNING

To reiterate, the purpose of this book is not to try and bridge the gap between science and faith, or science and spirit, as some have attempted to do so unsuccessfully in the past by drifting off into mysticism. The purpose of this book is simply one of trying to expand our view of reality. As stated by Michael Talbot in, *Beyond the Quantum*, "we have reached the edge of physical reality as we know it, and still something seems to lie beyond, something we cannot weigh or measure and still seems to have a profound effect on the physical world."

Many examples and expressions of that something have been presented in the previous sections of this book. Something that is going on that has so far been officially denied, overlooked or ignored. There is another reality behind physical reality, a more primary one which appears to bring the physical reality we experience, into being.

As viewed by physicist David Bohm, the reality we experience with the physical senses is a projection of a far more subtle implicate order that exists behind it. Unfortunately, in that regard mainstream science has closed its eyes to important evidence it does not want to officially recognize. Part of the problem is that, for the present at least, there seems to be no way to account for such phenomenon within the bounds of present theory which leaves science with the inability to formulate and incorporate such divergent concepts into the existing framework of reality. Additionally, this extreme hesitancy may be due to the fact that once that door is opened, it brings everything else that has been said about life's origins and purpose into severe question. If humans, animals, plants and all other living creatures all seem to have these other extrasensory abilities and can affect, alter and manipulate physical objects through "power of mind" alone, then what has science missed?

These things are not events that occur outside of

nature. They are not miracles or divinely instigated happenings. They do happen, they are real and they are also a part of nature. A part which is obviously not well understood, but all still a part of the greater reality of existence. Not only does it reinforce the idea and indicate that all of nature has some built-in drive towards creativity, it is also a clear indication of some deep, inherent, behind the scenes form of intelligence which drives everything that exists, something that the blind, mindless, pure random chance explanations of random evolution cannot explain and will never be able to account for since natural selection, the cornerstone of evolutionary theory, is an unintelligent, goal-less and mindless process which does not know the solution in advance. Even the smallest hint of creativity in the chain of evolutionary events thus becomes a frightening prospect to those who have committed themselves to such a non thesis. As for the rest of us, long term we need not worry. Blind, survival-of-the-fittest evolution is still a sterile and unimaginative concept. A house of cards that will eventually collapse because of its own "dead" weight and long term unsupportability. Unfortunately, in the meantime, it has done and continues to do considerable damage in those areas where it has been able to infuse itself into the psyche of the contemporary world.

Many scientists and philosophers who have accepted Darwinian concepts still seem to want to argue for morality, however. But, while convenient, without some deeper, more basic meaning to life, such contentions remain hollow and flawed. <u>Inventing sets of rules to play by has far less influence over the way people live their lives than a set of rules would that was derived from some higher truth.</u> Unfortunately, until that higher truth is understood in more detail, there is little reason to abide by much of anything except self generated presumptions.

For the accepting, religion hands down some very specific mandates. Thou shalt not.... and, thou shalt not .... and .... Some of these make sense in today's world, some do not and, for the most part, are arbitrary, inflictive and overbearing. Instead of providing reasons for following them, at least something more logically compelling than the blind threat of hell-fire and damnation, they are simply empty pronouncements with little real reason to be obeyed. In the end, however, it is always a matter of personal choice. Regardless, the end goal here is to show that life does have a higher meaning and purpose. Not one of servitude to a deity, or one reserved to keeping the gene pool alive, but one of personal fulfillment and spiritual evolvement. Once that is understood, morality and what constitutes constructive choice in that new context can be effectively discussed. Until then they are only careless declarations, entirely subject to individual opinion. To get beyond that impasse it is necessary to extend our present concept of reality into places where both religion and contemporary science in general have thus far refused to go.

While the predominant view point of science is one of a mechanistic, blindly evolving universe, there are still a few dissenters who are beginning to speak out. For example; in the words of Paul Davies, "The universe is revealed in a new, more inspiring light, unfolding from its primitive beginnings and progressing step by step to even more elaborate and complex states," and, "The far reaching philosophical implications of the new physics should not be ignored....the new physics has room for a meaning to existence."

These are cautious statements in their own way but important ones. Other scientists take the risk and also make bold remarks. They say things such as...

"The reason there are similarities between the way we think and the way the universe is logically constructed is because there is some higher intelligence that has done that creation. The massive amount of coincidences that it took bring the universe into existence is an argument for intelligent design, and so on." Sir Fred Hoyle, author of *The Intelligent Universe* states that scientific evidence shows that the universe is governed by some sort of inter-locking intelligences. Take one simple, but not so simple example, a single living cell. The mathematical odds against all the right enzymes coming together which are necessary to create just one single cell in a few billion years are a staggering 10 to the 40,000th power. In other words, it is essentially impossible without some intelligent outside help.

Here, of course, it is most important to realize that that help need not be "God." Most certainly not in the terms that "God" is usually thought of. It could be instead that things in the universe seem to have some inherent built in organizing principal of their own that leads forever towards levels of increasing complexity, a concept that would transform the idea of God into something else entirely. Unfortunately, to say that life appeared on earth through seeding from outer space, as has also been proposed to sidestep that impossibility, really answers nothing either because the entire universe is not old enough to beat the odds and create life somewhere else in space without some kind of striving intelligence behind it to also help things along.

Paul Davies circumvents the concept of intelligent design by providing a different explanation as to how it all might have begun. He writes, "The key to achieving this seeming miracle is *quantum physics*. Quantum processes are *inherently* unpredictable and indeterministic..... In the world of the quantum, spontaneous change is not only permitted, it is unavoidable."

This alone does not explain the bigger picture, however, because the mathematical odds for the creation of a single cell are still the same regardless of the degree of spontaneity that exists in nature unless that spontaneity is something more than purely random. So, when Davies adds the idea that at the fundamental level, things are not only spontaneous, they are also <u>self organizing</u> and that the ability of the physical world to organize itself seems to be a fundamental, and deeply mysterious, property of the universe, it is here that he has hit upon something very important. While Davies restricts himself from saying anything about the source of that power or property, he does say that it seems that nature has a built in creativity all its own which makes it able to produce an ever increasing variety of complex forms and that is one very large step to make.

Taking that idea a little further then, it is this creative power that has either led to intelligence in the universe or, that intelligence was always there right from the beginning and that the creativity that expresses itself in living forms is a direct result of that intelligence. Karl Popper, the philosopher, lends some cautious support to this idea by saying "the greatest riddle of cosmology may well be... that the universe is, in a sense, creative." Likewise, in his book, The *Self-Organizing Universe*, Erich Jantsch presents the idea that nature has a touch of its own free will and is capable of generating novelty, giving it the potential for partial self-determination.

So where does all this lead? Is there a "cosmic blueprint" as Davies asks and explores in his book, *The Cosmic Blueprint,* posing the question without actually answering it? Certainly religionists believe so, as he acknowledges, except they claim that the universe is all part of God's predetermined plan. The difficulty with that view, however, is that if there is a God in that sense, and God already has a plan which is in the process of unfolding, than where in that is there any room for free will, self determination and true creativity? Without that, life is almost as gloomy a prospect as life being a complete accident and without any meaning at all, in which case the individual is either burdened with creating the delusion that life has a purpose and reason or giving up in despair.

This, unfortunately, is the approach taken by Viktor Frankl, the doctor who spent several years in a Nazi concentration camp during World War II and wrote the book,

Man's Search For Meaning, where he elaborates on the view that man's primary motivational force is indeed, his search for meaning. As seen from this text, Frankl was another individual who was willing to accept the stark, "life is an accident," hypothesis of science. Life could have meaning in spite of that, however, he claimed. To have that, though, one had to be willing to reach out and give it one by making life have some intrinsic value solely of its own. This value, or usefulness, when seen in this light, becomes a forced matter wherein functioning for the benefit of society in ways where each person has dignity and value becomes ones only salvation.

Without question, there are those for whom such an aesthetic is quite enough to carry them along and certainly if an individual dedicates their life to becoming of value and service to others, that alone can become very rewarding. Perhaps even sufficient enough to obviate anyone from seeking greater clarification about deeper issues. As for all the rest, that is where trouble begins. In particular for those who do not understand who they are and what they are doing here, the ones who live in a personal philosophical void. All too often they fall prey to misguided ideologies and end up as pawns in the escalating battles of growing religious and political strife. In the extreme they become the ones who blindly shout death to everyone who does not conform to their insane views, brothers and sisters included, and become mankind's greatest enemy in the war for survival.

It is an afflicted situation. The world does not need another religious splinter group. (It is estimated that there are at least ten thousand of those in existence already) Or another pseudo-science of the spirit, or to be further intimidated by limited scientific theories that refuse to look at all those other aspects of the natural world that so many people intuitively know exist. But, until we can get to the point where that side of reality is openly acknowledged and studied in depth, all we can do is to see what other

139

valid conclusions can be drawn from the largely narrative pool of examples previously given and see what develops.

IN THAT REGARD

Here is the thing and it is extraordinary. It is called consciousness. The predominant scientific view chooses to see consciousness as a property that emerges once a certain level of biological brain complexity is reached. On the other end of things, consciousness is seen as the primary reality and source of all being. "Pure consciousness" is said to show itself in all things. Matter and living beings are seen as patterns of divine consciousness. For the mystical minded the claim is made that "true" consciousness is only experienced in non ordinary states of awareness such as meditation or acts of creativity which implies that if you don't meditate or do artistic works you will never be blessed to experience it. Too bad. Regardless, however, being logical, consciousness either shows itself in "all" things or it does not. Choosing to meditate does not in any way elevate one individual above another in some elite way. As for what makes some consciousness "pure" is also very unclear but if the words "pure" and "divine" are deleted from the above definition, then we have something of at least partial importance.

Additionally, concepts of consciousness are further muddied by creating artificial divisions and levels of consciousness. Freud divided the mind up into the conscious and the "unconscious" while Jung added "collective' unconscious to the mix. Others want to pile a collective consciousness and collective mind on top of that. But, because people share certain mental concepts and symbology does not make them collective and universal. As we have seen and shall see, one ability of individual consciousness is to be able to access and communicate with the consciousness of others. That does not make it collective. Furthermore, "unconscious" is a very poor choice of words for describing certain parts of the brain/mind. Subconscious is far more appropriate. Everything mental is somehow available and accessible no matter what else

141

may be piled on top of it. Conscious attention shifts constantly. What is aware in the "mind" at one moment slides into the subconscious at the next, replaced by something else again, on and on. As for deciding what "mind" really is, that too, can lead to controversy.

The most limited and unimaginative but rather prevalent definition of mind is the one that states that mind is the pattern of organization exhibited by the brain, another non-statement to be sure. Regardless, Darwinian biologists, neuro scientists and others are very adamant about that without realizing how narrow the concept is and how such a definition is incapable of explaining anything but the very minimal aspects of biological function. For those living things which have one, the brain is in control of the autonomic nervous system which regulates the involuntary actions of the heart, lungs, glands and digestive system, along with a whole range of other vital functions that maintain life on the basic level. But then, lodged somewhere in the brain, there is also a built in store of information called instinct. And what else could instinct be but an acquired body of data obtained through trial and error survival history and stored in the genes? Instinctive or otherwise, added to that there is also the drive to reproduce. Where does that come from?

Cell division alone does nothing to increase the chances for survival of the cell that somehow divided, and having offspring does nothing to further the immediate survival of the individual. It does, in fact, decrease the offspring bearer's chances during gestation. Out of this then comes the very limited concept that the only purpose of reproduction is to pass on information. Cells die, genes die, plants and animals die but as long as there is reproduction, the information survives. And with this thought in mind it is easy to sink into the intellectual trap which leads to the conclusion that the only reason and purpose the entirety of life has is to insure the survival of the information contained in the genes.

Of necessity, such an argument implies purpose which then defeats the entire concept of randomness, a major cornerstone of present evolutionary theory. To what purpose? If this is what it is all about then information, in and of itself, must not only have a life of its own, it must also have motivation and need, along with a high level of intelligence behind it to have so cleverly invented such an extremely complicated, self centered survival scheme. Above all, somewhere in there it also becomes necessary to conceptualize, to realize that there is not only just a "now" but also a future. Without some concept of "future," there can be no drive to survive. And then, piled on top of all that, the proponents of such a view still ask us to believe that it all happened by accident. Apparently ingenious as genes had to have been and must be to have come this far, the question is still, what is the point?

If it is as they say and genes by themselves are so smart and selfish and the only thing of importance in the entire universe is the survival of the gene, how did that come about? Brainless genes exhibiting intelligence, making value assessments by deciding that it is somehow important for them to survive at all costs and coming up with the will power and determination to survive in a meaningless universe, sounds like instinctive meaninglessness. What level of complexity did it take to make them intelligent enough to find a way to perpetuate, but not bright enough to see the pointlessness of it. And what level of complexity does it take before some conglomeration of molecules develops the "instinct" for survival? And if living is meaningless to begin with, why would anything of any level of complexity even care if it survived or not? It wouldn't, so what is being overlooked here? Regardless of how it is approached it still seems clear that genes, like everything else, are also a part of a much larger scheme? A much larger scheme wherein everything cooperates with everything else on the fundamental level so that the entirety of creation can seek growth and fulfillment. Ultimately it comes back to a much more expansive concept of "mind" that extends beyond the simplistic notion that *mind is nothing more than the pattern of organization exhibited by the brain.*

Researchers have been studying the excised brains of well known individuals like Walt Whitman and Albert Einstein for years, measuring dimensions, counting cells, looking at the structure, clearly believing that the answers to all their questions lie somewhere in the physical makeup of this organ. To date, however, what they have discovered is essentially nothing of significance regarding genius or character because they are stuck with the conviction that electro-physical-chemistry can explain everything. That does not mean that some nineteenth century scientists were literally correct when they declared that a vital force or eternal soul was responsible for thoughts and the thinking process but they were certainly more correct than the "meat machine" advocates of toady. Until it is recognized that no matter how much brain scan data is collected and no matter what the level of resolution, brain function will never be satisfactorily explained until it is understood that the "mind" also exists and is in addition to the brain.

The most senseless thing one can do is to cut off someone's head immediately after death and preserve it in liquid nitrogen, thinking that at some later date, when the technology for doing so exists, a new body can be cloned, a transplant undergone and the person gets to live again. This mentality reflects some grand misconceptions as to what life is all about and what makes living things alive to begin with, which in turn leads to an exaggerated fear of death. It begins by assuming that there is nothing more to life than brain cells and that the information stored in brain cells is the entire source of being and defines both one's mind and essence. Bottom line, you are nothing but a stack of data. But you can't just preserve the DNA because all that will get you is another human body. One with a brain, of course. But a brain without the information accumulated from the life just lived, so that won't work because the original identity is lost.

It is easy to see where such arguments come from, however. Some species of frogs, for example, along with other creatures, crawl down into the mud in the fall of the year and become frozen solid in winter and would be declared clinically dead upon examination, only to return to life when the temperature rises. So, is being in a complete state of stasis the same as being dead? Apparently not. Such things also happen in the plant world and in the world of microbes but most people don't consider them to be alive in the sense that primates and humans are. But still, let us not forget that plants and other lower life forms which don't even have brains at all, are fully capable of responding dramatically to human thought via some link as yet undiscovered and undefined. All in all, even though it is repetitive to say, there is beyond a doubt, another dimension to reality entirely. A dimension that would support the concept of "mind" being something that exists independently of "brain" or physical form.

Mind is where the blueprints really exist for physical form, brain included if the life form has one and it is not necessary to quote the unitarity principle of quantum physics which says that information is never lost, therefore you, we, everything is eternal. There is already enough evidence to show that even though the body has mortality, the person, the identity, the consciousness and mind continue to live with eternal validity, independent of the physical body and the brain. What happens from the molecular level on up is one immense cooperative effort on the part of everything that physically exists to manifest in physical form at one level or another in a creative effort to expand its awareness and spiritual growth.

Consciousness as we know it does not come into being because the brain has expanded to some tipping point collection of cell complexity. It already exists in its own greater reality, seeking its own fulfillment. And, as we have seen when expressed in the physical world, among other things it has the ability to react with and influence physical matter. Reading between the lines, that ability should lead one to believe that physical matter must also has some degree of awareness in order to respond to thought. As, physicist, Freeman Dyson said, ... mind is already inherent in every electron, and the processes of human consciousness differ only in degree but not in kind from the processes of choice between quantum states which we call "chance" when they are made by electrons. Sir James Jeans stated, "Mind no longer appears as an accidental intruder into the realm of matter; we are beginning to suspect that we ought to hail it as the creator and governor of the realm of matter..."

John Eccles and Karl Popper both say that man has an intangible spirit or mind that controls his brain and Eccles sees a creative source or outside intelligence as the driving force behind human action. Aldous Huxley stated that consciousness is the fundamental building block of the universe and the world is more like a great thought than a machine. Nobel prize winner, Ilya Prigogine said that "this is the heart of the message.... Matter is not inert. It is alive and active." Going a step further a report prepared for the House of Representatives, Science and Technology Committee stated that recent experiments in parapsychology "suggest that there exists an interconnectiveness of the human mind with other minds and with matter, the effects of which could have far reaching social and political implications."

Alfred Russel Wallace, the Englishman who should have gotten credit for the theory of evolution, the same individual who later disavowed its truth, felt that it was "utterly inconceivable" that man's spirituality could have been a result of natural selection and that the highest extension of the mind was man's ethics and morality. Two of

Darwin's closest friends, Lyell and Hooker, who were also great scientists at the time, fully agreed with Wallace in regard to there being an outside agency or "superior intelligence" which guided the development of mankind. Lyell also favored the idea of a "designer" in the bigger scheme of things.

As additionally pointed out by Paul Davies and others, matter most certainly has some level of spontaneity and organization ability, both on the atomic level and the organic level. This would mean it has some level of awareness and poses the question. If something has awareness, how could it have awareness of things beyond itself without having an awareness of self? Can it have one without the other? It is another important question.

Coming back around we return to those major misconceptions regarding thought, reason, memory and other associated functions. The misconception that the brain and the mind are one and the same. While there is the physical brain, there is also the mind. The mathematician and friend of Albert Einstein, Kurt Godel, believed that mind was something separate from matter. John Bell of Bell's theorem said that beyond the brain is the mind. Seth, through Jane Roberts stated that "the brain organizes activity and translates events, but it does not initiate them. Events have an electromagnetic reality that is then projected onto the brain for physical activation. Your instruments only pick up certain levels of the brain's activity. They do not perceive the mind's activity at all, except as it is imprinted on the brain."

Regarding John Bell, he also said that the real world is immersed in and inter penetrated by a more basic reality that is invisible and non local. David Bohm stated that "there is a similarity between thought and matter. All matter... is determined by 'information.' Information is what determines space and time and that even the electron has proto intelligence."

Following this, intelligence would imply awareness or some degree of consciousness. And if something as basic as an electron has some level of intelligence, then so must atoms and molecules and everything else otherwise considered to be physical. On the macro scale, this would include all the planets, the stars, dark matter and all the rest and would mean that in the "Ghia" sense, planet earth is itself alive and aware. As to what else may be going on in the universe, it is literally beyond human comprehension but that doesn't mean we shouldn't stop and take a look at the night sky once in a while.

Coming back to earth, however, on the other end of the scale, it would seem there might be some complicating factors, conceptually speaking, at the bottom of it all. In that regard let's come back to electrons. First, electrons, like quanta of light, seem to have no real physical size. If so, how can something without physical size have a quality of awareness associated with it? But even if it did have measurable size, like protons and other particles, what happens when these particles turn ambiguous and behave entirely as dispersed waves instead, without physical component, which makes it seem that particles have the ability to be in two or more different places at the same time? Where does the awareness or intelligence that might be associated with something physical go when particles are exhibiting themselves as waves and do not have a specific location in space? Where also is the mind, spirit or soul of a deceased person located so that it can communicate with living beings in the physical world while being physically invisible and otherwise undetectable? Why can the clinically dead person, whose body is on the operating table, be able to look down on the scene and see and hear what the medical staff is saying and doing while none of them are able to see that hovering entity in return?

According to the skeptical, it couldn't be that living humans have an extremely limited range of perception, physically speaking. Appropriately, that part of it doesn't even seem to occur to them and they feel fully justified in saying that because they haven't, or can't, personally see or sense something, it therefore does not exist. In the least, by doing so they are overlooking the fact that there are a multitude of other creatures on the planet who can see, hear, smell, feel and taste things that are far beyond the range of human sensitivity and are obviously aware of a whole list of things humans aren't, including, according to some, the presence of none visual beings in the room. In this regard, some children have invisible playmates. That's the way parents describe them at least, which means that the parents believe they are pure figments of the child's imagination and otherwise non existent. But instead of trying to cajole the child into giving up such nonsense, ask the child to expand on their experience instead and what do you get? Or, ask an adult who can clearly recapture those experiences. It's a different story entirely.

Continuing, however, is consciousness a prerequisite for intelligence or are they different degrees of the same thing? Certainly not in the machine sense where computers display "artificial intelligence," something which is not intelligent at all in the strict sense of the word. But still, while the individual particles that make up a machine on the macro scale all have their separate intelligences and awareness, can they and do they combine in such a way as to become a "gestalt" wherein the whole is greater than the some of its parts? If so, then what level of complexity is required for a gestalt to gain the ability to become proactive instead of just reactive? What about the automobile that started by itself and ran over the owner who hated it? Some unfortunate coincidence that was, huh? Or, does a gestalt that results from being an automobile also have feelings and is it capable of volition?

While it doesn't mean that one has to have a love affair with their car or truck as some men do who give the thing more attention than they do their wives, the moral of the story might still be to at least remain neutral about that part of it. And, going a little further, what about the other implications of mind over matter? Can private expectations influence how long and how well one's vehicle will keep operating? Can you at least get it to stop dripping oil on the garage floor? And how many people have ever had a computer that they had best leave alone when they were in a foul mood so it didn't keep crashing or do unkind things to the work in progress?

"Mind" alone, as the singular driving force can, as we have seen, directly affect decay rates of isotopes, heat metal and a wide range of others things. Not just the minds of humans but the minds of cats and other critters can do this too. So, while it may be of different levels and complexities, mind is mind in a universal way and would also seem to be an underlying characteristic of the universe.

Some egocentric individuals claim, however, that only humans are blessed with consciousness and contribute all of the rest of animal and plant life to hard wired, instinctive behavior. A few also seem to believe that even humans are caught in the same trap, one of whom appears to be Stephen Hawking who has a reputation for espousing the dismal. But if that is true, where does the spontaneity and drive towards greater complexity as put forth by Paul Davies and others come from? There is a difference between randomness and spontaneity and to say that spontaneity is a hard wired characteristic of everything from particles to people, violates reason. Putting that aside, however, let's get back to human consciousness.

Human consciousness as used herein has, as a minimum, mobility. It can be projected elsewhere by its possessor. It also has the ability to remotely access information on levels that are not provided by the normal five bodily senses. This information can be from the present as well as from the past and the future. It is not restricted by time which should also be providing us with some serious clues as to the structure of time itself. What it is, and is not.

P.C.W. Davies pointed out that no physical experiment has ever been performed that detects the passage of time. Flowing time is not a quality of the world itself, but a psychological illusion and Einstein said that; "for us believing physicists, the distinction between past, present and future is only an illusion, even if a stubborn one." And, in looking at all the major equations of physics from Newton to Maxwell to Einstein, they are all symmetrical in time. Factoring in the outcome of the famous "Aspect" experiment along with the studies of Helmut Schmidt which show that the past can be changed from a position in the present, there should be no reason to be surprised at the ability of consciousness to transcend time and navigate through it.

Additionally, if the past is not fixed and immutable, then how could physicists from the Stephen Hawking school of thought ever hope to calculate backward to the beginning of time in terms of the "Big Bang" and thereby create a "theory of everything" that is meaningful? They could not. Furthermore, there cannot be a theory of everything until 'everything' is at first recognized. That includes the phenomenon of consciousness, the implications of which are profound. The many attributes of consciousness are not only every bit as real as everything else in the physical world, they extend far beyond the limitations of that world into a greater, much less understood reality as yet largely unexplored.

Regardless of all else, it can be stated that science will not have a clear interpretation of reality until it can develop laws which explain the ability of the consciousness of one living thing to communicate with another and to have observable interactions with matter. As for the rest of the population, they must lift concepts of consciousness out the realm of the eerie supernatural, the weird and paranormal and learn to integ-

rate the idea into everyday life that consciousness and its ability to react with matter is a fundamental characteristic of the universe. Beyond that it appears that everything has some minimal level of awareness and exhibits attributes of consciousness, making consciousness an all pervading truth about the universe.

Mind over matter violates present laws of physics but since mind can directly influence matter only means that the present laws are in error and incomplete.

"The universe is, and you can pick your terms, a spiritual or mental or psychological manifestation and not an objective manifestation. There is presently no science, religion, or psychology that comes close to even approaching a conceptual framework that could explain, or even indirectly describe the dimensions of that kind of universe. Its properties are psychological, following the logic of the psyche, and all of the physical properties that you understand are reflections of those deeper characteristics. Again, each atom and molecule-and any particle that you can imagine-possesses and would possess, a consciousness. That idea must be the basis for any new scientific theories that hope to achieve any success at all and lead to an acquisition of true knowledge." Seth

After all, if a woman can create a visible ghost with its own budding personality and a group of people can create an invisible entity capable of communicating and moving heavy tables around by itself, what else should that be telling us about the abilities of the human mind to create and how limited our thinking is in that regard, especially when it comes to self.

All humans receive and deal with psychic information all the time. The difficulty is in learning to listen, recognize and bring it up to the conscious level so it can be utilized. As to how all this is possible, we can only speculate, since for most people it is a very poorly developed ability. However, if one person can pick up on the thoughts of another or send information to them, then this occurs somehow. On the quantum level everything is claimed to have an electromagnetic reality. Although not interpreted in those terms, that reality still exists on the macro level. So where is ESP in the electromagnetic spectrum? Or is there still another form of energy and energy transmission that is as yet undiscovered? Whatever it is, it is there somewhere and saying it one more time, just because present technology doesn't have the capability to sense it, that does not mean it does not exist. Regardless of all else, there is a lot more going on than much of contemporary science and a large number of skeptics would like to admit.

By analogy, if we accept the view of the world as postulated by those members of the scientific community, the main line physicists and the Darwinians, we have what amounts to a flat, two dimensional, very cold and barren landscape. But if we add the attributes of consciousness to the mix, then suddenly we have mountains and valleys and rivers and trees and flowers and all the rest. Then if we acknowledge that the so-called "dead" come through on rare occasions, showing their presence in the physical world, that thought expands outwardly with vast implications. Clearly life has a far greater meaning than the one mainstream scientific starkness has restricted it to. It has an immense complexity and depth and a spontaneity that constantly expresses itself, over and over in the beauty of creation, making it clear that behind the physical reality we often make the mistake of limiting ourselves to, lies a far greater reality. One which brings a higher meaning and purpose to everything from the sub atomic particle on up to the vastly complex things that can be created from those particles. Or waves, or energy fields, or however one chooses to describe them.

No matter what, however, regardless of all else, there will still be the eternal pessimist who may reluctantly acknowledge these things to be true, but still.... Maybe there is a cosmic blueprint, maybe there is more behind the scenes than we previously acknowledged but what does that prove? Maybe, once we understand it better, maybe we will still discover that, that too, had an accidental beginning? What can be said to that? Not much. Some people are determined to be miserable no matter what, and end up having missed some of the greatest gifts life could have bestowed on them along the way because **beliefs about the nature of reality limit the believer's ability to see, participate in and understand that reality.**

But, letting that go and getting back to consciousness, it can be said that imagination and curiosity are also characteristics of it. So, too, are varying levels of spontaneity and creativity. Motivated by curiosity, the imagination can travel anywhere within or beyond the universe. Imagination is not bounded, consciousness is not bounded. Likewise, consciousness is not a singular thing. It is in one sense, a phenomenon. It is more than awareness. It is also more than likely a characteristic of something else. Consciousness implies freedom of choice, intelligence, memory and a desire to express itself. Beyond that it is somewhat impossible to describe, if for no other reason than because of the limitations of the thought process and the inability to achieve an undistracted objectivity when trying to do so. Nevertheless, realize that there are literally an endless, ongoing series of possibilities in regard to creativity, innovation, invention and change in almost every aspect of human involvement. But it goes beyond that......

Since consciousness is the source, not only of inventiveness, but of the universe itself, then there must be an essentially infinite variety in the types, levels, intensities, groupings and complexities of consciousness, all with their own kinds of awareness, attitudes, desires, motivations, comprehension and sets of rules which apply where they choose to manifest. If for no other reason, these conclusions are a fallout of the tenets of physics which acknowledge sub atomic particle awareness.

Even on the physical plane, however, there is more than one set of rules. The physical body does not appear able to walk through walls. The individual in the out-of-body state, however, while still consciously retaining an awareness of the wall, moves as effortlessly through it as light through a window. The body, meanwhile, left behind, continues to function and maintain, preserving its integrity and revives when the consciousness returns. And once returned, the consciousness is sometimes quite able to get the body to do things under extreme situations which far exceed its normal performance ability. In one documented situation previously cited an individual was able to survive several hours submerged in near freezing water without hypothermic death or permanent side effects. He did so merely through a change in mental focus. What must it be like to be a polar bear? Here, where the only thing that kept him alive was his state-of-mind, another set of rules had to have come into play. Ordinary people in the right state of mind can walk barefooted on hot coals, others are capable of tremendous feats of strength and endurance under drastic circumstances, defy all the odds and go way beyond what are considered to be normal limitations of the physical body. This being the case, then perhaps when some other individual completely believes he can walk through the wall in his physical body without harm, he will be able to do so.

To continue with consciousness, however, everything that has consciousness must of necessity be aware of its own individuality to some lessor or greater extent, as well as have some awareness of its participation in the bigger scheme of things. There is identity. Using humans as an example, there are many kinds and levels of consciousness necessary for our lives, all involved in a great cooperative scheme. If not, life would be impossible. As a minimum, there is the awareness of the sub atomic particle, then molecular consciousness. Of much greater complexity is cellular consciousness. Cells, in turn, combine in specialized ways to form organs and other bodily components, obviously all in communication and cooperation with each other in ways that exceed the limitations of biology alone. This suggests a body consciousness forming around them like a complex electromagnetic field to take command and bring about the desires of the body as a whole, as motivated by our own consciousness. This level of consciousness which is akin to identity, is a characteristic of all life forms, plant and animal.

The idea that the identity consciousness does have mobility and can indeed leave the body under certain conditions is not a new premise but a very old one that has only recently been rediscovered by some members of the medical profession. If correct, then consciousness (in this case, the identity consciousness), while it may appear to reside in the body for the most part, is something separate from the body. It can also be referred to as simply "the consciousness," the mind, the psyche, the spirit, or maybe even the soul, if one prefers. Whatever it is, it is the essence of us and what this mobility points out is that there is full awareness in terms of sight and sound along with memory, in or out of the body. And after death.

In the near-death situation the identity consciousness returns to the body after the body has been resuscitated by the medically adroit and continues to dwell there. In other cases where the body has been revived but the consciousness has left and not yet returned, the person is in a state of coma, with just the body consciousness in charge. If the identity consciousness returns, the person revives more completely, even though they may now be limited in function due to injuries that may have been sustained. If they lost their legs in an accident, they will no longer be able to walk. If certain levels of brain damage have occurred, they may be limited in other physical areas, but not because the mind is no longer intact. It is. As with a computerized control system where damage has occurred to the interface circuitry between the computer and the device it controls. The operating system is still intact but the mechanism is no longer able to carry out its purpose because the hardware has been damaged.

If the body does not survive, or more likely, the higher identity consciousness does not want it to, this consciousness departs the body and continues on with the rest of its more eternal journey; quite possibly to return in a brand new body to start over and learn another set of earthly lessons somewhere else. Whatever the full extent of this phenomenon, there is one reassuring thing about it and that is that dead is not dead after all, as many might worry. Dying is but a transition. Alive, the body adheres to a psychically imposed pattern or mental blueprint and a set of rules it must abide by while living. Even though the material that the body is composed of changes constantly, the pattern maintains its own dynamic integrity. If it did not then there would be no body. It would not have a cycle of growth and it would not be able to maintain itself or to heal itself along the way when injured. While the form itself exists in the space-time continuum, the pattern for it exists outside of that framework - THE BODY IS A PROJECTION, THEREFORE, INTO THE THREE DIMENSIONAL FIELD. Illusion, perhaps, but much more than holographic. And as for those transcendent blueprints, where did they come from to begin with, one might properly ask.

From God, many will answer because God created man in his own image, they will proclaim, which is still a better answer than saying it was all a monstrous accident. But still, looking around, seriously.... Well, God certainly has an endless imagination and a sense of humor both and there is certainly some solace in that, if that is the way it happened. But what else could it be since it should be clear by now that there is far more to the story than accidental, random mutation and natural selection? Perhaps we each had a hand in the creation of our own blueprints. Of course in doing so, there had to be some over riding guidelines. First, all the raw material the body is to be constructed of must come from planet earth and once in existence it must be able to sustain itself from that which is environmentally available. The creating entity, you, me, us, must also accept the life/death cycle imposed on the situation going in, hopefully understanding the necessity of it, along with all the other implications of being "human."

Having said this, the reader is left to follow this chain of thought alone. Or not, as the choice may be. If done, it would be of value to remember the fact that mind can influence matter, therefore, once the body is in existence on the physical plane, the owner of that body has some control over the physical makeup and operation of that body while it is alive, probably a lot more than most people recognize or are willing to accept. If we had a hand in the blueprint to begin with, then surely we also have some ability to make changes to it, providing they fall within the limitations of physical existence.

Unfortunately, for far too many people who are either unaware of evidence to the contrary or simply don't want to acknowledge it, they are saddled with the idea that when the body dies, they die and dead is dead. There is nothing beyond that. Therefore, for those who insist that that is the way it is but aren't very happy about it, they speculate that if we can learn to preserve the body through some non degenerative process, we then stand a good chance of being revived at a later date, to live again. Or, as previously cited, another school of thought even goes so far as to say, why spend money trying to freeze and preserve the entire human, just cut off the head and preserve that. In the meantime, other old ideas continue to prevail. The body, when seen as some kind of living machine, becomes weaker with time, slows down, gradually wears out and eventually begins to fall apart. This includes the brain and the mental faculties. Or do they?

Suppose that as a youth you had purchased a new automobile that had appealed to you - say, for example, a 1968 Ford Mustang. Then you were involved in an accident and the entire front end had to be replaced; bumper, grill, radiator, fenders, hood, wheels and other associated parts. Next, someone rear ended the vehicle. More parts were replaced. Later, the engine wore out and was exchanged, along with the transmission, tires, brakes, hoses, seats, and more. To carry the analogy further, suppose that eventually every part on the car was at some time replaced and that the car you still possessed no longer contained even one simple component that it had when it left the factory, not a single screw, bolt or washer. Assume also that each new part added was manufactured at some date later than the original, stretching out over the years. Now the dilemma. The car still looks like a 1968 Mustang and according to the Motor Vehicle Department it still is. But is it, really? If not, what then? A later day replica of itself that still conforms to the original blueprints!

As humans would repair the cars they drive, so too does the human body renew itself. A portion of our nutritional intake provides fuel to the muscles and brain so we are able to carry out the tasks of living while the rest is used to repair and replace. In the process our blood and body chemistry goes through profound change. Every day cells die by the millions as new ones are generated to take their place, new ones that somehow evolve from the food we eat, transformed into something living which is every bit as much a part of us as was that which had been replicated. The skin, in particular, is regenerated at a prodigious rate. So is the blood, the liver, the spleen and other vital organs. Thus, within a period said to be about every seven years, every last atom and molecule and cell in our whole being has been replaced at least once and, for some parts, much more often. So, like the hypothetical automobile just a few short years later, we have a 1968 model, John or Jane Doe, only now the being is no longer hypothetical. It is real, it is us. And a strange us it is.

Every second, every minute and every hour of every day we slough and shed. If we should somehow live to be fifty or more, it is at least the seventh new "us" we have had in a row.

Either way, the question must still be asked. If "we," as living beings, are our bodies but we no longer have even one original atom or molecule left in our bodies or one single cell remaining alive from the beginning, then who or what are we but an ever changing, self duplicating replica of ourselves? And wherein lies the master set of blueprints for that accomplishment. In the genes? Maybe, but only partially because there are some major discrepancies with that idea also. And what exactly is the aging process if we are constantly being renewed? Is it nothing but another illusion, the appearance of change superimposed on a physical structure composed of elemental particles that are themselves all billions of years old which eternally rearrange themselves, over and over again. In spite of that, however, the thing of most importance is that in the period of one human lifetime, our own memories, feelings and emotions all persist and appear to be consistent in their own evolution, even though they all began in brain cells long since dead and disappeared.

Then, as if that isn't confusing enough, consider that the atoms and molecules themselves are not solid chunks of matter at all but are at least 99.999 % pure empty space. Relatively speaking, the nucleus of an atom is equivalent in size to a ping pong ball in the center of a football field with the electrons moving around it out at the ends of the field with nothing but void in between. Then further consider the idea that the protons, neutrons, electrons and other basic particles of the atom may not be particles at all but simply the wave phenomenon of a complex energy field and then what do we have? What exactly is the essence of "Us" after these considerations? What is the "I" that is me and the "you" that is you?

Although it may appear a little absurd at this point, the biologist, of course, will still argue that as long as the same synaptic connections are continued in the renewal process of the brain, regardless of what the deep physics of the brain may be, that there is no problem. If this be the case then "we" (our identity) is nothing more than a series of interconnected electro-chemical conductors inside our skulls, a complex set of biological wires that are constantly being replaced with the instructions for doing so buried in the DNA of each cell, faithfully replicated. Yet every cell, we are told, has the same DNA and, therefore, the same potential to be any one of the other many hundreds of different kinds of highly specialized cells elsewhere in the body. If so, why do we never find skin cells in the brain or brain cells in the gall bladder or liver cells in the big toe? To control things on this level we are forced to again come back to the idea there has to be a higher generation of blueprints. And again, where is such a master plan hidden? Somewhere in there, we are assured, evolved out of the great accidental happening that once crawled out of the muck and became us, in there in the baffling chemistry of things. Perhaps so, but another difficulty still remains.

As stated, the bio-chemical approach to life must, of necessity, postulate that consciousness can only arise out of a collection of interrelated brain cells. But just what the magic number might be to create this threshold effect has never been scientifically verified, however. How could it be in a world where one school of psychologists argues that animals are not even conscious at all. Purely instinct driven meat machines, they have no self awareness because, if you put a mirror in front of them, they do

161

not look in it and act as if they recognize themselves.

Perhaps what the animal does not have instead, is an inflated ego. Maybe its attitude is that it sees what it knows to be a counterfeit reflection, so why be concerned about it. Just because it does not make faces at itself or try to groom itself in some self centered way does not mean that it is not aware of itself. Sounding like a biblical tale, this great honor has been reserved solely for humans. Humans who do not wish to acknowledge that any creature that has an awareness of any other creature must also have an awareness of self in order to do that. The antelope does not always run from the lion, only when he knows the lion is hungry, which in addition to instinct, requires judgment and awareness. If anyone should still have any remaining doubts about the matter they need only ask anyone who has ever had more than a superficial relationship with a pet, be it dog, cat, monkey, mouse or goat.

Beyond that and back to humans, a reminder. You are not a physical being who has a soul. You do not have a soul. Instead you are primarily your so-called soul and you have a body and with that we come to the subject of reincarnation.

Even though the concept of reincarnation may defy the logical skepticism of some people, belief in life after death has been almost universal since the earliest of times. Still a tenet of many major religions today, reincarnation was also a part of Christian thinking in its beginnings. Lots of people, including many who were famous, believed or believe in reincarnation, along with the Dali Lama and his followers as well as millions of Hindus and others around the world. Still, as we know, that alone proves nothing and does not make it true. There are cases on record, however, which defy other explanations.

When General Patton went to Africa in World War II without ever having been there before in this life, he knew the locations of towns, oasies and other landmarks that lay off in the distance out of sight that did not exist on the maps available at the time. Another of the best documented reincarnational experiences is that of writer Tim Stewart and his wife, with whom he reunited in a later life. Under hypnosis, Stewart became aware of his former self, William Max, killed in the war in 1942. He was able to go back to Max's home town in Pennsylvania, knew the landmarks, the history, his former relatives and friends, all in great detail. He also knew what happened in England where he was stationed in the war. It is an astounding story, one we are beginning to hear more and more. Even so, if one chooses to discount or deny reincarnation as an explanation, these events still go far beyond the possibility of just coincidence. One could not coincidentally make up a story like this that could be validated so accurately. The details had to come from somewhere. If they did not come directly from some larger pool of personal past memory that these individuals were able to access, then, in the least they would imply an unusual psychic ability to access the information through both space and time of someone else's life. Either way, either explanation goes beyond the limited concept of reality held by the skeptical. At the same time, however, there is still a need for a word of caution.

Many hypnotists will do a past life regression for others, for a fee, of course. They will attempt to lead the subject back through time into a past life while under hypnosis. Because hypnosis is a state of narrowed focus and high suggestibility, however, the subject is somewhat vulnerable and in a situation that could easily become fraudulent.

Not so long ago therapists went through a period of doing childhood regressions in an attempt to recover early life memory and trauma and created an immense scandal in the field. Leading the patient back, the wrong question, the smallest hint or suggestion, the subject trying to be co-operative and helpful, along with a therapist with the wrong, pre-imagined diagnosis to begin with and very

quickly there were wild accusations of childhood molesta-
tions. Fathers, grandfathers, uncles and friends of the family had taken advantage of the child. This is not to say that
such things don't happen. They do and the proportions are
disgusting but not every person in therapy is there because molestation put them there. Regardless, at the time
some large scale scandals were created by inept counselors and it is a fact that a hypnotist can easily lead
people to create an imaginative reincarnational history. So
can living in a New Age community. Having lived in one
for several years I met a number of women who all insisted they had all been Cleopatra in a past life. Or an
English queen, even a Mary Magdelon or someone else of
elevated importance but never a housewife or other ordinary citizen and none of it verifiable , even in a minor way.
These are the things that muddy the waters and cause
more serious minded people to scoff and summarily dismiss the entire subject without further investigation. That
does not change the fact that there are cases that stand up
under scrutiny, however, and indicates that the subject deserves further investigation.

When considered in the larger view, one human life
span is an extremely short period of time. Each individual,
regardless of who they are, is also limited to viewing life
from one unique perspective. Their own. Although individuals can gain understanding and feel compassion for
their fellow humans, one person's life is not another's and
another person's experience is at best, second hand to
one's own, with different rewards and consequences. It is
the story of the white man who dyed his skin and went to
live in the ghetto so he could find out what being black
was like under those circumstances. But it is not the same.
Underneath he was still white and he could get up
and leave any time he wanted. He wasn't truly black and
he wasn't trapped there until he died and that is far different. The only way he could really have known what it was

like would have been for him to really have been black under those conditions. In a broader perspective and regardless of the length of a person's life, what they might have been exposed to in a single life time is but one word on one page of one book in the entire library of Congress in terms of the all the separate possibilities one might have been born into instead. And, considering that it is scientifically clear that all of life has a built in spontaneity and drive towards greater complexity, which is the more reasonable prospect? That we are given one life and one only and then the light goes out and we are totally and forever extinguished, or that we live one single life and then spend the rest of eternity trapped in the limbo of heaven or hell, or it is a much larger narrative with a far greater purpose wherein we can return over and over as many times as we choose, always into a new situation to help expand our view of life and the universe.

With this as part of some more multifaceted picture, the individual or entity can now directly witness and feel what it would be like in the extremes of rich and poor, prejudice, hatred, peace and tranquility, the horrors of war, male and female, good health or deformity, this human race or that one and much, much more. The opportunity is endless. It also has to be optional. If it were not then there would have to be some equivalent of God somewhere taking notes, making mandatory assignments, judging progress and handing out demerits for poor performance. Some feel this must be the case, however, because they have invented "Karma." Their attitude is that if you don't get it right in any one life time, you carry this burden with you, over into the next life and have to keep repeating things until you graduate and are allowed to move on. This concept of karma buys into the, "man is a flawed being and needs to be punished," negativity of religion. It also implies that "suffering is good for the soul."

What they fail to understand is bi fold. First, that little is learned without making mistakes. At least not as well and much sooner forgotten than if there were consequences to one's actions. Of course, some are slow learners and do things the hard way, regardless. Like marrying over and over again repeatedly. Either stubbornly picking the same worst type of person possible for them to be with or refusing to look closely enough at themselves to see that they are impossible to be with themselves and shouldn't be marrying anyone until they have gotten their own behavior under control, which brings us to the second item. The real lesson to be learned from suffering is that it is almost always somehow self imposed and largely unnecessary, something most people would probably disagree with. All too often they see themselves as victims trapped in their personal situation and fail to see that there are always options. Sometimes very few and very difficult, but there nevertheless. Inertia, fear, lack of imagination and laziness keep them where there are and the trap is self imposed.

Yes, but what about the innocent victims of war? Are they not put upon? Why would anyone choose to be born into such a hellish, hazardous situation? That would seem to be completely senseless. But then, why not? Perhaps they were the oppressor in some previous existence or they want to witness the horror first hand so they can go on to work against it later. And as for those who voluntarily choose to pick up weapons and go off to engage in battle, well, it may just be some misguided search for glory only to find that none exists, or, it may just be some display of madness. For the newborn coming in, it is always a personal agenda and a do-it-yourself project. One's life is subject to being part of some predetermined master plan but the plan that exists is self generated. Unfortunately, there are few guiding hands along the way, no student counselors, no score keepers and some become lost in the process. It doesn't have to be that way, however.

If there were greater understanding as to why we are here to begin with, that would certainly help. As stated previously, life does not come with a book of ultimate truth. But still, maybe that too is one more reason we are here. To face the multitude of challenges and help write it in the process.

Whatever happens, whatever we individually choose to do, it is all about choices freely made. A person can also choose to "opt out" on their life somewhere along the way if they get severely side tracked, choosing disease, accident or suicide to short circuit the process. Again, free will decides so, not only does one chose their parents through prior mutual agreement but they also accept the place and country of the parents to be born into. And, yes, the time period.

While astounding at first conception, the theory of relativity seems to be one of the more fundamental truths of the physical universe. Time wise, everything is relative to everything else. Jump in a spacecraft, travel fast enough and you can land somewhere in the future. And if you could attain a velocity approaching the speed of light relative to the location you took off from, you could end up far into the future of what you left behind, but, still in your own present. So, let's say that not only did you take off from some specific geographical location on earth but also came back and landed at the same exact place in the future. If then, in doing so, that same place was actually still in existence to land on, then thinking that through, that could only mean that the future already existed.

Without doing all the calculations let's say, for example, that relative to his departure time, the space traveler was only gone a few years of his own time but was traveling fast enough to carry himself many decades away in the future such that, upon landing, all the people he originally knew were long dead and buried. For those who stayed behind, however, and continued to still be alive after those original few short years, they would have no awareness of the spacecraft landing because, for them it wouldn't have happened yet. Additionally, for the time traveler, the past he experienced before leaving would appear to be long gone. Except it isn't, not for the people left behind who are still living there.

In this imaginary scenario we could also have not just one, but many different space travelers all leaving at the same time but each traveling at a slightly different velocity and thus scattering themselves out through time into the future. In conclusion, therefore, with the theory of relativity accepted, past, present and future all exist at once and do so in a way that is non interfering. Why not? Some of the conjecturings of physics hold that some sub atomic particles can only be explained as moving backwards in time. So where did they come from except from a future that also exists in the present.

Other particles may also be moving faster than the speed of light and if particles have awareness as indeed seems to be the case, then what is the nature of reality for them, zipping about as they do? Perhaps for them, time is simply a human illusion. Perhaps traveling through time for them is somewhat analogous to traveling through space for us. And, coming back to physics, it is a recognized fact that electrons for one, seem to be able to be in more than once place at the same time, so where do they find the time to do that? And if that is true for electrons, what else is possible? Perhaps archeologists, anthropologists, psychologists and all the other branches of science which aren't doing so should be talking to the right physicists, the ones who have taken the "time" to try and conceptually understand the real meaning of time and its implications even though as yet, they haven't had sufficient time to figure it all out in detail and don't seem to want to take the time to carry those implications over into everyday life.

But still, taking some of the ramifications of time into account, there is still much that can be said as a result. If past, present and future all exist at once, then they are so co-mingled that it would be possible for there to be more that one possible year, 1940, for example. Or any other day or year or point in time that can somehow be accessed. Worlds within worlds, within worlds, a situation which would allow all variations of a theme or situation to be played out. Probable worlds starting out for each individual which come into personal shared existence based on the choices made along the way. And, if this was the situation, then in this regard, there was not just one singular outcome to World War II, for example, or for any other major event. It is possible that in one case Germany won the war and those people who chose that path of experience then had to learn to deal with that. Once again, a singular universe or a multiverse?

So too, would be the idea that space may be just as big an illusion as is time. Space, while seemingly empty visually, is not. Physics speaks of the 'known" universe, which is that part of everything which can be seen with telescopes. The bigger the telescope, the more light that can be collected from farther out in the universe and the bigger the known universe becomes. The known universe, however, is not very well known at all. For the most part it is a hypothesized summation instead, but one which is still very interesting. In that universe, ordinary matter, that which is detectable, only makes up for 4.9 percent of the total amount necessary to make things behave as they seem to do. Dark, undetectable matter makes up for another 26.8 percent and dark energy contributes the additional 68.3 percent necessary to make our theoretical universe balance out and what, if anything, does that have to do with everyday life back on planet earth?

HIGG'S TO YOU TOO

On July 4th, 2012 the existence of a particle called the Higgs boson was confirmed. The grossly mislabeled "God particle." At least it was according to the extensive media coverage the event received at the time. But was it really? All too often it seems that who gets the Nobel prize is far more important than the complete truth. And the truth is, they are still arguing about it, along with the real significance of whatever it was that seemed to present itself during the experiment, putting modern physics in somewhat of a crisis. For now, at least, nature has thrown scientists a curve ball and that is as it should be. Some people don't see the humor in that, however, because they have staked their careers on their own favorite theory. But, even though there is far more verifiable evidence for the existence of telepathy, clairvoyance and many other psychic phenomena than for the existence of a so-called Higgs particle, the data seem to support the fact that something was indeed discovered. That something also had a mass of 126Gev which fell somewhere in the correct range for the, until then, theorized particle. But, and this is where nature didn't seem to play fair. According to an early documentary presented by a scientist who was a participant in the experiment, the witnessed particle should have had a mass approximately 15Gev higher, or one 15Gev lower than that which was determined and then life would have been much simpler.

The lower particle mass would have confirmed the idea that there was just one universe. The one we seem to be living in. The higher particle mass, however, would support the idea of a "multiverse." That means many parallel worlds, if you will, weaving in and out of each other. Most mainline scientists strongly reject such a concept, however. First of all, other than pure theory, they have no evidence to support such an idea and no way to experimentally verify it. Not yet, anyway. Additionally, they also say that the multiverse is an <u>unnatural</u> explanation for what's out there because the entirety of creation happened purely by chance, making a multiverse necessarily impossible to come by.

But.... is that really true? Theoretical physicist, Laura Mersine-Houghton, points to the non-uniformity of background radiation in space as proof of the existence of other entangled universes. She thinks that the traditional concept of a single, lonely universe makes no sense. And what about you? Are you sure that when you walked out the door this morning that you walked out into the exact same world that you did yesterday?

What if on a deeply subconscious level you have been coming to the conclusion that you really didn't like the way things seem to be going in today's world, what then? Well, maybe that would be the start of an entirely different chain of events for you.

Perhaps somewhere in there the world news might seem to take a small turn and the people you thought you knew might have a slightly different slant on things than you always thought they did. You might even find that some of your memories about past events were somewhat incorrect. Some things didn't happen quite the way you thought they did. This tiny detail and that one, all soon forgotten as your life moves down another path. How would you really know for sure? How do you really know it hasn't already happened and continues to happen? This choice, that choice, leading you in different directions over time, bringing experiences into your life that provide you with challenges you would not otherwise have. Or, more simply, just to expand your concept of reality.

What if it was a particular bright sunny day instead? You had a good nights sleep, you are feeling just fine and your mind seems quite clear as you are driving down the freeway mid morning on a Sunday and there is almost zero traffic in either direction. You have also not been behind the wheel long enough to have slipped into highway hypnosis either when suddenly you see an automobile come racing up behind you, close enough so that you can clearly see the man driving and his woman passenger. Then, at the last moment it pulls over to go around and pass. Except that it doesn't. It is not behind you, it is not along side of you, it seems to have completely disappeared. Startled, you pull over and stop. It is not in the ditch either and the nearest off ramp is still a few miles ahead down the road. How well do you trust your senses at a time like that?

Well, as long as the theorists are tossing things out there which can't be proven, why not join in on the fun. If there are parallel universes or universes intertwined with our known one, what would they be made of? Our dark matter and dark energy? Maybe. Unfortunately, if everything was just linear, the number of other universes possible would be limited to about twenty and a half and what good is half a universe, even if universes appear to be infinite in extent? But what if there was a great deal of sharing going on instead? Sticking with planet earth for now in trying to make a point, how could it be possible for automobiles from one universe to be traveling down the same freeway at the same time as those from another without colliding with each other and what would it take to make the freeway common and viable to different realities at the same time? Or for people from different universes to be walking on the same beach together without bumping into each other? Or......?

At this point most logical individuals would probably be thinking that only an extremely crazy person would even ask such questions and that anyone who then attempted to answer them would be loonier still, so why go there? On the other hand, try and understand string theory. Or, better yet, get someone who claims to have some understanding of it explain it in an understandable way and tell us what affect it has on our everyday life. Ask them about all those extra spatial dimensions, too, and ask them what that has to do with your ability to walk on the beach. And, while you are out there walking around, think about the fiber optic cable that might be buried underground beneath your feet, used for the transmission of information. Phone conversations, internet information transfer, fax machines and a phenomenon all its own.

At the core of the cable is the thing that makes it all possible. Single strands of glass of very small diameter, the important aspect of which is the amount of data that can be transmitted down this tiny little pathway. It is upwards of a million million bits per second. What this means is that literally thousands of different phone conversations, along with Netflix movies and a whole lot of other stuff can be flowing back and forth on this single fiber at the same time. And, because of the way it is chopped up and encoded at one end by what is known as multiplexing, and decoded and put back together at the other end by demultiplexing, the loss in fidelity is essentially zero for all <u>humanly</u> considered practical purposes. Still, if any one signal was slowed down by several orders of magnitude and re examined, it would be found to be full of gaps.

While real, these gaps become irrelevant in the over all sense because the response times of whatever is on the receiving end of things, the human ear, the television set, the computer screen, the printer; all are to slow to notice. It is the same as when we go to the movies and watch the big screen where people and things appear to move smoothly about. In reality, however, if we slowed a typical movie down we would clearly see that nothing is actually moving at all. What we have is a series of still pictures all taken in sequence instead, all with a short time lapse between each one where the screen goes dark. The only reason we don't notice this is because the response time of the human eye is too slow so it doesn't see the gaps, and blends the series of still photos into what <u>ap-</u>

<u>pears</u> to be a smooth flow of action. Television basically works the same way, except that the gaps between the separate frames of screen information are put to use to carry other information necessary to generate the picture on the screen.

By the same token and with a little innovation, the gaps between frames in a theater movie could also be used to create and hide a movie within a movie which could also be viewed with a little signal processing. The viewers could also sit side by side and neither would be aware of what the other was experiencing. With that as a goal in mind and properly engineered, there would be no need to build multiple theaters, just one would do because there would be movies within movies within movies, all shown at the same time in the same theater. The particular movie the viewer would see, the one the ticket was purchased for, would depend on which head set he/she was given with its selective pair of glasses to look through and earphones to pick up the right sound track. Here, in cases like this, it doesn't matter what you are seeing, it only matters what you think you are seeing. At other times, however, it may important that we know the difference and where does that lead except back to Higgs boson, what its mass really is and what that implies.

As previously stated, there are two schools of thought regarding the big picture, neither of which can prove themselves to be right at this moment. Universe or multiverse. Which is the true reality? On the surface, having one universe would seem to make things a lot simpler than a multiverse ever would. At least at first glance. But what if the multiverse were a multiplex-verse? Then what becomes possible? As a beginning, there is a lot to work with. First, there is all that dark matter and dark energy out there which are the two different faces of the same thing. Or, the two faces of something even more basic which is as yet undetectable in the physical universe or universes. Next, there is the duality of nature and the fact

174

that particles can indeed be in more than one location at the same time. But how many places? That is the unknown and so far impossible thing to determine. Then there is the concept of multiplexing and demultiplexing, along with that of frequency sensitivity, only on far grander levels than ordinarily considered. Additionally remember that as humans we are extremely limited in terms of our sensory equipment. Other living things can "see" farther into the infrared and ultraviolet portions of the spectrum than we and can also hear, smell and taste things we aren't even aware of but in larger terms, they are also very limited and have their own narrow interpretation of reality just as we do.

Moving on, let's visit something solid next, only on the atomic level to remind us that solidity is as big an illusion as everything else, maybe one of the biggest illusions of all. Looking at an atom up close and personal, what do we see? Mostly nothing. In terms of the size we attribute to an atom, the amount of actual matter that occupies that space is far, far less then one percent of the volume of space the atom seems to be taking up. Then, regardless of where we find the atom, we also see that it never comes to rest. Whether it is trapped in an array of like atoms to form an element like gold, or it has combined with different atoms to form a compound, they are all in constant motion, perpetually. They vibrate, so to speak. Add energy in the form of heat and they vibrate more. Add enough heat and they break their bonds with their neighbors and the substance melts. Subtract heat and they vibrate less. Subtract enough heat and the bonds again become weak and solids fracture. That is somewhat beside the point, however, for now. What is important is that everything we see as solid is also transparent at some wavelength of radiation or to some size of particle. Light passes through glass, microwave through plastic, x rays through steel, neutrinos through the entire earth.

There are not enough examples here to build an entire theory on but with some inspired imagination we might be able to see how something could be worked out. Start with all that dark matter and dark energy. Where is it? Certainly not "out there" all clumped together somewhere, but distributed throughout all of space. It surrounds us. We move through it without even knowing it. We can neither see it or sense it. Nor can we build instrumentation to do so with present technology because maybe our own universe is not "on" all the time either but has gaps in its actual presence just like the pictures on the theater screen. As a result, any instrument one might construct has the same limitations and cannot sense what is in the gaps because it is also "off" during those periods. Then, using all the stuff of the dark matter and dark energy, somehow multiplex it into those gaps while also using some of it to insert into multiple gaps so it is shared and what do we have but an infinite number of possibilities or seemingly separate universes all intertwined but basically inaccessible to each other on the physical level. On the out-of-body level, however, the spirit, the entity, the consciousness, the basic us, can move through walls unimpeded and travel to other physical locations in what appears to be instantaneously. As for crossing boundaries into other universes or realms, some claim that with practice, that can also be done when in the out-of-body state. Robert Monroe, *Far Journeys, Journeys out of Body* and, *Ultimate Journey.* One word of caution needs to be given to those who would attempt such a thing, however. If you believe in demons in your normal state, you may well find demons in your other travels, the why of which would take another book to explain.

Certainly, what has been suggested as to how a multiverse could be possible is far from being the entire narrative but if the multiverse theory is ever somehow proven, indirectly of course, by slamming particles into each other in underground tunnels or whatever else it takes to convince the gods of science, then the ramifications become endless and it will take more than a mindless accident to explain the complexity of that situation. Instead, any explanation would seem to require the existence of a vast intelligence and imagination to bring it about instead, where conscious intent is the driving force behind it all.

Meanwhile, having taken a little time to pursue some of the timely aspects of space and time as misunderstood components of reality, it is time to return to a further discussion about the many reasons for choosing reincarnation.

Some reincarnations may be cases of role reversals with close individuals. One time a parent, one time a child or other varying complicated relationship with some significant few, down thru the past and future. The possibilities are endless, all of which brings up even more questions. An important one is, if reincarnation is true, then why aren't we consciously aware of a larger view? Why the veil that hides the bigger truth?

While rare, there are cases of people with provable memories of other lifetimes but they are limited in scope. At some level of development, however, it would eventually all come together but until that level of perspective is acquired, the individual can only gain the most if the immediate life-time drama is taken seriously. Having a role in a play or in a movie which might be quite moving for the actors is still a different experience than the same thing being played out on the street. Even though we may well know on a deeply subconscious level that we are eternal beings and don't really die, we need to learn the consequences of our actions on this lower level in a very direct way for them to be truly meaningful, before we can move on.

As for some individuals, they seem to come into the world with a ready made, very clear sense of purpose

right from the beginning. The majority of people, however, do not and that can present its own problems and
confusion. Why not me? Why do I feel so lost and confused, they ask. Why don't I have a clear path and reason
for existence? Why don't I feel more important? What's it
all about? Even so, privately, most people still have some
sense of life's hidden dimensions even though they may
be completely unable to verbalize and explain them. They
may not have a clear idea as to what it all means but they
still feel that there has to be more to it than meets the eye.
They certainly hope so, they want it to, otherwise, what's
the point. But how to figure it out? It seems impossible.

There is a way, however. One which can only be approached in general terms since any cook-book list of possibilities would be volumes long and still incomplete,
making the reader the only one fully qualified to analyze
the specifics of their personal situation, look for clues and
fill in the blanks. All in all, it begins by taking an objective look at one's personal situation. Were you born in a
country with a stable government and some level of freedom or was it a country in turmoil and oppression or
maybe at war? It might even have been somewhere in the
jungle close to nature under conditions most would consider to be primitive, or somewhere in the arctic, faced
with survival in the extreme.

And, yes, primitive people share the same gene pool
as the rest of the human race, they have the same brain capacity and intellectual potential as everyone else, as
demonstrated recently by the lost boys of the Sudan who
walked half across Africa to freedom and later immigrated
to America where they were able to learn and adapt, many
of them finishing college in the process.

At any rate, if a stable political situation was the
choice, then you must be here to work on issues or goals
that could not be achieved under duress. Of course one
could say, if you have a choice, why would you want to be
born anywhere else? Particularly in a place undergoing

the extremes of war or great social upheaval. For some, however, there is an intensity to life under such conditions that might not exist elsewhere, just as there might be for those who live in a highly active earthquake zone or in the heart of tornado alley or under the shadow of an active volcano. Some people make it even more immediately real by base jumping off high buildings or the sides of mountains or trying to break speed records, deep diving records and a whole lot more. That doesn't necessarily mean they have an active death wish, it means that they want to live on the edge and if they should die in the process, that's okay.

Regardless of where a person was born, it doesn't mean that they have to spend their entire life there. Some shorter period of time may be enough. They get it and leave, as they should. Others become caught up in the madness, however, such as that of war and get trapped there. Or they get stuck in other situations they can't seem to get out of and fail to fulfill some greater potential. It may be considered sad but in the bigger scheme it is never an unforgivable disaster. Nothing is an eternal tragedy. Nor is there some outside penalty imposed upon the individual by the universe. It is enough to become aware of the mistakes and move on. Looking back, they hopefully come to realize that they, themselves made bad choices and could have done things differently. What they choose to do about it at that point is also entirely up to them. Free will reigns on both sides of the curtain that divides the physical world from the non physical. Additionally, there is not some cosmic mandate and drive for ultimate perfection. The thought of ultimate perfection is in itself, undefinable and has no meaning in this context. If it did it would signify a finality, an end. And, to have to exist in a final state of forever perfection would be just as boring and destructive as spending eternity in heaven. An open ended universe is much more stimulating and challenging than any idea of completion. That outcome can't be proven either but intuitively it seems to come a lot closer to the truth.

Leaving that behind, next consider your parents and the subsequent dynamics of that situation. Maybe you were even an orphan and never knew them. One could hope to learn a lot from that if they didn't get bogged down in self pity. The same would be true if a parent, or both parents, were completely uncaring and neglectful, resentful of having a child or were cruelly sadistic or somehow perverted and abusive. Then an assessment of one's life becomes very difficult because, how does one look at that with much objectivity? Sometimes the damage inflicted is so severe it can twist the individual's outlook into a lifetime burden that forever distorts their view of the rest of the world and they become unable to see beyond it all. Regardless, blanketed as the challenge may be, it is hidden in there nevertheless.

As opposed to the extremes, a person may also find themselves in a very low key environment instead. Life is simple and has its own benign rhythm to it. Days in the sun on the sandy beach without any attempt to live up to the arbitrary standards of others. One does not have to grow up and "amount to something." They do not have to conform and "fit in." They do not have to work, pay taxes, salute the flag, chase the "American dream," or follow any other prefabricated misconception as to what life should be all about if they do not want to. The only rule is, do no harm. To oneself or to others. Happiness is far more important than suffering. Everyone has a right to be here. The same and equal right as everyone else, regardless of social, economic, political or intellectual stature and a simple life living off the land in tune with nature can be far more rewarding and beneficial to the development of the human race than any accumulation of wealth and power.

Regardless of the confusion that seems so prevalent, there would also seem to be individuals with very specific talents or strengths who show up at crucial times in history where they may be of service. A Franklin D. Roosevelt and a Winston Churchill. A Martin Luther King, a Nelson Mandela, a reincarnated Dali Lama, Michelangelo, Copernicus, Newton, Nikolai Tesla and Albert Einstein. It may also be a great musician, composer or opera singer, mathematician or athlete; people possessing extreme ability whose lives give great inspiration to others, demonstrating the greater potential of the human race as a whole. Can their existence be explained as nothing more than benevolent accidents?

Can random evolution explain a Mozart? Absolutely not. Not in the framework it propagates. So, where do these almost super-natural abilities come from? Offensive as the idea might be to some, reincarnation is a better explanation by far. But is reincarnation an ongoing, forever thing? A recurring cycle that goes on unbroken, also for eternity? While certainly not as boring, that too, would become as dead ended and maddening as being forever trapped in heaven or hell, something impossible to take very seriously because one cannot imagine it having a purpose. Not so with reincarnation if we realize that on every level of earthly life, we are the cooperative creators. Not only of our physical selves but also our environment and our private and public destiny, personally and communally with all the necessary freedom for learning to get it "right." Individuals experiment and test with their own lives. The race as a whole experiments en masse with larger concepts. War and peace, human rights and the rights of nature, equality and discrimination, self aggrandizement and charity.

Often, because of the complexity of the issues involved, the conglomerate can become fragmented and at odds with itself, however, constantly repeating the same old mistakes, failing to see, for example, that war is a most ineffective way of resolving issues and that over population is destroying the environment we live in. Political and social repression also compound humanity's problems along with distorted ideas of what is more important than what in life.

Above all, industrialized countries like the United States tie success to household income and an ever growing gross national product. Business does not want a declining population because a declining population is a declining market and bad for business. Far too many religious groups do not want a declining population except for those they disagree with. Neither do many ethnic or family groups. They see breeding as the easiest way to gain control over ideologies and political systems alike. It is their one hope to gain power and dominance and perpetuate themselves long term. Meanwhile, too many politicians and people of influence stand silently by because they do not want to offend anyone. Better to let things go on as they are, even if larger and larger portions of the population end up dying prematurely from respiratory disease, poisoned water supplies and contaminated food. Religious arguments that connect birth control to not being pro-life merely reflect a stupendous misunderstanding of the entire conception process while the fertility clinic does not see the hidden wisdom in the in-ability of many to conceive.

And then there are the highly limited attitudes of some scientists and certain major philanthropists. They don't even mention birth control as a solution to the growing problem. The answer for them is to improve agriculture, produce more food, generate more electricity and eradicate disease. Nothing could sound more humane than that. And as for far visioned scientists, well again, forget attacking the problem at its roots and look to the future. Instead of limiting population growth, their proposal is to expand the search for other inhabitable planets somewhere else out in space that we can migrate to. And to accomplish that we will also need, yet to be invented, propulsion systems and vastly larger space vehicles to do the transporting.

Unfortunately, hindered by limiting concepts of space travel, any such journey could not be completed in a single lifetime. As a result the space craft would also have to be completely self sustaining and able to provide life support for several generations of humans to achieve such a goal. The proportions of such a venture are equally stupendous. To solve the population problem this way is not a question of a few thousand, or even a few million individuals selected to be carried off planet earth. To be effective it has to be on a scale of billions. Additionally, all of this has to be accomplished in an expeditious manner, soon enough to prevent the race from poisoning and polluting itself into oblivion or decimating itself into extinction through warfare in the meantime.

But while scientists put forth such proposals, no one else seems to take them seriously, as indeed they probably should not. Sadly, on a more realistic level, few people ever took the environmentalists seriously either but they have been speaking out for well over a hundred years, telling the world that what is happening now, would happen, well in advance. And while they should have been listened to, far too many with the power to influence change vehemently disagreed on religious grounds or interfered because they felt it would adversely affect the economic situation. Theirs, of course. Additionally, and for the most part, the general population either didn't get it or just didn't care. They would rather have a new car than breathe fresh air any day.

Regardless, what should be clear by now is that climate change is real and will continue to become more extreme. More than likely it is a situation that cannot be remedied during the lifetime of anyone presently living. Even if polluting emissions were completely halted today, the atmosphere would still not return to normal for at least a century. Secondly, of course, billions of people in other parts of the world all want what the industrialized nations already have. Goods and services no matter what the cost to the habitat, with cities in India and China now having the most toxic environments on the planet. In the short term it seems extremely unlikely that humans will ever be able to invent their way out of this problem, leaving birth control as the only presently viable solution and good luck with that. Finally, of course, there is the bigger fact that those who have done the most to create the world's problems and are in a position to provide the most help, are also the ones most determined to want to keep things exactly as they are. And then, in a bigger perspective, the next obvious question. If the planet is already grossly overpopulated, why do more people keep reincarnating into it? Shouldn't they know better?

Humans, unfortunately, are widely separated in terms of their intelligence, knowledge and wisdom and have widely diverse individual wants and needs, along with free will and are not always inclined to look at the bigger picture. At the same time the race as a whole has its own agendas and a proclivity for experimentation. And, while some things should be more than obvious, there seem to be times when the only way that knowledge can be assimilated is through direct experience. Some things have to be learned the hard way before they can be properly integrated into the consciousness of enough people to make long term changes. How badly can the planet be overpopulated before it completely threatens species survival. How extensive of a war can be fought before the fear of extinction takes over and moderates our behavior on a global scale. How much religious extremism can be allowed to express itself before we are on the brink of sinking back into the Dark Ages? How extremely lopsided can a nation become in terms of who controls all the money before it becomes completely dysfunctional?

At what point do we have to stop being so self centered and uncaring about the bigger picture?

Beyond all that it must be realized that a "dead" person is not necessarily any more intelligent and wise than they were when they were living so they aren't able to make any better decisions either way. As for the living, we are where we are because this is where we have progressed to. Certainly we should be capable of doing better. Regretfully, it keeps coming back to same thing.

"Now, for the first time in history, man can perceive that the idea of the unity of the human race and the conquest of nature for the sake of man is no longer a dream but a realistic possibility..... Yet modern man feels uneasy and more and more bewildered. He works and strives, but is still aware of a sense of futility with regard to his activities. While his power over matter grows, he still feels powerless in his individual life and in society.... While becoming the master of of nature, he has become the slave of the machine which his own hands built. With all his knowledge about matter, he is ignorant with regard to the most important and fundamental questions of human existence: what man is, how he ought to live, and how the tremendous energies within *man* can be released and used productively." Eric Fromm.

The potential and the promise are still there, however, painfully slow as the process appears to be, which brings us back to another major question. Is there such a thing as absolute right or wrong? There apparently is for those who believe God has spoken to a chosen few and allowed them to pass on his message but, other than that, such a thing does not seem to exist. In the final analysis we are not judged by some set of rules or commandments sent down from on high, we must come up with them ourselves. In order to do that it must be realized that in the end it is strictly about the individual. Anything that violates that concept violates life itself. Believing that there is such a thing as doing something for the greater good at the expense of the individual is a corrupt way of thinking. In the end it also sets everyone, including the proponents of such an idea, up for arbitrary extermination. In the extreme it can lead to genocide, as some hopefully remember with regard to Hitler, who decided that the extermination of six million Jews was for the greater good of the rest of the human race.

The same logic was also used in Russia and China on an even greater scale and in Rwanda, Kosovo and a multitude of other places around the globe on a lessor scale. It is still going on in the middle east after long years of illegal US intervention where the never publicly admitted need for crude oil and a personal animosity on the part of the president was the bottom line cause for invasion. An almost unprecedented, criminal abuse of power, all at the expense of innocent people.

Furthermore, not one bullet fired or one bomb dropped during those wars had anything to do with "protecting America's freedom," as many would try to lull us into believing. Instead, as a result of going to war in the Middle East, the freedom of Americans was placed in far more jeopardy than ever before in history, along with that of western Europe and other places around the world. All that can be seen of this over-riding atrocity now is that portion where "America's heroes" returned home missing arms and legs and half their skulls, physically and psychologically unable to integrate back into society, committing suicide in droves at rates that far exceed those lost in any actual combat, just a very small portion of the hidden cost of it all.

Unfortunately, until such atrocious behavior has been publicly acknowledged and openly dealt with, we are a nation hiding from the truth, our conscience muddied and not at peace with ourselves, thus more likely to commit further compromised acts of injustice in the future. Where is the heroism in that? All that has been demonstrated thus far is that there is still something seriously wrong with our approach to problem solving on the world stage.

Undeniably, however, there is another side to it all. The world is definitely still in chaos, an ongoing theme and nothing new about that. Dictators, despots and mad men keep rising up regionally and continue the slaughter. But it is different this time and has a far more sinister side to it. It is not just about a leader or a nation here and there that is out of control. Far more rudimentary, it is about religious righteousness and fanaticism instead. Something which cuts across all borders with outrageous fervor and deep seated spitefulness. Granted that eventually, with the use of enough boots on the ground, all backed up with enough remotely guided drones and hi-tech weaponry, such movements may eventually be suppressed into a less harmful state but any victory achieved through force alone is never a final victory. It simply drives the perpetrators back into their caves where they wait, plan and regroup. A non-victory where the flames are never really out, that smolders and seethes to one day reappear with far too many innocent people caught in the middle.

But why does this have to happen to begin with? That is the question we should be asking and only through an understanding of the basic issues involved can there ever be bi lateral solutions that will allow peace to prevail. As stated by Chris Hedges in his magnificent book, *War is a Force That gives Us Meaning*, the fact that the US went into the Middle East in Kuwait and Iraq sent the message to the world that the US thinks it has the right to go anywhere and do anything to any nation any time it wants. And, it can do it without justification, to suit its own agenda, and the people of that region be damned. No wonder certain factions of the world population are outraged and offended. They have a right to be.

A territorial war can be won with bullets and bombs and when mad men go to war there is little that can be done except to retaliate in self defense. A war fought over ideological issues is an entirely different matter. Suppression is not victory. No one ever wins an ideological war with weapons.

After thousands of human lives and trillions of dollars, all that has really happened is for old fanatical groups to expand and morph into new ones, some with better organizational skills and even more hatred driven determination. But why and where do they come from? Here is how Jane Roberts' Seth describes them.

"Basically a fanatic is a person who believes he is powerless. He does not trust his own self-structure or his ability to act effectively by himself. Joint action seems the only course, but a joint action in which each individual must be forced to act, driven by frenzy. or fear or hatred, incensed and provoked, for otherwise the fanatic fears that no action at all will be taken toward 'the ideal.' Through such methods and through group hysteria, the responsibility for separate acts is divorced from the individual and rests upon the group instead, where it becomes generalized and dispersed....... Fanatics have tunnel vision, so that beliefs not fitting their purposes are ignored. Those that challenge their own purposes, however, become instant targets of scorn and attack."

"Fanatics cannot stand tolerance. They expect obedience. A democratic society offers the greatest challenges and possibilities for the individual and the species, for it allows for the free intercourse of ideas.." and this is the major reason why democracy becomes the fanatics' prime target because the fanatic always fears conflicting beliefs and systems that allow them to surface.

Fanatical groups are also composed of people who believe the end justifies the means, no matter what, and most of its members are people who will die for a fanatical cause because their own life is barren without it and they have no other real cause to go on living for. Additionally, again quoting Seth;

"Fanatics are inverted idealists. Usually they are vague, grandiose dreamers, whose plans almost completely ignore the full dimensions of normal living. They are unfulfilled idealists who are not content to express idealism in steps, or wait for the practical workings of active expression. They demand immediate action and they want to make the world over into their own images. They cannot bear the expression of tolerance or opposing ideas. They are the most self-righteous of the self-righteous and they will sacrifice almost anything - their own lives or the lives of others and will justify almost any crime in the pursuit of their own ends."

But, how to better deal with it? Perhaps the lesson should have come from history. The Romans tried to extinguish Christianity and look how that turned out. Left alone it might well have died a natural death long before it became a world phenomenon. Perhaps if the United States had practiced some restraint and taken time to gain some perspective after 9-11, things might well be different. Too late for that, however. If dignified resolution cannot be found in the light of day, the battle will be fought surreptitiously in the dark endless night of prejudice and misunderstanding. As for finding that dignified resolution to begin with, that becomes nearly impossible because of the radically different basic philosophies people run their lives by, most of which have little or nothing to do with the real truth about our origins and reasons for being here. Difficult as it may be to believe, fundamentalist religion is still somewhat of a reaction to, and a rebellion against, the meaningless world of scientific intellectualism. Over the top and horribly twisted, of course. But still...

Be that as it may, it is a most unfortunate situation and while it should be possible for all people to come to agreement about something so fundamental as the basic meaning of life, the probability of that happening in the foreseeable future is essentially zero. In the meantime the situation is not entirely without hope. Regardless of all else, it would not matter what people believed individually or how disparate their views as long as they could all agree on one very simple issue. That issue concerns itself with human rights.

Consider what Albert Einstein said in an address to the Chicago Decalogue Society just nine years after the end of World War II.

"In talking about human rights today, we are referring to the following demands: protection of the individual against arbitrary infringement by other individuals *or by the government;* the right to work and to adequate earnings from work; freedom of discussion and teaching; adequate participation of the individual in the formation of his government. These human rights are nowadays recognized theoretically, although, by the abundant use of formalistic, legal maneuvers, they are being violated to a much greater extent than even a generation ago. There is however, one human right which is infrequently mentioned but which seems to be destined to become very important: *this is the right, or the duty,of the individual to abstain from cooperating in activities which he considers to be wrong or pernicious.* The first in this respect must be given to the refusal of military service. I have known of instances where individuals of unusual moral strength and integrity have, for that reason, come into conflict with the organs of the state. The Nuremberg trials of the the German war criminals were tacitly based on the recognition of the principle: criminal actions cannot be excused if committed on government orders; *conscience supersedes the authority of the law of the state.* The struggle of our days is being waged primarily for the freedom of political conviction and discussion... "

190

In another statement Einstein also said this. "External compulsion can, to a certain extent, reduce but never cancel the responsibility of the individual... Whatever is morally important in our institutions, laws and justice can be traced back to interpretation of the sense of justice of countless individuals. Institutions are in a moral sense impotent unless they are supported by a sense of responsibility of living individuals. Few people are capable of expressing with equanimity, opinions which differ from the prejudices of their social environment. Most people are even incapable of forming such opinions."

As Einstein stated, it all comes back to personal responsibility. Unfortunately, however, much of what is wrong with the world comes from failure to accept that responsibility on an individual basis. But in the end, when all is added up, the one question that needs to be asked the loudest is, what is more important than what?

"We make ourselves worthy of living by making ourselves *competent* to live. If we default on the responsibility of thought and reason, if we turn our backs on reality and facts, thus undercutting our competence to live, we will not retain a sense of worthiness. If we betray our integrity, if we betray our moral convictions, if we turn our backs on our own standards, thus undercutting our sense of worthiness, we do so by evasion; by the refusal to see what we see and know what we know, we commit treason to our own (correct or mistaken) judgment and thus do not retain our sense of competence." Nathaniel Branden

MORALITY AND MEANING

"The growing doubt of human autonomy and reason has created a state of moral confusion where man is left without the guidance of either revelation or reason. The result is the acceptance of a relativistic position which proposes that value judgments and ethical norms are exclusively matters of taste or arbitrary preference and that no objectively valid statement can be made in this realm. But since man can not live without values and norms, this relativism makes him easy prey for irrational values systems." Erich Fromm

Even though life may not have an absolute right or wrong associated with it, if life still has a larger meaning. Then, by definition, there is a certain morality attached to it. A higher, more universal morality rather than a range of separate, arbitrary, culturally related rules which people abide by or ignore to serve their own needs.

Fortunately, while many choose to self centeredly interpret the situation that way, it still seems that the vast majority of people still retain some built in, individual sense of right and wrong, warped as it may be at times. Most people inherently want to do the right thing even though it is all too often not very clear as to what that right thing is. And while they may intuitively suspect that there is some bigger truth involved, science and religion have so effectively derailed and twisted their thinking that most people no longer have a clear idea about much of anything philosophical. Once so undermined, it becomes very difficult for people to find their way back to trusting their own thoughts.

As a starting point, however, even if people were not able to conceptualize it well or verbalize it clearly, if they were somehow assured that life had a higher, more intrinsic meaning and started to live accordingly, they would have a much more focused and fulfilling life. Regardless of whether or not that could be effectively proven to anyone who chooses to adopt the classical scientific view still does not change the truth, whether acknowledged or not. Even though a scientist would adamantly insist that science only declares as fact those things which can be rigorously proven to be true, it is still a false claim. Science has made some serious blunders down through the ages and still continues to do so with its pronouncements about the physics of the universe and what is considered to be the resultant reality and often ends up with its own form of dogma. Beliefs instead of facts, misconceptions instead of truth which, once accepted, are used to build upon in an attempt to carry science forward. Eventually, however, somewhere down the line, a new group of people will have a good time rewriting all the textbooks.

Meanwhile, if your life is working for you and you are happy with the results you are achieving in terms of your own development, then that alone is enough. But if you find yourself living in that philosophical void described earlier and/or are in a position where your personal experience does not agree with what you have been told by the church, science, the medical community, politicians, psychologists or society in general and the many gurus who dominate everyday thinking, then there is a problem. The problem is not that you as the individual are necessarily wrong. It is more likely the other way around instead. For those who trust the ability of their own minds it becomes clear that a good deal of what we are exposed to in terms of popular viewpoint is in the least shallow, skewed and misdirected. Pat, mundane nonsense that gets passed along without discernment, more often myth than fact. It is also grossly insufficient and relatively meaningless in terms of some larger truth.

So here is today's dilemma, reiterated once again. **Religion, science and philosophy have all floundered in a critical period of earth history where mankind, which now has the power to annihilate itself and is des-**

perately clamoring for answers, is almost equally convinced that no viable answers are possible. As a result modern man/woman is psychologically and spiritually adrift.

Beliefs about reality are not necessarily attributes of reality, however. They work, not because they are undeniably true but only because they are widely accepted. Fundamentally and for the most part, the belief systems of the separate individual are ego fabrications built up as a response mechanism for dealing with the world. They may often have little or nothing to do with any bigger truth and, once established, may well prevent the individual from seeing the truth or from accepting it in a useful manner. Regardless, in the operational sense, for better or worse, these erroneous fabrications become that person's truth.

But again, where to turn and who to believe? Everything institutional is strongly entrenched. Church, government, the medical profession, the scientific viewpoint regarding human origins. For those in control, any search for some greater truth that questions their power base is all too often seen as a threat to be dealt with, right or wrong, and they will take all the steps necessary to protect their position.

With this considered, in the course of history, how many dictators or rulers of nations have ever stepped down voluntarily? In the last one hundred years of human history alone, how many innocent people would have been able to live out their lives in a more normal fashion if it hadn't been for the actions of just a single mad man here and there along the way? It is a fair question which also serves to point out that the general population is equally involved by allowing itself to be manipulated and victimized by its own ignorance and gullibility, otherwise such wayward leaders would never be allowed to come to power to begin with. Even worse is what happened within the Catholic church in recent years? Bad enough that priests were raping young boys while the hierarchy turned a blind eye and did its best to cover up the scandal. Far worse is the fact that when it eventually came to light, large numbers of the congregation turned their heads and made excuses for the sick behavior.

Such abuse of power and perversion does not need to be stupidly forgiven, its perpetrators need to be individually held accountable on the personal level instead. Across the board. Political, religious, governmental, business, financial. It doesn't matter. Criminal is criminal.

MOVING ON

Interesting as some of these diversions may be because of their direct affect on everyday life, they are all still secondary in their own way and here we return to reiterate what was stated in the early chapters of this book.

"At the top of the list of serious problems facing the modern world, the lack of a cohesive, unifying philosophy of life that serves to give human existence meaning is the most grievous and burdensome. This is true simply because all other problems facing the human race derive from this primary factor. Interrelated but caused by this lack, there are extreme religious differences and ideological insanity. There is also nationalism and war, hunger, pollution, global warming and extreme over population to name a few."

Simply put, a unifying life philosophy can only be achieved through an increased awareness of what has been largely denied, overlooked and distorted by science regarding the origins and meaning of life and by an outward rejection of the very limited dogmatic pronouncements of religion.

Religion, as usually practiced, is basically about the power that can be obtained through the control of other people's thinking. Some choose to take their holy books literally, which is impossible because they contradict themselves. Taking what religious leaders promise in their sermonizing literally is something else. Text derived or not, their railings are bound to create deep disillusionment if listened too seriously. Little wonder that so many followers end up blaspheming God when life's tragedies are imposed on them. Unless someone is betraying their own mind by believing so, God does not come out of hiding and personally take an individual by the hand in times of crisis. Nor does God take sides and play favorites, one person or group of people at the expense of another. Additionally, good people still die in spite of all the prayers that have been said in their behalf and prayer has not, will not and can not ever bring peace on earth all by itself. It may be a place to start as a way of declaring one's good intentions but unless it is followed with dedicated action, it is without merit and brings home the point that something is seriously lacking with regard to organized religion as presently put forth and there is great danger when institutions try to force individuals to disown their own internal truth.

Quoting Jane Robert's "Seth," we have the following.

"Man's "subconscious" knowledge is becoming more and more consciously apparent. This will be done under and with the direction of an enlightened and expanding egotistical awareness that can organize the hereto neglected knowledge, or it will be done at the expense of the reasoning intellect, leading to a rebirth of superstition, chaos, and the unnecessary war between reason and intuitive knowledge. When, at this point now, of mankind's development, his emerging subconscious knowledge is denied by his institutions, then it will rise up despite those institutions and annihilate them. Cult after cult will emerge, each unrestrained by the use of reason, because reason will have denied the existence of rampant subconscious knowledge. If this happens, all kinds of old and new religious denominations will war and all kinds of ideologies surface."

These words were spoken back in 1977 and, more and more as the years pass, we see religious splinter groups turning to violence as a way of asserting themselves, proving the statement to be true.

Hate is an intense emotion and a common enemy can serve as a strong, unifying force amongst people, making them feel that their lives have a meaning and purpose that would otherwise not exist and it is useful for as long as the emotion can be kept alive and directed. Sometimes it even becomes a part of the group or national culture and can be passed on from generation to generation, re infused and fanned by those in control to promote their own sick agendas. Petty criminals and terrorists, manufacturing hate and artificial enemies to further their own misguided ends, all made easy because the messages of religion are muddled, the words of philosophers conflicting and the summations of science are dismal. It is the dark side of humanities legacy that extends far into the past.

Meanwhile, in recent times the world has seen Catholics and protestants kill each other in Ireland. Serbs and Muslims killed each other in Bosnia, Hutu massacre Tutsi in Rwanda while Sunnites and Shiites continue to battle throughout the middle east, and lately Muslims slaughter Christians in central Africa. On and on, it is all the same where meaning is lost in warped confusion. And now, a relatively new theme on the world stage that seems guaranteed to generate a mad following is the, "death to decadent America," slogan that is used as a battle cry. It is yet another zealous banner of self righteousness embellished with shouts of, "God is on our side," that has accounted for most of mankind's greatest atrocities. And where does it end?

The threat of death does not deter war and conflict. Instead, it often adds excitement and intrigue to the game and raises it to another, more daring level. Additionally, people with little or nothing to offer in a peaceful situation can gain importance in conflict and often don't care if they die in battle because they know their lives are already dead ended anyway. No matter how it is viewed, however, there is no honor in that kind of death. Unfortunately, war and armed conflict are so rampant and ingrained that much of the world population seems to have forgotten that there are other ways of resolving things. Meanwhile, all it will take to place the planet in serious jeopardy is for some extremist group to gain control of some country's nuclear arsenal and use it in a suicidal attempt to end it all, uncaring about the outcome. Or, in lieu of that, a continuing escalation of what is already under way, driving the world back into the dark ages once again.

Could such a thing happen? Absolutely. That battle is already in process. It has been going on in one way or another from the beginnings of human history but has severely escalated in recent years. More than land, resources and money, it is about control over the minds of others and it is here where a difference in opinion can cost a dissenter their life, remembering that what makes its way into the mainstream of human consciousness determines the future of the entire race. It is not a battle for America's soul as the evolutionists would claim, however, and it does not matter if the United States continues to be a world leader in science or not because that alone is far too narrow an issue. Not only is it self serving and nationalistic, it misses the point. There are a lot of other people in the world besides Americans. Granted, however, that if the freedom of Americans is in jeopardy, then to an extent, so is the entire world. But it goes beyond that. If the freedom of any group of people, large or small is in jeopardy, then potentially, so too is the rest of the world. The battle field is not limited to one country in North America or in the middle east. The battlefield extends to everywhere there are people. It is a battle for the "soul" of the entire human race in all of its ramifications.

Then, as if this was not bad enough, we are forced to deal with other forms of twisted thinking along the way. Not that of scientists or religionists but of philosophers who say such non-helpful, non-meaningful, totally off the track things as, "we are more likely to be artificial intelligences trapped in a fake universe than we are organic beings with minds in a real universe." Beyond that and equally convoluted is the stream of non-logic which seems to have begun with Samuel Butler who said that "the hen is only an egg's way of making another egg." This, in turn, leads to, the body is nothing more than a gene's way of making another gene. In other words, a body, the person, animal or plant, does not live for itself. Instead, it's sole purpose is to perpetuate the genes, a statement popularized by other equally distressed writers of the present day.

At first glance such a proposal is so logically disruptive and convoluted that it is almost impossible to respond to. Obviously exactly what its proponents wish to achieve with the game they choose to play. Don't be fooled by it, however, because it's only purpose seems to be to deliberately not make any sense and to provoke, which it does poorly. If survival of the gene is all there is to it, then genes must not only have some level of consciousness and individual awareness of their own. They must also have consolidated intent and must be extremely clever over-achievers who are more intelligent than the end product they help create to have invented such a complicated way to continue themselves. A way which, by itself, violates all the premises of the basic evolutionary theory these exposers claim to advocate. As a result, the selfish gene proposal is just another sarcastic, attention getting version of that old, life is a meaningless accident, scenario.

Be that as it may, however, in the final analysis one thing stands out above all the rest. There is no enduring happiness when life has no meaning and **there is a difference between life being meaningful to the individual and understanding the larger concept of life having a higher meaning.** Many people become deeply involved in life's activities, dedicating themselves to meaningful activity, often with great purpose and never question the larger issue. Nor is that really important. The difficulty is with those individuals who are confused about what it is that they should be pursuing to begin with. Money, power and fame sought only for the sake of same more often than not lead to end of the road disappointment and it seems a waste of a lifetime learning such a simple thing.

But, for those so minded, the career, money, power or whatever else it may be, becomes the entire definition of their personal identity and they are left without a deeper sense of self to fall back on when difficulty arises. Lacking a clear understanding of life's cycle and real purpose, many people develop an intense fear of dying and will do most anything to extend the process as long as possible. Lacking the same insight, those in medicine, along with friends and relatives, insist on keeping others alive at all costs, quality of life be damned, even if those last days are spent hooked up to a machine. And for what? It is not for the benefit of the terminally ill, it is for the living who don't understand the essential process and won't let them die in peace and continue on with their eternal journey.

ARE WE ALONE

If we are to properly examine the issues of origin and meaning, we are also compelled to give some consideration to that other question. Are we alone in the universe? Are there other life forms out there somewhere? And, if so, do any of them have some level of conscious awareness, such as that exhibited by humans? Is it more rudimentary or more advanced, and how does one go about finding out? To that end, some people established an organization called SETI where SETI stands for, Search for Extraterrestrial Intelligence. To make it appear scientific in nature, radio-astronomer, Frank Drake wrote an equation. This equation was an attempt to determine how many civilizations might presently exist in our galaxy which have evolved to the point where they could communicate with electronic signaling, something we, if we listen carefully, might be able to pick up. Then, if something were ever detected and their Technology Taskgroup feels confident enough that the senders of those signals won't jump in their spacecraft, come here and abduct all our scientists, we could respond to them and set up an intergalactic chat room.

The Drake Equation, unfortunately, allows almost endless possibilities for guessing what the values of the variables in the equation might be, which renders it almost useless. But regardless, it still indicates that the answer is not zero. Far from it, there should be anywhere from thousands to multi millions of planets out there that could and might support intelligent life, none of which is trying to get our attention at the moment. Not electronically, at least. As a result this brings up what is called the Fermi paradox which asks, "where are they?"

That whole idea presupposes that, as yet, there is a complete lack of observational evidence to support the idea that there are other intelligent beings elsewhere in the universe. This is true because apparently no one in the elite group associated with SETI has seen them or heard from them. Nor have they visited planet earth. Absolutely not and anyone who says otherwise is highly suspect for a variety of reasons. But are they right?

Granted that the entire issue of UFOs is one more area where delusional and/or attention starved individuals come forward to swear they have been abducted by aliens or are channeling them or having their babies or helping them conduct experiments. There is also an abundance of photographic material showing fuzzy lights in the sky along with numerous non-professional organizations which have given themselves the power to decide which of these bits of evidence deserves to receive their stamp of authenticity, which, by itself, adds absolutely nothing to the ongoing arguments about whether or not UFOs and ETs really exist. In the end there is little difference between these clubs of amateurs and that group of scientists who only see what they want to see, see what they are willing to accept and nothing more, even if it is nothing. Furthermore, as far as both groups are concerned, if there were indeed extra-terrestrials who chose to make contact with humans, it would have to be them personally because they, or someone in their intimate little group, are the only human emissaries qualified enough to be so privileged. Therefore, if someone else should make that claim, it couldn't possibly be true because they, themselves, weren't personally included in the experience.

Pretending to be an expert on Ufology or an ancient astronaut theorist is one thing, however, and claiming to be the last scientific word on extraterrestrial life is another and here is where the SETI-ites break a most fundamental rule of good science. The essence of that rule says, check the facts and complete a comprehensive investigation before making all inclusive statements. In particular, just because someone might wish it to be true, it is nevertheless extremely neglectful to make the claim that there is absolutely no evidence for the existence of extra-terrestrials. For one thing, are these people completely unaware that ex president Jimmy Carter claims to have seen a UFO, along with several American astronauts, scores of highly credible commercial and military pilots and literally millions of individuals around the world. Beyond that a National Geographic survey found that 77 percent of all Americans believe that there are signs that aliens have visited earth.

Considering all this then, how could anyone be as poorly informed as the SETI-ites? Additionally, in a case like this, before judgment can be passed and the claim made that there is no evidence of ET's, those accounts that contradict that need to be proven to be wrong. At least the more significant ones. And as for that large portion of the scientific community actively choosing to deny the existence of extraterrestrials, perhaps it is as someone said. They don't want it to be true because if some group of beings from outer space was advanced enough to get here then the implication is that earth scientists would not be the most intelligent beings in the universe. Such an idea also presupposes that scientists are the smartest people on earth to begin with. This, however, is absolutely not true.

Without a doubt some scientists are among the most intelligent people on earth but pursuing a career in science does not necessarily make one bright and perceptive. Scientists are like any other professional group. Some are highly intelligent, some are abominably stupid, draw twisted conclusions and make very bad decisions just like doctors, lawyers, businessmen, politicians, psychologists, humanitarians and all the rest. As a result, even though some of them think that they should, scientists should not have the final vote on anything when it comes to human and world affairs. Nor should anyone else. Granted, there are good reasons why some segments of the population shouldn't be allowed a voice in some matters but in larger terms, we are all in this together. And, above all, governments do not have some divine right to deprive their citizens of information when it comes to something as important as the existence of life elsewhere in the universe. Even though it is hard to envision how such a wide consensus could be achieved amongst world governments, if one were a conspiracy nut, here is where a master conspiracy could easily be formulated. As a minimum there are photos of Swiss Airforce fighter jets chasing UFOs and the record books contain many accounts of military encounters both in the US and elsewhere, but that evidence is officially denied to the public. Why? Because some few individuals have arrogantly decided that such information would create severe panic on the part of the general population and therefore needs to be withheld.

Regardless of that, everyone still knows that it can't be suppressed forever. And, heaven forbid, what if the ETs preempted the process and set down in full view in some highly public place? Then what? How would the authorities explain their deceit in that case? They couldn't. Meantime, what?

Perhaps somehow SETI will get lucky and that would be a door opener. But even though that probability is essentially zero, it has already been established that a huge number of other solar systems exist elsewhere in space that have planets which should be able to support life forms so we should keep searching and cataloging those anyway, doing spectroscopic analysis and whatever else is necessary to confirm the findings. Additionally, keep probing our own solar system, especially the planet Mars. We already know it has water on it, that most basic of life's ingredients, along with an atmosphere and who knows what else that might be life supporting. And if we can't confirm it remotely, surely an upcoming manned mission will find some microbes. Maybe even a few fossils.

Once something of this nature has been confirmed, the bigger announcement can finally be made. There is life out there because science has said so. Furthermore, if life indicators exist on Mars, then life most certainly has to exist elsewhere in the universe. This is true because many of those millions of other planets are much more like earth in composition and far more capable of having advanced life forms on them than Mars. And with that being difficult to argue against, the general population can continue to be spoon fed small amounts of facts at a time so that people can slowly expand their thinking in preparation for the final revelation.

Having said that, would organizations and/or governments actually put such a plan into effect? To be sure, they are certainly capable of it and, if this is the case, it is a contrivance decided upon by the few, based solely on their own limited personal judgment as to what is better than what for the rest of us. Meanwhile, standing off to the side, there are also one very large amount of people who are saying, "good grief," who's kidding who? Tell us something we don't already know. As for all the rest of the population, the one's in the middle, what do they do under the circumstances, since the entire subject is still shrouded in deep controversy.

Granted that no craft from outer space has set down on the White House lawn as yet and allowed photo ops before inviting world scientists on board for a check-out ride to the moon and back. Granted also that no one who has seen a UFO can explicitly prove that what they saw was of extra-terrestrial origin either. At the same time, however, it should be more than clear by now that this great multitude of people did see "something." Additionally, many of those somethings also appeared to have completely violated the laws of physics as presently defined by earth scientists. They would have had to, otherwise how did they get here? That does not mean that because they did, what was seen was simply an illusion. It could as well mean, as discussed earlier, that present laws of physics are incomplete, just as most any theoretical physicist would be willing to admit.

In addition to visual sightings, however, these craft and their behavior have also been recorded on film, magnetic tape and memory cards alike and are there to be viewed. Of course some of them have undoubtedly been faked and anyone can use that as an excuse to summarily dismiss them in their entirety. But what if we took the same attitude towards "science?"

Stem cell scientist, Dashiki Sakai committed suicide because he was found to have fraudulently over stated his laboratory findings. A diabetes researcher fabricated data in nine different published reports, a social scientist almost completely fabricated published data and the list of other, claimed to be scientists from around the world who have done the same thing is a very long one. Such fraudulence also goes as far back as the days of Darwin where coffee stained monkey and human bones were put together to fake a genetic "missing link" discovery but does that mean that the rest of us should automatically reject everything put forth as science? So, being aware of that, let's go to Switzerland where, by far, some of the best possible evidence for the existence of visitors from outer space exists. While doing this bear in mind that there is one serious problem with regard to this material. That is that, there is just too much of it. It is too clear, too explicit and too overwhelming. So much so that it seems to offend the experts in the field. But, for those who don't need this outside authentication and approval, it is there for review. At any rate, what we have in Switzerland is a man named Billy Meier. Billy Meier has been having contacts with his visitors since he was only a boy and has been photographing spacecraft from as far back as 1964.

The photo evidence that Meier has accumulated is not of just a few fuzzy lights in the sky, either. Nor is it limited and contrived in ways that should have been obvious to those who have been duped by others. Instead, it consists of hundreds of mostly full color photographs of spacecraft, both at a distance and as close as that of one craft sitting in front of his house, sharply focused and full of detail. One picture even shows a Swiss military jet in the same frame as a disk shaped space craft. There is also movie camera footage of multiple craft, a copious amount of contact notes and much, much more and it is there for review for those open minded enough to take a look. All this evidence was obtained by Mr. Meier working almost entirely alone. Furthermore, Meier was an extremely poor individual with nothing more than the equivalent of a grammar school education with the further handicap of having but one arm. Additionally, most of his photographs were taken long before the arrival of desk top computers and graphics programs and would have been impossibly expensive to create his photo evidence that way at the time they were first presented. Even today it would take a level of expertise hard to come by and difficult to conceal. It is an important issue. One of enough significance that judgment should at least be reserved until after having done a comprehensive examination.

Billy Meier, however, has never tried to convince anyone to accept any of it. All he has done is to have shared his material and his experiences with those who would make the effort to examine and listen and let people draw their own conclusions, keeping in mind that the evidence obtained by Mr. Meier can neither be proven to be true beyond a shadow of doubt, nor can it be proven to be false to the same degree. So, left with this enigma, any reader who has not had their own personal experience is left to draw his or her own conclusions about the entire subject. Meanwhile, Billy Meier has done exactly what he set out to do. He has helped to create a UFO controversy, pure and simple.

The photographic evidence alone would have done that but there is still more to the story. It is in the information passed on to Billy in his meetings with his visitors and recorded in his contact notes, much of which is also quite important. One example of this was a documented early warning about ozone depletion in the upper atmosphere over the south pole before earth scientists had become aware of the problem. Other warnings were given about the unknown side effects of atomic bomb testing and nuclear reactors. Beyond that there are the statements about what are considered to be the two most serious problems facing the human race today. The first is overpopulation and the second is the status of earth's religions. Both of these have been touched on elsewhere in this book but that doesn't mean they don't deserve some additional thought. As for further messages given by Billy Meier's visitors in the contact notes, they make it clear that his visitors are not here to either share or flaunt their technology. The message is primarily a spiritual one instead. Earthlings are not ready for great advances in technology, least they badly misuse them to further personal power because the present state of their spiritual development lags far behind the technology already in use. Regardless, these visitors have decided not to openly show themselves as yet. Their mission is also not one where they feel the need to prove their existence to all the skeptics just to prove a point. This was stated by Billy Meier's primary contact, a woman named Semjase:

"General public contacts are not in our own best interest at this time and besides, they would not convey a correct significance for the state of mind in which we are now in." However, she also stated that ... "On many occasions space travelers have visited your Earth from other stars, sometimes from very distant systems, like ourselves. On occasion accidental contacts which are unique may take place with earth people." (Note that according to these visitors there are at least 108 different civilizations that have made earth contact thus far.)

Therefore, if this is true, does that mean that it is a matter of grave concern? Are we in danger of being invaded from outer space? Some would think so. On the other hand if they can indeed get here from elsewhere in the universe and they had such intentions to begin with, they most certain would have been able to do so long ago so maybe we can set that paranoid thought aside and consider this additional quote.

"We, too, are still far removed from perfection and have to evolve constantly, just like yourselves. We are neither superior nor super-human, nor are we missionaries.... but we have taken on certain tasks such as, for example, the supervision of developing life in space, particularly human, and to ensure a certain measure of order. In the course of these duties we do here and there approach the denizens of various worlds, select some individuals and instruct them. This we do only when a race is in a stage of higher evolution. Then we explain to them that they are not the only thinking beings in the universe."

If indeed there are other conscious beings out there, something which the odds are far more in favor of than against, along with there being more than a single group from one sole location in the universe, then the religious views of most people require some deep reflective reconsideration because we are by no means all alone. There was a period of time when Meier's visitors considered openly showing themselves but decided against it because, in their opinion, the spiritual progress of humans was making a backward turn. (no kidding) As for themselves, they do not have "religion." Nor does anyone else throughout the universe that they have had contact with, of which there are many others. Religion is peculiar to earth alone. Nor do they believe in a God or a Creator. Instead it is the "creation." Physical matter is the embodiment of thought or idea. Mind or spirit is the greater reality from which the universe emerges in expression.

Be that as it may, however. One thing we have been granted is the right of self determination. As a life form and race of beings we can choose to take a broader view of our earthly situation and strive for improvement or we can continue down the road we are presently on that could well lead to our own destruction.

PRELIMINARY ANALYSIS

Spending the many hours it took to accumulate and compile the evidentiary findings presented in this book is one thing. Trying to extract and formalize pertinent conclusions is another. Regardless of any conclusions drawn, however, this book is not an attempt to establish a new school of thought, doctrine or ism. It does not need a label or a following of missionary minded devotees. It is not a plea, either, asking people to change or abandon some existing lifestyle or system of belief. It is a matter of choice instead. As was previously stated, "the search for genuine truth about the natural world" has to be an all inclusive search if we are to ever arrive at the "whole truth" and not some limited edition of what that truth might be. As a minimum it needs to include that which has been labeled paranormal, metaphysical and supernatural for lack of better words. Nor does it matter if ninety nine point nine percent of the examples could be written off as coincidence.

If there were just one verifiable case of one individual being able to raise the temperature of a block of metal by thinking about it, or change the decay rate of a radioactive isotope, or receive one scrap of verifiable information from the deceased, or have some source of invisible energy move a table, or bend a spoon, or be able to receive information from the future about an upcoming disastrous event, or any of the rest of it, it would still prove one thing. That singular example is still very much a part of reality and must be given due consideration if we are going to arrive at some least amount of the "genuine truth." It is not a, one in a million, situation however. These psychic/paranormal events happen by the millions instead. Mostly minor, many blurred by the background hassle of everyday life, too often dismissed as coincidence or imagination, they occur nevertheless and they are real. Accepting that as a starting point, what does that tell us and what else could we hope to learn about the greater reality we live in?

First, as quantum theory also brings to light, it tells us that any purely mechanistic view of the universe is incorrect. It also indicates that it will take much more that multidimensional string theory to explain the situation.

Secondly, while acknowledging that some living things do evolve physically over time (while others do not) there is a huge gap in understanding and in being able to account for the rest of the story. If nothing else, consider the Mozart phenomenon where some child with extraordinary talent or ability is born to very average or even below average parents. A composer, a ready made opera singer, an exceptional mathematician all bursting onto the scene at a very early age with extremely rare abilities. What kind of genetic accidents are these? Technically speaking in terms of gene theory alone, the leap required is orders of magnitude too great and the odds of these things happening make them absolutely impossible. But they occur irregardless, not once or twice in the entire history of the race but actually fairly often.

Then recently discovered, another rare human ability. There is a very small group of people who exhibit the extreme in memory function. Pick any day of their life and ask them where they were, what they were doing and what else was going in their personal life and they can tell you, including what day of the week it was. They literally remember everything. That alone is somewhat remarkable in its own way. Not as useful, however, as the memory of someone like Nicola Tesla who memorized the entire list of logarithms and antilogarithms which, before computers, were used to mathematically manipulate very large numbers. To do this Tesla had to remember thousands of numbers. Not only did he remember them, he could also look thru the logarithm tables mentally, find the ones he needed and do the required calculations in his head. An extremely handy ability at the time in his research and engineering, long before computers came on the scene. But still, for those who remember their own past in great detail, here is the thing.

One of these individuals is a twelve year old boy who has an identical twin. He has this ability, his twin does not. Identical twins, same genes. Why one and not the other? The variation is too extreme. Strict genetic theory says that can't happen. Except that it did. How is that possible? It can only be possible if there is something more to identity than genetics. It can only happen if everyone has an identity independent of the body they inhabit. A separate, psychic, psychological and spiritual identity. There is no other way to explain it. Another example as to why evolutionary theory needs to be radically modified and downgraded as an explanation for how we got to be what we are.

To be teaching evolution in its present form in the classroom is every bit as horrific as the Nazis teaching children about the superiority of the Aryan race during World War II. Granted, the story religion would tell if it were allowed equal voice and time would not be much closer to the truth either, primarily because it is a far more complex situation than any religious explanation is able to account for. However, call it God or call it something else, the concept of a creative force bringing the universe into being is still one small step closer to the truth of the inherent spontaneity and inbuilt creativity finally being recognized by some members of the scientific establishment than is Darwinian evolution. Not literally in six days and nights in the biblical sense but in broader terms on a more profound scale. Furthermore, if those religious sects that avow it could strip the ideas of original sin and, man is a flawed being, from their dogma, then the message given would be far more positive and beneficial than the one evolutionists espouse. While it would remain childish in scope and severely lacking intellectually, it would still be a more accurate scenario than that promoted by the accidental universe advocates.

Additionally, while many would be reluctant to extrapolate the body of information given earlier that far, it none-the-less proves that life has far more dimensions to it than most of science would grant, especially the evolutionists. Unfortunately, the majority of people settle for beliefs they are comfortable with and then spend their time closing their minds to the rest of the world to support those beliefs, making short term changes in outlook difficult to come by. It is also not a situation where suddenly, as some new age gurus would have us think, there will be a harmonic convergence and the vibrational level of the whole planet will rise and carry the entire population into a higher state of universal consciousness which will bring over-night peace and well being to the world simply because we have moved from one astrological age into another. And this is where many would-be psychics have also failed badly.

Predicting the future regarding mankind's spiritual development, they have stated almost in unison that by the year 2000 humans would have greatly increased their awareness, attitudes and concern for others. The veils would be lifted from people's minds. People would understand better who they were, where they came from, and what their fundamental spiritual nature was. Almost like the second coming of Christ, a new resounding environment for earth was to have come into being. Earth was to have undergone a self-cleansing process to overcome the distorted vibrations man has created over the centuries. A geological upsurge would also have happened to halt unbridled technology and materialism for the safety of all mankind.

This scenario somewhat correlates with the Hopi Indian prophecies for the *Great Cleansing*. Only here the cleansing of the earth can be initiated by a dance ritual. When the time is right, certain members of the tribe begin the dance and the world will be purged of its evil. That, too, is somewhat akin to the Tribulation and Rapture of Christian fundamentalism except that the now long overdo reappearance of Christ would serve to trigger the event. What all these viewpoints have in common is an image of man as a flawed and debased, fundamentally weak and sinful being, unfit to be alive wherein civilization is ultimately damned. Such a perverted view in turn leads some to believe that the only path to salvation lies in personal suffering, sought-after or self-inflicted.

Unfortunately it doesn't matter how many fishhooks one chooses to insert into their back or how many skewers they run through their arms or cheeks or how long a hunger strike they endure or how much ceremonial tea they drink or how long they meditate, none of it leads to a meaningful understanding of the greater scheme of things. While these practices may eventually bring the individual to an altered state of mind, they do not bring about a grand, magical inner awakening some would call enlightenment. Unfortunately, when trying to connect science and religion in an attempt to show that life has meaning in spite of what science purports, some authors drift off into pseudo East Indian philosophical mumbo jumbo under the assumption that they are saying something meaningful. They can talk about the *Atman* and *Brahman, pure consciousness* and all the rest but none of it explains a thing and the *Brahman* does not come to know itself in all of its dimensions through self centered human perception, whatever that might possibly mean.

It is also hard to believe that anyone could learn anything useful through self denial in a search for blissful *non being* by attempting to separate themselves from all human emotion, desire and physical pleasure. Others, however, simply seek *perfection,* whatever that is supposed to imply, believing that that will lead them to *Nirvana* where they will then be absorbed back into some grander whole which will solve everything. It doesn't matter what the belief system. It can be anything from atheism to pantheism or anythingism. One can revel in it or submerse themselves in it so thoroughly that they lose their identity, but none of it brings a person any closer to the real truth of existence. It is only by stepping away from the shrine or stepping outside the laboratory and leaving the dogma behind, whatever its nature, and taking a sincere look at what else is happening in the, not so ordinary, everyday world that we will ever be able to see beyond that which has so limited our perception. And to begin that journey let's not start by assuming man is an inherently flawed being. If we cannot see man as being born into a state of grace then let us at least try and see ourselves born into innocence.

MORE CONCLUSIONS

Repeating again, life does not come with a "Book of Ultimate Truth" to help one get through the maze. The result is that large numbers of people are left feeling mentally and spiritually adrift in a confusing world of chaos, suffering and grave injustice that only seems to get worse as time goes by. Unable to live with uncertainty, however, far too many give up and settle for deceptive answers that are easy to hide behind along the way.

This does not mean that better answers do not exist, however, because they do. As shown, the evidence surrounds us. All we need do is take a clear look at it. The most important aspect of this evidence is that it shows that life on the planet is not accidental and therefore meaningless as science would have us believe, but has great purpose and reason. This purpose and reason, however, has nothing to do with heaven or hell or some grandiose God who created man in his own image. Our origins have far more significance than that and there is a a greater reality that exists behind the scenes of the physical world we live in. There is also significant evidence to show that consciousness is an all pervading truth throughout the universe and there is such a thing as eternal validity of the self, or soul, as some would use the word.

Physicist, Paul Davies, stated that "science itself cannot reveal whether there is a meaning to life and the universe, but scientific paradigms can exercise a strong influence on prevailing thought."

There is certainly no question about that. Look at the disparaging influence the evolutionary paradigm has created. And, in that regard, "the present laws of physics are inadequate to deal with complex organized systems like living things," Davies also states. "Biological systems have a hierarchy of organization which requires a new form of explanation," and that "he has been at pains to argue that the steady unfolding of organized complexity in

218

the universe is a fundamental property of nature...... We seem to be on the verge of discovering not only wholly new laws of nature, but new ways of thinking about nature that depart radically from traditional science."

As a case in point, this book gives numerous examples of phenomena that traditional science has chosen to exclude from serious consideration even though they exist and are therefore very much a part of "nature." We do not need new ways of thinking about them, however. We only need a full recognition that they truly exist and proceed from there. One aspect of this concerns what Davies calls, the cosmic blueprint. Here he asks, "if every molecule of DNA possesses the same global plan for the whole organism, how is it that different cells implement different parts of the plan? Is there, perhaps, a 'metaplan' to tell each cell which part of the plan to implement? If so, where is the metaplan located? In the DNA? But this is surely to fall into an infinite regress."

These questions are much the same as asking, where is the mind and individual identity located? By now it should be clear that the mind and brain are entirely different things. The mind, or perhaps the psyche, is what we are. Spiritual, non physical beings who manifest their physical body. Not a chance happening, but for a reason. The mind, we, present ourselves thru the brain and the body but are separate from it. If that was not the case then the operating room, out-of-body experience would not be possible nor would projections of consciousness. It would also be impossible to have information transmitted from the deceased to the living, either directly or thru an intermediary. Additionally, it once again brings home the point that cannot be over emphasized. Dead is not dead after all. Something else is happening instead and it is not the classical religious view either.

Without actually saying it, some major religions promote the idea that we are born but once, live a microscopically short life in terms of eternity, die and, depending on the affiliation, go to some equivalent of heaven if we have lived correctly, go to hell if we haven't or, for some, end up with a stop over in purgatory. The astounding part of this story is the wide and differing range of prerequisites required to make it into heaven to begin with. These may vary from having been kind and considerate to those around them, loving their deity and not blaspheming god, to denying and despising their physical needs and enduring endless, self inflicted suffering to coming full circle by strapping a bomb around themselves and blowing up innocent people. What gives one a pass into heaven in one context can just as easily send them to hell in another. And for the lucky righteous, the rewards of heaven also take on different hues. The Christian heaven, while probably sexless, has the sounds of harps playing, streets of gold and immense banquets of food while for those on the opposite end of the spectrum, seventy two virgins await to fulfill one's needs. As for those others who spend their lives in suffering, who knows what their reward will be. Perhaps Nirvana. Let them be re absorbed into the cosmos so perhaps they can start over and have another chance at getting it right the next time around.

And what, pray tell ends up on the other side? One's soul? In what condition? If a person is demented when living, are they demented in heaven and what possible value could be gained from spending eternity in heaven in that condition? What joy could be gained from spending eternity in heaven in any condition if it was nothing more than some replay of physical life since most concepts of the soul also seem to include bodily desires and values. Food, the glitz of gold, sex with a virgin. Then what? One can only eat so much no matter how exotic the meal and a virgin can only lose their virginity once and lose their desirability. Then what does one do for the rest of eternity. Besides, while virgins deserve a place in heaven too, what kind of heaven would strip them of their virginity just to please some madman who hated himself so much he became compelled to take that hatred out on others? No wonder a large number of people say they would prefer to end up in hell instead where it is not so contradictory or tedious.

One lifetime lived according to the rules and the reward is endless, eternal boredom. One lifetime of breaking the rules and it is punishment forever. It would seem that for those religiously minded individuals who believe in life after death, the concepts of heaven and hell need some serious revision. If nothing else, since they are all essentially worshiping the same god, there should be some level of agreement about such things because, once again, they can't all be right.

PERSPECTIVE

On a larger note, why, of all things, is there the need for religion to begin with? According to Compton's Encyclopedia, "thoughts of death lead necessarily to the development of religion. There would be no need for religion if no one ever became ill or died. All religions attempt to answer such basic questions as: where did the world come from, what is the meaning of life, why death and what happens after, why is there evil and how people should behave."

Then the same reference clearly states that the existence of religion is rooted fundamentally in human ignorance. "People do not know the origin of the world, why there is death, or the answers to other basic questions. Explanations must be devised on the basis of complete lack of evidence... All acceptance of religion is based on pure faith, not on the weight of evidence or the reaching of reasonable conclusions... If belief is the key to religion, it is also the chief problem. If religion were a form of knowledge, then its teachings would have to be supported by visible evidence that could be supported by everyone...But there can be no evidence...that a supreme being created the universe. Nor can there be evidence of life after death. These and other beliefs are not open to verification; they are matters of faith."

All right. Since the encyclopedia is considered to be a reliable source of information , should it be accepted as the final voice of authority in this matter? If no one ever became ill or died, would not people still wonder what the meaning of their lives might be? And while there may be no direct evidence that a supreme being created the universe, there is a growing body of evidence to show that is was not created by accident. There is also a large body of evidence to show that there is indeed, life after death, a thesis favored by religion but one where there is an outrageous amount of disagreement as to what that actually entails, almost all of which is disappointing to anyone who has given it more that a passing thought. And that is the key. Thought and due consideration. Recognizing that, what is the fundamental difference between a Darwinian evolutionist and a scripture reading religious devotee? Except for the fact that they are quoting from a different bible, there is none. Both groups prevent themselves from arriving at any higher truth because the foundations they have chosen to build on are both fundamentally flawed. For one thing they both assume the worst about human nature, each in their own way. Religion asserts that people are born into sin, live in sin and die in sin and in the end this non-truth is every bit as destructive as the meaningless universe dogma of science where the only purpose and drive of living things is for self survival, all at the expense of everything else. **As a result both create an anti-life, mental climate that keeps humans from achieving some higher potential of excellence.**

What religion has failed to see is that if ideas of hell fire and damnation were abandoned, most people would still be decent because, inherently, most people are relatively decent to begin with. Unfortunately, that side of the human race is sometimes difficult to see because it gets so grossly distorted by media coverage of events. Truthfully, however, the great majority of the world's people are behaving themselves to the best of their ability most of the time. It is the very small minority that gives us all a bad rap. Regardless, without the silly, contradictory confusion thrown at them by the righteous, they might even be more decent because they would realize they were living in a world without being lied to about important issues. One can argue all they want, but somewhere logic, reason, common sense and intuition all have to come together with that which is claimed to be truth. Overwhelmingly, religion does not meet that test. If it did, religionists would not point the finger at those who question their views and claim them to be possessed with the devil or that they are the "Anti-Christ," or something equally wicked. If religion was correct, its practicers would not have to try and destroy the disbelievers because religious beliefs would stand the test by themselves.

The same holds true for Darwinism. What science fails to see is that the universe is accidentally impossible and that instead of a blind, self centered drive for nothing but pure survival, there is great cooperation amongst all species, all of which are inter dependent and necessary to each other for overall survival and fulfillment. This includes humans.

Regardless of all else, however, one's personal opinions about reality that are based on what religion or science might put forth should never be an excuse for bad behavior. Undoubtedly, a world free of religion, without all of its artificial differences, would be a much less conflicted place to live in.

So would a world where science didn't jump to conclusions before all the evidence is in and take the dimmest view of life possible

At the same time one cannot deny that science's discoveries can and do have social and philosophical implications. Unfortunately, scientists as a group seem to love making attention getting, grand extrapolations when it comes to things of possible technological value but adamantly insist on taking the dimmest view imaginable of all things more fundamentally related to human existence, and are quite prone to jump to conclusions before all the evidence is in. It is not about trying to silence members of either group, however, as the Darwinians have done to the creationists. It is about what science should be all about. Remaining skeptical and doing its best to separate fact from fiction.

Meanwhile try and keep in mind that we are all in this worldly situation together, standing on common ground, united beneath the skin because <u>we are all the</u>

chosen people. Additionally, in the context of reincarnation, a good many people have experienced both the roles of male and female as well as those of different racial backgrounds. But perhaps not enough. Racial prejudice still abounds and it is loathsome and criminal both. It is not only a display of ignorance but a sign of deep seated fear and self hate turned inside out, projected onto others by those who find it easier to hate someone else than work on their own weakness and lack of maturity. As Philip Wylie, author of An Essay on Morals, said almost seventy years ago that, even without reincarnation, "Each snobby Anglo-Saxon may (already) be part Jew and part colored man. Has this inexorable circumstance been made clear to every moppet old enough to clutch the Star Spangled Banner? And does he know what a torrent of Asia beats in his veins?"

Probably not but, setting that aside and coming full circle with the rest of it, here are those old questions revisited. Did God will Hitler to execute six million Jews, did God cause Stalin to kill sixteen million Russians and the Chinese Communists thirty million of their own people? Of course not. But, it did happen. Therefore, if not directly willed, at least most certainly allowed, if those are the terms we are forced to think in. And without the approval of all the victims, many who had to have prayed desperately to be saved. But, obviously, God wasn't listening to them. Why not? And then too, what did the families and friends of all those victims tell themselves to make it okay once it was over? That it was ordained by a supreme power and therefore all right? Were those the kinds of answers the holocaust survivors also placated themselves with? How could that be, especially since Hitler, himself, made the overt claim that he and his mission to purify the race were "blessed by God." And what about the Crusades and all the other religious conflicts that have taken place down through the centuries and appear to be escalating? What about the fact that in a recent ten year period alone, more than 100 wars were being fought around the globe, eighty percent of them due to religious differences with both sides praying for God's blessing and assistance, placing God in an extremely difficult position indeed. And since, "They are all God's children" and everyone involved in the conflict is either his son or daughter, how does an all knowing God figure that one out, especially when the best course of action would have been to sidetrack the war right from the start and keep it from happening. But for the believers, God obviously does not have the power to prevent war, only the power to decide who becomes the winner.

Likewise, on a lesser level, murderers continue to assert that God instructs them to commit horrific acts on his behalf, making anyone who claims to have a direct line to God highly suspect, understanding however, that not every one who professes religious faith is guilty by association. But the question remains. How many people would kill other people just to defend their belief system? Even in situations where their own lives were not threatened or at stake? And why? Unfortunately, far, far too many would and do, even though they have to set aside a core tenet of their belief system that says it is sinful to kill. Surely, this must be some disconnected form of insanity.

When it comes to belief systems, there are other forms of insanity that show themselves in defiance of reason and simple common sense also, unbelievable in the extreme. For example. In a city in India there was a town that had a statue of Jesus mounted on the outside wall of a building. At some point Jesus began to weep and it was considered to be a miracle. People collected the tears. They anointed themselves with them. They even drank them hoping for some revelation or healing or private miracle all their own. Then along came a skeptic who took a careful look at the situation and found a leak in a sewer pipe which let the water seep through the wall and drip out of Jesus's face. Astounding enough, but some devout believers refused to accept his conclusions. Instead, the discoverer of the truth was convicted of blasphemy and forced to flee the country for his own protection as some of his accusers insisted that he was trying to deprive them of their right to believe whatever they wanted.

While this case is unusual in it's particular aspects, it clearly demonstrates how totally illogical some individuals can become and to what lengths they will go to protect their misconceptions. In the same vein, however, it is neither fair or equitable to restrict any criticism to some poor uneducated individuals elsewhere in the world when the same phenomenon exhibits itself just as strongly in other areas.

In the final analysis, however, it is not our wayward belief systems, in and of themselves, that are to blame for the situation we find ourselves in. It is the neediness, naiveness, gullibility and intellectual shortcomings of the individual that allows them to to exist in their present forms.

One might be astounded by the inane stubbornness and absurdity of some human who would do most anything to keep from accepting the fact that he allowed himself to be duped and drank toilet water in the process. But, technically speaking, there is little difference between that individual and one who has allowed themselves to become indoctrinated into the mindset of other more formalized religious and political systems. Indoctrination has a way of short circuiting the thinking process to the point where the individual not only becomes unable to process the truth but no longer even cares about it. And once their delusional misconceptions become an integral part of identity, or ego, that individual is fully capable of sacrificing the lives of others and their own to protect their fantasies and the organizations that promoted them. This is what keeps religious and political hierarchies in place and allows them to prevail at the expense of those it

227

claims to want to help. But, it is not all bad, however. To the contrary.

Idealistically speaking, the church, the temple, the mosque, the house of worship, provides a gathering place where people can come together and do more than just say their prayers and go home. Hopefully it helps to build a sense of community, commonality and sharing that extends outward and makes life more bearable for those who participate. Companionship and guidance, solace and support in times of tragedy, validation, unity and a sense of belonging to something bigger than just themselves. It may also provide a charitable out-reach to others less fortunate. Food, clothing and shelter for the disadvantaged, sometimes at the price of a small sermon but often not. A lot of basically very decent people coming together, trying to make the world a better place. And they do. It is this level of charity and cooperation that keeps society functioning as well as it does. While many would consider them to be an acts of foolishness, the the generosity and sacrifice of some in order to help others who are even more disadvantaged is often astounding no matter what they may or may not believe in. Truthfully, many religions can and do encourage this kind of behavior and do deserve considerable credit for promoting it. At the same time, however, it is not a quality that comes to people solely through religion. It is an inherent quality of human nature which some people are capable of expressing once they set aside their misplaced value systems and allow themselves to see what is more important than what. Nobility is not about righteousness, it is about humanity.

Sadly, though, on the more ordinary level, far too many people have a more pressing need to identify and affiliate with groups that are more extreme and far less generous. The street gang, the hate group, the cult, the militia and back again. Belonging and recognition. Us

228

against them, and a common enemy to focus on. Fear driven people who wish to be feared in the process. Recognition is the thing, no matter how achieved. Negative attention is better than no attention at all and some people simply behave badly because they would otherwise be ignored. Whether factual and realistic, or misconstrued, misleading and just plain wrong, once this sense of identity, this set of beliefs about self is formed, it is difficult to change. So too, is the world view of the individual, the group and the nation. If it is healthy it can be of benefit to the individual and those within that sphere of influence. If it is unhealthy and destructive, the individual and those who are within reach, suffer the consequences.

Once a rigid sense of identity is locked onto, however, the real problems begin. There is nothing more impenetrable than a closed mind. It is air tight, waterproof, logic proof, bullet proof and more. It is what keeps individuals chained to prejudice and allows them to commit atrocious acts against others. It is what keeps systems of government and religious institutions in power. As should be clear, the basic goal of religious systems, like governments, is to perpetuate themselves, even at the expense of those who follow. It is not always about truth or honor or decency or what is best for the individuals. It is what is good for those on the top of the pile. Take, for example, the country of North Korea. It is a closed, cruelly oppressive, inhuman and barbaric place. The citizenry has been and is constantly being totally suppressed in an all consuming way for no other reason than to appease the infantile ego of a dictator who follows in the footsteps of his father and grandfather. Isolation is the key, however, and that is no longer as easy to impose as in previous generations. Information has a way of penetration even the thickest of walls and it is not much of a prediction to say that the tyrant's day are limited.

BEYOND THAT

When it comes to personal responsibility in areas outside of such very bizarre and extreme situations such as North Korea, however, more sane judicial systems draw clear lines in this matter. Acts that harm others are criminal. The Nuremberg trials after World War II expanded this concept by saying that it doesn't matter whether you were acting under orders or not when you committed the crime. No excuse, that is not forgivable. On the physical side of things in the US at least, one is also not allowed to harm themselves. If the suicide attempt fails, a person can be locked up for observation. As for mental or moral suicide, however, there are no laws against that. There is no culpability for leading other people astray ideologically either, unless they commit criminal acts in the process. But these are people who, for the most part, have never learned to think clearly to begin with. Impulses, ideas and random thoughts are one thing. Learning to think clearly and logically is something else. Being observant, analyzing and drawing conclusions based on reason takes concentrated effort. Thinking is often hard work and few ever learn to do it objectively and well. Blessed is the independent thinker, however, who is able to read between the lines and see beyond the distortions and lies and aspires to a higher code of conduct, particularly in situations where human rights are being trampled on.

Not only are the extremes of animosity and hatred, religions failure, they are also philosophy's failure and science's failure. And, since philosophy and science are also products of the human mind like religion, it is humanity's failure. Somehow, for whatever reason, almost all of the world's great thinkers in the last several hundred years have failed to come up with anything that is in any way very satisfying or redemptive regarding life's importance and higher meaning. Rigorous as have been the many arguments put forth, pessimism and negativity are still the keynote. Because of some great vacuum or inability to carry logic an additional step forward, this is all the mainstream intellectuals have been able to put forth thus far.

What they have not seen, do not see and apparently do not want to see is that a greater reality does exist behind the physical reality we too often limit ourselves to experiencing. But, accepted by the skeptical or not, the problem is not that proof of this greater reality does not exist. Scientifically recognized or not, it does. But it lies in areas that the mainstream science of today has consistently restricted itself from going and refuses to venture into because the answers reveal themselves in ways that science is, for the most part unable to verify according to their self imposed restrictions and guidelines. Advanced as science may seem to be, it is still in many respects very limited in scope and ability. Even the very minor example of being unable to measure and assess the nature of the energy involved in just the transmission of thoughts alone, proves that.

While the "laws of physics" may appear to be fundamental in nature, they are not. Physics is primarily the application of mathematics. While mathematics itself, within itself, is necessarily rigorous, the "laws" that mathematics supports are nothing more than useful mental constructions which appear to explain how things work in physical reality. Because they often seem to do that, they are endowed with more importance than they really deserve. Physics may be able to describe and predict the behavior of a few million molecules of gas trapped in a jar, both on the individual and mass level, but it is unable to explain exactly what a molecule is or what sustains the basic structure of atoms and keeps them from winding down and degenerating back into nothing more than a collection of fundamental particles lying in a heap somewhere after billions of years of banging into each other, combining and recombining without loss of energy in the process.

But, be that as it may.

Conclusively, however, after all is said, when it comes to furthering our understanding of the other dimensions of reality and the greater truth, science still remains in a better position to put the pieces of the bigger puzzle together than either religion or philosophy. The answers are not hidden in ancient scriptures or scrolls or Kantian meanderings from the past but lay within reach of the inquiring mind in the present, if we choose to use it fittingly. And that is climactic, the future depends on it. Here again, it all comes full circle, back to the individual and what individuals are willing to do.

As Nathaniel Branden stated: "To use our consciousness appropriately in any given situation is ... neither instinctive or automatic. We are not wired so as to always choose awareness over blindness, knowledge over ignorance, fact over delusion, truth over falsehood. The design of our nature contains an extraordinary option -- that of seeking awareness or avoiding it, seeking truth or avoiding it, focusing our mind or unfocusing it. In other words, *we have the option of subverting our means of survival and well being.* It is at the most fundamental level that the issue of honoring the self first arises: Shall I assert consciousness or flee from it? Shall I take responsibility for consciousness or pretend no such responsibility exists?"

Elsewhere Branden also states; "We live in a psychological age - or at the beginning of one. It is doubtful if at any other time in history there has been so much awareness on the part of so many people that often they do not know what they feel, what they long for, or where they are going." This he calls self-alienation. It occurs for several reasons. First, "most parents teach children to repress their feeling and emotions. They teach unconsciousness as a positive value, as one of the costs of being loved, found acceptable, regarded as 'grown up.' Furthermore, emotionally remote and inhibited parents tend to produce emotionally remote and inhibited children, not only through their overt communications but also by their own behavior, which signals to the child what is proper, appropriate and socially acceptable. Parents who accept certain teachings of religion are likely to infect their children with the disastrous notion that there are such things as "evil thoughts" or "evil emotions." The child may be filled with mortal terror of his or her own inner life."

Going beyond what Branden says, many people superstitiously still believe that there is such a separate thing as "evil" at loose in the world. That it is a driven force, in and of itself, personified by the mythical devil, waiting to jump out and possess. Even worse, for some it is an alternate side of their own being, hidden within the self and therefore to be feared and constantly fought against because moral weakness may set it free and place one's soul in jeopardy. Others, however, take advantage of such an idea and use it as a handy excuse. "The devil made them do it," they say, sidestepping personal responsibility, fooling no one but themselves.

Equally damaging is the concept of original sin. It deprives one of hope. What is the point, they say. Humans are an inherently flawed, lowly creation that cannot trust its own feelings, intuition and good sense. They cannot live life freely and unburdened. Paying penance is the only salvation and that can only come about by disowning ones flawed self and giving up their soul to some unnatural belief system. One such popular system goes so far as to state unequivocally that happiness cannot be found in earthly life at all, and that we are born only to fear, fight and die.

Certainly a person can accept such a viewpoint if they choose and with enough faith then deprive themselves of the much more fulfilling life they could otherwise have. But it has nothing to do with truth. It is just another subjective device used to maintain control over people's thinking and rule their destiny.

Meanwhile, other people are surrounded by a more generalized fear of almost everything in life and, as a society, America is a fear promoting and fear ridden nation. The world is a very unsafe place, people state with equanimity, almost determined to make that the truth. What is not seen, however, is that fear often attracts that which is most feared. Fear created the cold war and the arms race between the US and the Soviet Union after World War II and fear drives other nations to develop weapons of mass destruction. Fear keeps us locked into a situation where we are forever far more willing to give up personal freedoms for the sake of security and, now that the threat of terrorism has become more prominent in our world, it becomes a powerful psychological tool in the hands of government to manipulate its people. Such thinking can easily degenerate into a dangerous cycle because by nature, who else would a fearful citizenry want to lead them than paranoid people who are more than willing to use force for the preservation of their own greater good?

Fearful people can also be very vocal and fearful groups of people create organizations that promote even more fear. Some do it with misguided good intent, others do it for profit and often it is for both. ie; the medical/pharmaceutical profession and the military-industrial complex, trite as that may sound. The cancer society, the heart institute, a foundation for every disease, prevalent or not. The Russians, the Chinese, the Arabs. Awareness saves lives, they claim, but by the same token the generalized negative climate that prevails in our society creates more problems than it solves. Beyond that there are so many other things to fear also and it is a long list that can interfere with healthy living. This uneasiness derives from the larger myth that "the universe in general is a very unsafe place" and it most certainly can be viewed that way if that is the choice. Some people even sit up nights worrying about being hit by an asteroid or a piece of man made space junk falling out of the sky and spend their time trying to convince the public and the government that we need to endow the space agency with more scope and capability to deal with such remote possibilities. Hopefully their fears are not universal enough or strong enough to draw that which they spend their time fearing to come and collide with earth and harm the rest of us.

More realistically, however, there are far more practical things to worry about for those who feel they need to spend their time that way. Loss of job or income would be high on the list, along with getting ill or having an accident. Then we can move on to someone poisoning our drinking water. Not a lumber mill or a chemical factory or a city upstream dumping raw sewage into the river but a bona fid terrorist. A terrorist may also carry a bomb onto the plane or the train we are riding on, or blow up the building we work in, or place one in the stadium or along the parade route and, yes, these are clear probabilities. But that is not the question. The real question is, how probable?

What is the actual probability that any of these things will happen to any one particular individual at any one time? How many millions of people fly, take the train or ride in buses and cars every day? How many billions of passenger miles are accumulated without incident? How many millions of people attend sporting events every year? As always the tendency is to shine a bright light on the few casualties that occur and dramatize them instead of focusing on the billions of people who go through their lives without those kinds of incidents. Statistically speaking, the world is a very safe place to live in and would be even safer if we dwelt on the good rather than become obsessed with the bad.

Trouble is there to be found, however, if a person insists on doing something stupid or irresponsible. There are also hardships at times, but the objective is to learn from them. Be like the cat who is aware of the vicious dog who lives down the street and don't climb that fence. And don't kill yourself worrying about the possibility of the dog getting loose until he starts to growl at you personally. Above all, do not project negativity into the future because that alone may set the stage for mishap. It is like the woman I once knew who had a dreadful fear of being stopped by traffic police, so much so that her anxiety caused her to drive too slow and too cautiously which turned out to attract the very attention from the police she did not want. If she could have just relaxed, trusted herself and driven more normally, the problem would never have occurred. People do this in many other respects also, subconsciously setting themselves up for trouble, many times in far more serious ways than ending up with a traffic ticket.

On the other side of that, I have also known several women who traveled the world alone without negative incident, some into very out of the way places but they all started out with confidence and self assurance, trusting their own judgment along the way and arrived home safely. Life has its risks and it is important to take a few, trusting that the universe will grant you what you seek. But, as the saying goes, be careful what you ask for. You may very well create the drama you think you don't want or need. Above all learn to listen and trust your own inner voice. It exists for a purpose and will keep you safe if that is your choice, provided, of course, that you don't also embrace some other belief that makes you feel like you don't deserve to be safe that defeats it.

In addition to that issue is the one about other people. No matter how you may feel about the other people in your life on the personal level, the fact is that you have very little control over their actions in the long term. The people we care about, children especially, can be provided with love, guidance and good example, or not, as also happens all too often, but in the end they are still here for their own reasons, just as we all are, and on their own life's journey.

If we care about them we can also lend financial assistance, moral support and perhaps even inspiration and encouragement to pursue their own dreams but ultimately, they are who they are and that is that because they may also have appeared on stage to pursue goals that are in entire opposition to our own. And sometimes they want nothing more than to be allowed to find their own way. Next to child abuse, there is little that is more tragic than parents who reject their own children because they have different goals than theirs. They reject their own children for lots of other reasons too, quite often because the child finds it difficult or impossible to accept the rigid, narrow minded religious or cultural views of the parents. Here we have the example of the man who tried to run his own teenage daughter down with his car and kill her because she was friendly with a boy with a different heritage. We also have the teenage girl who was thrown out of her home and ended up on the streets of Las Vegas as a hooker because she didn't want to read the bible at the dinner table. Then, when the poor child ended up in the morgue, her parents excused their behavior by claiming it was the daughter's own fault because she turned her back on God.

On the opposite end of such distorted thinking there are other people who loved their child dearly and lost it early in life and their world turned completely upside down and inside out. What kind of all loving god would take away someone so precious and delightful, so full of life and promise? Disease is difficult enough to understand but when that person loses their life due to some wanton, stupid or vicious act of another it can become impossible to make sense of and lead to extreme bitterness and an end to faith. And, unless a person was very simple minded, it would seem to come across as very insulting to tell parents to visualize their little lost child up in heaven holding hands with God as one popular talk show host recently did. If that is the best answer a person can come up with at such a sad moment, it would be far better to admit a lack of understanding and remain silent. Other than that, what else is there to say? Sorry about the loss, sorry about the pain, that's just the way it is. God's will or grand mishap. There is nothing that can be done. Try and get past it.

But wait! Let's not forget the fact that, among other things, people can contact the physical world from beyond the grave, as has been so clearly demonstrated? What about that? As we have been saying, dead is not dead after all. Maybe not, but that process still appears to be so totally irreversible. The pain of their going is still an ongoing ache and we miss them terribly. Still, if dead is not really dead, then somehow we will all get to meet again and what a happy reunion that will be. But why did they have to leave in the first place? Why couldn't we all just go on living here on earth forever?

Physical death implies birth, however, just as birth implies death and there are reasons for this ongoing cycle. Some don't see it that way, however, and state that if they didn't get old and run down, they would like to live forever, clearly not understanding the implications of what they are saying. Having specific lifetimes in the physical world is a spiritual necessity. Prolonging one's lifetime beyond some limit would be just as damaging to the spirit as spending eternity in heaven or hell. Based on what the average person is able to deal with and continue to learn from, there is no real point in extending present life expectancies. If there was, people would automatically live longer. Granted, the average individual certainly has the potential to acquire more knowledge, expand their comprehension, further their creativity and become far more advanced intellectually, psychologically and emotionally than they presently do. Unfortunately, though, most people stall out somewhere along the way and start winding down long before they might otherwise need to if they had learned to think in broader terms earlier on and not become the victims of the myths surrounding the aging process.

Others come with a different mission in mind, however. Their lives are usually more intense and specific so they purposely end early, when the goal has been achieved. Here we might use someone like John F. Kennedy as an example. How do we make sense of what happened to him?

On the surface he was a person of high intelligence, full of energy and drive, very charismatic with great leadership ability and a unifying figure that inspired young and old around the world in a time of need. Perhaps few remember but one thing he taught the nation was that a person with a different religious background was not a threat to their views. Initially many protestants felt very strongly that a Catholic president would somehow affect their religious freedoms but it was just as mindless as the fears expressed by many whites when the nations first black president was elected. And then Kennedy was assassinated in the prime of his life. It seemed so senseless. But let's try to see it from a different viewpoint.

First of all, as difficult as it may be to accept, no one dies until they are ready to do so. Ridiculous, some would scream. If that were true then why can't I live forever, they may ask. Well, the truth is, you do. You are an eternal being and you might well remain in the physical realm a lot longer than you think possible but somewhere along the line you will realize there is little or nothing to be gained by prolonging any one lifetime beyond some point and, with a little reflection, that becomes clearer on a conscious level as we age. Inherently, of course, that wisdom is already there on a deeper level and we go with that when the time comes when we know we are done for this time around. So, as we shall see for Kennedy, the stage was set. But how to do die? We all have to make the transition from life to death somehow. People choose the way they want to go. Some feel they need to use their death to make a statement. They martyr themselves for a cause.

Others couldn't care less. They have an accident because it is quick or they go quietly in the night. Sometimes because there life has been complete and sometimes just to put an end to their faulty judgment or because they feel stalled out and don't feel they can keep up the pace of early accomplishment. Maybe even to get themselves out of a dead ended physical or psychological trap they have fallen into through drug addiction or because of some other seemingly unsolvable problem. Maybe the hopelessness of fighting in a war. For others, however, fighting against a terminal illness becomes the final challenge, the last chance to show the world some bravery. These people get diseases that are debilitating, painful and prolonged which family and friends can rally around. As for Kennedy, however, he was in some sense a martyr. Still in his forties, a renowned, respected and idolized world leader, why would anyone choose to give that up? It had to have been without his permission. Except it was not. But why would anyone make that choice? It doesn't make any sense.

Not true, however, because it made complete sense to him. Clearly, he wanted his death to make a bold statement. But to do that he needed a collaborator in the form of Lee Harvey Oswald. Contradictory as it may seem, however, there was no coincidence here. For everyone who wishes to die a violent death there is someone who will step forward and take it away from them for their own notoriety and it all came flawlessly together right down to the point with Kennedy, himself, insisted on riding in an open limo with the top off, making himself the highly visible target he was. But again, why?

Not knowing all the facts, we can only speculate, but if we take the man off his pedestal, what else do we see? As an individual he showed the world what a person can do on the personal level with his rise to power and he was worshiped by many as the very articulate new voice of hope in a troubled world. As a president he stood firm against the Soviet Union and keep them from establishing Cuba as a missile base. But then he also saw our troops fail miserably in the attempted invasion of Cuba at the Bay of Pigs.

On the personal side he was a family man. On the surface, it was the story of Camelot. Wealth, power, influence, a loyal wife and children, extended family. But there was also Marilyn Monroe, the sexy movie queen behind the scenes, along with innumerable other philanderings and surreptitious friends. So then, on the personal level he was also every bit a fraud. And too, what about the world situation? Could the youngest president ever elected bring real peace to the world? Could he end poverty and hunger? Could he even solve any of the more everyday problems in just the United States alone? If nothing else could he just drag big business into the courtroom and end some of the distressing practices his own father was guilty of in his acquisition of wealth? Then, too, what was wrong with the general population? Why do they always look to their leaders to fix everything? Why don't they step up and take responsibility? Educate themselves, become better informed, get involved?

Kennedy might have been bright and aggressive but he didn't have the life experience or the accumulated wisdom to handle some of the bigger issues that faced the nation and the world at that time. Sooner or later he would be up against his own limitations and in serious trouble. If he had lived, his life might well have ended in personal failure. But if he died when he did, he would die as a hero and an inspiration. Of course, while this explanation may not be entirely accurate in all the details, it does

241

provide some perspective when trying to reach an understanding in situations that would otherwise be difficult to comprehend. The special pain associated with untimely death is still real and difficult, however, but it is somewhat alleviated by also knowing that when it comes to those special people in your own life, you will all meet again, both on the other side and quite possibly in more lifetimes to come, playing different roles. In the meantime, for the still living....

The life you are experiencing now should best be looked at as an opportunity. When it is over, what is it that you can take with you? Not money, or power, or fame or all those exotic collectables, the jewelry, the closets full of unworn clothing, none of it, so why are they so important to some people while they are here? Purposely chasing money, power and the accumulation of material goods, solely for the sake of possession would seem to be the result of an unfortunate personality defect.

Nevertheless, nowhere in the entire process is there anything that says a person has to live by the rules of conventionality, either. It is a personal right to live one's life any way one chooses and, as long as it is done without bringing harm to others, it doesn't matter how it is played out. If it feels right and provokes some level of passion, there is much to be gained by the choice no matter how odd or extreme it may seem to others, whether it is living in a penthouse or in a mountain cave. Medical doctor to voodoo healer, great philanthropist to moocher on the corner. Or, model citizen. Not by coercion or peer pressure, but through desire.

On the other side of it, though, remember that where you are at, at this moment in time, is exactly where you have taken yourself with the decisions you have made thus far, both before birth and after. It is either with choice or by default. Certainly we can blame others who may have abused us, cheated us, failed us, or done other harm-

242

ful things to us but as has been said, it is not what has been done to us that counts but what we do about what has been done to us that matters. Granted, sometimes the things that have been done to some are so severe that they become life crippling in the extreme but we must attempt to look beyond that. Understanding deeper reasons does not in any way diminish or excuse anyone's bad behavior, our own included, self destructive or otherwise, impossible as it may be to avoid. But that is where the challenge lies, waiting to be worked on.

The companions to this, the what has been done to us, are several. First, what have we allowed someone else to do to us or to others when we were in a position to do something about it and let it happen anyway? Next, what have we done to others that was harmful to them and, what have we done, or are doing, to ourselves that was, or is, physically, mentally or morally harmful? And finally, what have we done about that? Transgression is transgression. If you believe you live in a meaningless universe then you may well believe that the only penalty is in getting caught for illegal acts and anything is excusable if you don't. Unfortunately the base premise is incorrect. There is a higher meaning to life and that changes everything.

No, we do not receive a bi annual report card as to how we are doing along the way and there is no final examine at the end of the road. God does not judge you. There is no heavenly panel of moralists with a check list. Friends and neighbors don't take a poll. People still pray and plead with their god, however, but no one answers and in the end the only accountability that really matters lies entirely with one's own conscience and ends with personal integrity. Even though some people are very good at playing hide and seek with themselves on the conscious level, the truth is still there and has a way of eventually expressing itself, adding to or subverting the individual as they move through life. Mistakes are made, but that is part of the process. Short on wisdom, not enough information, constantly evolving situations make mistakes inevitable and some of them are irreversible.

Some things can not be taken back and, in spite of what some might say about finding peace in forgiveness, some things are still unforgivable and we should not pretend that they are. A murderer does not deserve forgiveness. How the victim's family and friends deal with the aftermath is up to them but it seems fair to say that life was not meant to be spent in ongoing mourning, either. That dishonors both the victim and the survivor. But, in the end, regardless of all else, the only accountability, the only morality that really matters is that which adds to our own spiritual development and growth.

"It is not for the purpose of satisfying the wishes of a supernatural being that we need a code of moral values, nor for the purpose of satisfying the needs of our neighbors. Morality is a practical, *selfish* necessity. Alone on a desert island, an individual would face constant alternatives requiring moral choice: to think or not to think; to perceive reality, identify facts, and act accordingly, or to sulk and pray; to work and produce, or to demand a miracle that would spare the effort; to act on independent judgment, or to surrender to terror. The fact that we live among other human beings should not obscure the intimately personal nature of our need for a code of ethics. Our self esteem requires it, our happiness requires it, our life requires it." Nathaniel Branden.

In the end, while we can fail others in their expectations of us, the only failure that matters is when we fail ourselves and that only happens when we abdicate our responsibilities to ourselves. It doesn't matter who we disappoint along the way as long as we don't disappoint ourselves. And when we do, the object is not to become sidetracked by guilt or disappointment, but to learn from it. Guilt, in particular, has a way of compounding the problem and perpetuating the mistake. It also leaves us open to manipulation and control from those with an outside agenda.

God does not judge humans and mistakes do not make a person sinful. Right or wrong, humans judge humans, but the only judgment of real importance is how we learn to judge ourselves. Few people are capable of seeing themselves with enough objectivity to do that wisely, however, nor of seeing that the difficulties they find themselves in have been set in motion or allowed to happen through their own actions. Regardless, the idea is not to beat oneself up for past mistakes but to learn to avoid them in the future, and the only purpose guilt should serve is to remind us not to repeat those past mistakes in the future.

Letting guilt become a form of self punishment is self betrayal. Guilt can also produce fear and fear is debilitating. We become afraid to trust ourselves and afraid to take the risks that are necessary for real fulfillment. Unfortunately, much of that comes from the culture we live in. We are bombarded with messages that tell us that we cannot trust our own judgment about almost everything, from how to spend our money, to what clothes to wear to the party, to when it is proper to even voice an opinion. We are also told that we need a political analyst to tell us what they think the president really said in his latest speech because we who sit at home and listen aren't capable of that, which is why he is there doing it for us instead. We have even come to the point where we need experts to do post mortems on sporting events and tell us how to interpret the action.

Most damaging of all, though, are those who insist they know what is best for us on the personal level. How much sex we should be having, how many hours of sleep and when, how much water we should drink, how many vitamins to take. Flu shots, checkups, organic foods, the list is long. Above all, don't trust your own judgment for a minute because you are not an expert, even when it comes to yourself. You couldn't be feeling as good as you think you are because there has to be something going on inside your body that you are unaware of and if you don't ......

In today's society, even experts consult other experts when they step out of their own area of expertise. Eventually it spills over into all other aspects of one's life. People become immobilized, afraid to make choices based on desire or intuition or even using their own reasoning process for fear of getting it wrong. As a result they shut down, limiting and cheating themselves out of rewarding experiences and adventures they could otherwise have for fear of making a mistake. But mistakes are part of the process. There is no other way to achieve self improvement. And more often that not, mistakes can lead to a success that could not have been achieved without them. The real value not only comes from admitting one's mistakes to one's self and acting on that but also from firmly keeping in mind that while mistakes are unavoidable, we also do a far larger portion of things right every day of our lives than not, or we wouldn't even be here. In that regard, t**he goal in life is to become largely independent of the opinions, habits, and judgments of others so that one's inner equilibrium does not depend on such an untrustworthy foundation. Any real security is found within.** Additionally, be again reminded of what Winston Churchill said. "There are no experts, only varying degrees of ignorance," while also keeping in mind the following.

"You will not find yourself by running from teacher to teacher, from book to book. You will not meet yourself through following any specialized form of meditation. Only by looking quietly within the self that you know can your own reality be experienced, with those connections that exist between the present or immediate self and the inner identity that is multidimensional. There must be a willingness, an acquiescence, a desire. If you do not take the time to examine your subjective states, then you cannot complain if so many answers seem to elude you. You cannot throw the burden of proof on another, or expect a person or a teacher to prove to you the validity of your own existence. Such a procedure is bound to lead you into one subjective trap after another." Seth

Too many people want easy answers, however, when they are not there to be found. They will most certainly not be found by listening to someone who lauds themselves as being an awareness coach or a meditational and intuitive earth energy gardener who uses quantum touching and matrix energetics along with alchemy and sacred geometry to heal your chakras and elevate your consciousness. You also don't need to find a sacred mountain to climb or spend a week in a sweat lodge to purify yourself or fast for thirty days in a row, or drink unsweetened organic tea for the rest of your life. You cannot become enlightened by jumping into a polluted river and letting yourself be dunked by a swami or by getting on your knees in front of a plaster statue of Jesus or spending fifty years in a monastery analyzing moldy old holy books. It takes a different kind of effort.

Everything begins with the individual and change only comes about when enough individuals come together and make it happen. As stated previously, the world is in crisis. But that is nothing new. The world has always been in crisis in one way or another. The only difference is that now it is much more critical because of its proportions and fundamental nature. If religion in its present forms prevails, we will sink into a bombed out, computer aided repression of the human spirit to a degree never seen before. And if the Darwinian stance regarding our origins and the meaningless, meaning of life prevails, we will be just as doomed. Probabilistically, however, this is less likely to happen than the other possibility because the inquiring minds of other scientists in other fields will continue to dig deeper and will eventually investigate all those previously shunned phenomena that keep occurring on the fringes of everyday life. Then, when the results are in, there will be only one logical conclusion. Life is not an accidental happening and we do not live in a meaningless universe.

While there will still be room for argument as to what the purpose of life really is and exactly how we should be living it, the one thing that is certain is that science has thus far been terribly wrong in its limited assessment and has created a tremendous rift between the many segments of society. Furthermore, no matter what scientists say about value judgments being outside of their frame of reference, science still implies that values are therefore without basis and the reasoning qualities of the mind are purposely directed away from any inquiry and exploration that would bring about acceptable evidence for such values. In reality, however, human experience is not limited to those events which science can explain and humans generally live by the very values science chooses to ignore.

Additionally, hard as it may be to understand, the resurgence of religious fundamentalism is in its own way, a very skewed reaction to the misconceptions of science regarding the meaning of life. Yes, it is extreme and dangerous but not unexpected. In trying to dominate world thinking by imposing their opinions on the rest of society, the Darwinians have alienated vast numbers of people who understand on a deep, intuitive level that fundamentally, when it comes to life, science has gotten it all wrong. That doesn't make fundamentalists right either because, for them too, it's also an all or nothing game and on the personal level, religionists don't want to be found wrong any more than scientists do.

Being wrong scientifically can be career limiting and

harmful to the ego but being wrong in terms of religious faith is a threat against one's fundamental being, the person's very soul, if you will, and some of these individuals will damn well go to war to defend their beliefs. Like it or not, terribly wrong as the extreme fundamentalists are in assuming that force is the only solution to the problem when trying to resolve these deeper issues, the more moderate religionists have gotten it a wee bit more correct than most scientists. Without this recognition and some basic understanding of why people will fight for their beliefs and why some people become terrorists to begin with and why hatred sometimes runs so deep, little will be resolved in the near future. There is hope, however, and everything leans in that direction. As always, it still comes back to the individual.

SUMMARY

There is a battle going on, no doubt about that. And, if "Science" could eventually convince the majority of people, Americans especially, to fully accept the Darwinian version of things, that would be just as damaging to human progress as would a consolidated, unyielding view that the entity "God" was unquestionably responsible. For scientists to take the position that only evolution can be taught in the public school is one thing. Certainly it would be impossible to teach all the religious variations regarding creation and it is not in the best interest of the school system to do that. But to not even allow a teacher to point out that that view is controversial is another. Being repetitive here, it is a battle over the soul of the individual, all right. Both in America and everywhere else in the world, the danger being that should either side win and these extreme views spill over and completely dominate politics and government, then real human progress would be in serious jeopardy. To force any one concept of reality on others is dictatorial and Hitleresque and to assume that the only available choices are religion or present day science is about as narrow minded and unimaginative as it could possibly get.

Self created or otherwise, our view of reality is still carrying us down a road that presents us with somber questions about our racial future. It is a time for concern, to be sure, but it must be an intelligent concern, not a fear based one. Contrary to what the religious doom sayers continue to state, the apocalypse is not upon us and it is not too late so we don't need to be chewing our nails over that one. On the other hand, however, the time has indeed come to embrace a more abstruse version of that which we call reality if the prospects for the future are to be pleasing. Life is more than mindless procreation. We have both a right and a reason to be here but we must learn to understand those reasons in terms that are clear enough to put into words and daily practice.

Looking at planet earth in an objective manner while knowing that there is another complete side to everyday existence, one might come to the conclusion that planet earth is the kindergarten of the universe. It is a place where most people are still learning how to share the toys and get along with each other in more respectful ways. Aggravating and frustrating as that can be at times, we still need to maintain respect for each other and try to understand our differences. To do that effectively we must embrace our own selves as fully as possible. Our feelings and emotions along with our logic and our intuitions, everything that makes us human. In the process, while it may seem like life is an entirely do-it-yourself project, it is still filled with many, more evolved, surprisingly generous and caring individuals, willing to lend a hand along the way when we are open to it.

In the meantime we must all learn to take responsibility for our own thoughts and actions. Everyone came here for a reason. That reason is uniquely one's own and is not meant to be sacrificed to someone else's value system in the process of development so honor that and try not to get sidetracked by the unscrupulous. Know more than anything that dead is not dead. Each individual is an eternal being on a self selected mission, a part of which is often just trying to figure out what it is and gaining insight. Is is not just about genetics and survival of the fittest and the gauge of success is not about about money and power but creativity and spiritual progress. One might also consider the fact that since, dead is not dead, that you will eventually end up having to face those you cheated, lied to and abused and have to live with the fact that you did.

Be especially aware of individuals you seem to have strong connections with, good or bad, because there is probably a reason why you have met up again. Interrelations between family, friends, acquaintances and even enemies are often complex. Also remember there are reasons why, for example, all the great Dutch artists showed up in the same relative time period, or an Immanuel, a Caesar, a Thoreau or anyone else who impacted society in a way that brought notice, came along when they did. It may even go so far as to have two old enemies show up to take opposite sides in a war like two of the great strategists of all time, General Patton and General Rommel in World War II, taking advantage of the conflict to play out some high level, private game of their own, which brings up that other point. Those we seem to have the deeper connections with. If we have not resolved the issues between us, we may well meet again somewhere along the way to bring things to a better conclusion.

Old lovers reunite and old enemies reappear. Some are forever bonds, some are just passing adventures. Often we will do things to help the growth of another and often they will do the same for us. Many times it will make little or no sense as to why the things that happen, happen the way they do, but in the end we will learn and understand why a loved one may have stayed such a little while or why things went the way they did at the time or why our own life took the turns it did and know there were self generated reasons for every bit of it. It all has a deeper meaning.

Ultimately, know that every life has its own importance in the bigger scheme of things, right down to the very last bird, butterfly or tree and in that respect it is not just churches, temples, sites and certain books that are sacred. Every thing that exists is important and equally sacred. And while some may lead lives that seem completely insignificant, they still add to the whole and have their own importance. One that is impossible to weigh in earthly standards. In the end, the greater reality is: no one, no human being, no animal, no tree, plant or insect, lives nor dies in vain. There is meaning for all of life, not a meaning that we have to invent, but a meaning that is behind everything. It is the essence of who we are, whether we choose to believe it or not.

We are not born by accident and as a species we did not evolve from pond scum. We were born with a purpose and that alone gives meaning to every single life form on this planet.

We chose to be born at the time, place and situation we find ourselves in and we are here to experience particular aspects of our greater selves in the lifetime we are now living. It is not about who has accumulated the highest pile of cash or material possessions, it is about what we have left when all of that is stripped away. What have we allowed ourselves to feel and to think, what have we learned, how high did we reach, what did we dare to try? What gifts did we share along the way, what awareness did we gain of ourselves and our bigger role in the universe? Did we allow ourselves to ask the bigger questions and stand in our own space, to be awed and mystified and yet remain trusting and willing to try and balance the life we are living against the greater destiny that awaits?

Unfortunately, for far too many that destiny is obscured by the overwhelming mass of conflicting, distorted and often downright false information people are exposed to from birth onward and forced to deal with during their lifetime because of the way it has become so deeply entrenched in the minds and institutions of the times. Once accepted, digging out from underneath it is usually very difficult. But it is possible and we should be encouraged to do so. It is done by re examining old and new ideas alike, reading between the lines and looking beyond the facade and the superficial. It is about becoming more spiritual wherein;

A SPIRITUAL PERSON IS ONE WHO PLACES THE PURSUIT OF TRUTH ABOVE ALL ELSE BY ATTEMPTING TO UNDERSTAND HIS OR HER PLACE IN THE UNIVERSE AND THEIR REASONS FOR BE-

ING HERE. To accomplish this, the seeking individual must first learn to become scrupulously honest with themselves about their own thoughts, feelings and emotions and not become sidetracked by either the easy promises of others or the fear driven proclamations about what will happen if you do not heed some edict.

Contrary to popular opinion, spirituality has nothing to do with worship or reverential attachment to doctrine or to ritual enshrouded belief systems. Religion, in the strict sense, is in fact the antithesis of spirituality and the true apostasy of human life. Thus there are no side entrances one can slip through by quoting scripture, performing ceremony or sacrificial rites or by having some priest bless you, some guru smudge you or new age shaman place a crystal on your forehead while pretending to channel the archangels. You cannot climb the great Pyramid of Cheops and expect the first rays of dawn to magically endow you with soul illuminating enlightenment and rebirth, either, as one popular new age guru claims to have done. Nor does spirituality come from adherence to rules put out by such people, nor from subservience of any kind, either mental or physical, nor from self imposed suffering. By the same token neither does it come from ego. Anyone who seeks adulation, pursues and preaches to a following, thinks of their admirers as a flock of sheep that they must administer to or feels the missionary need to convert others to their way of thinking has confused spirituality with their own mis guided self importance.

Likewise, spirituality cannot be gleaned from a study of astrology, mythology, the Egyptian Book of the Dead, the Book of Enoch, the texts of secret societies or so-called sacred geometry. Even worse are works that pretend to be the keys to everything, especially spirituality. Although some of these publications may have certain elements of truth in them, for the most part they are blatantly misleading. Being full of elaborately contrived conglomerations of sacrosanct mumblings and creatively meaningless terminology all strung together in statements which endlessly revolve outward about themselves in ever widening circles, the reader becomes lost. Unfortunately, even though it is quite meaningless to begin with, many do not see it to be so because it alludes to some grandly disguised insight and sounds profoundly beyond understanding. As a result many innocent, gullible and sincere people feel they can embrace and covet such meaninglessness anyway, be it channeled messages from the Pleidiens, Ashtar, the Archangels or great Uncle Willy, now long departed.

Along these same lines some people also feel that spirituality is some sort of commodity. IT IS NOT A COMMODITY. Spending five thousand dollars or more for the privilege of undergoing a three day intensive, enlightenment seminar is not going to bring you any closer to becoming spiritual. Nor will the certificate of attendance you might receive or even a degree from a college of divinity. In a similar fashion, neither can you become spiritual by having your aura or your colon cleansed or your ears coned. Acupuncture, core contacts, sound, color and light therapy will not do it, nor will metaphysical psychometrics, transcendental meditation, Reichian aqua energizers, holotropic integrations, visionary enlightenment, neurolinguistic programming, past life therapy, chakra tuning or other nefarious, misleading self indulgence.

It is never that easy, or that hard, depending on your view. Nor should it be. If there is any price tag on spirituality at all it is one of time and patience. Regardless of whatever else happens, however, the bottom line might still be said to be, there is no such thing as becoming spiritual. It is not a situation where one day you are not and the next day you are. It is not a state you magically cross over into. In a larger sense we are all "spiritual" to begin with. The idea is to become "more spiritual." It is a quest, not a condition. It takes both heart and mind, intuition and logic, emotion and reason, seeking to feel and understand

and to come to balance within and without, acknowledging the creative beauty in all things, from the microbe to the galaxy. In the end, of course, spirituality is not achieved by pursuing it but by allowing it to happen. Seek knowledge, truth and peace. Live, not with self centered greed but with involvement and human charity. Ask for wisdom. Learn compassion and understanding and when to mind your own business.

Finally, with all things considered, the spiritual path is not a path at all. One does not work at becoming spiritual. To become obsessed with its pursuit is also in contradiction to what spirituality is all about. So is denial or mistreatment of the body along with sensual or intellectual deprivation. Being spiritual requires one to understand the fact that they are first of all a spiritual being and that the body is the physical manifestation of that being. The individual who honors their body and lives with full appreciation of life's pleasures is, therefore, far more spiritual than a celibate priest, a reclusive monk or a person neurotically obsessed with diet. Because the flesh has its own treasure trove of wisdom, turning one's back on the life they have chosen can only lead to erroneous conclusions, both about life itself and whatever lies beyond life.

Regrettably, in this age of potential enlightenment, even though there is just as much proof for the spiritual side of reality as there is for the physical existence of the electron, many sciences refuse to acknowledge such a possibility so, once again the reader is reminded that, not only is the hidden reality as valid as the physical one, it is the origin of it and in this regard the life sphere is a place we come to by choice, picking a particular period of time and social environment to reappear in that is consistent with the goals we have in mind.

In any case, suffering is not a mandatory part of that life, either. It is only a part of life if we choose to be born into a situation that almost guarantees it or it occurs when we make bad choices or behave foolishly. And though some misguided individuals may spend a lifetime enduring self inflicted pain and mutilation in penance for imaginary misdeeds and shortcomings, God will not one day appear before them and take them in his arms. God instead, could only wonder how he happened to come upon such damned fools as these who do not love and honor their bodies and the life they have come to live. The purpose of life is not to spend it "Glorifying God" as some people would have us righteously believe but to freely live that life with honor, decency, love and creativity. Nor is life to be spent fearing God. Nor does fearing God make one "good," as in the expression, "He/she is a good, God fearing person."

How can anyone claim to love a God that does such frightful things that one must live in fear of that God. Why reincarnate into a physical body if you are going to turn your back on that same body in denial and confusion and spend it living in fear? Birth is a new beginning. It is also a chance for something else. Quoting Kierkegaard who founded modern existentialism, something which has its own severe limitations but has this truth, "... so much is said about wasted lives-but only that man's life is wasted who lived on, so deceived by the joys of life or by its sorrow that he never became eternally and decisively conscious of himself as spirit." In other words, a spiritual being. In that respect, remember that:

LIFE BEGINS IN AN UNBURDENED STATE OF GRACE. What we wish to do with it after that is up to us. The purpose of choosing to reincarnate is not to endure punishment, but to learn. If pain can provide the learning situation we need, so be it. Learn the lesson and then learn to leave the pain behind and move on to include that other mountain of evidence that science would like us to exclude and decide for yourself, who is right and who is wrong. The facts are verifiable if we refuse to be intimidated by the experts and realize that there is a solid foundation for hope and inspiration in the challenging world situation of today. There is good reason to act with decency and honor because, without that, we only end up discrediting and dishonoring ourselves.

Additionally, be encouraged to live the life you have chosen more boldly. Learn to trust your own mind and your own intuition. You won't be getting on an airplane that is about to crash if you are not ready to die and you will not be home on the day when an asteroid hits your house and you won't be trapped in a mall when a gunman shows up and starts shooting if you don't want to be. Above all, stopping being so afraid. Fear can easily attract the very thing feared. Do not limit your thinking to the ordinary and do not buy into the myths about aging unless you want to limit your ability to function fully, long before necessary.

Don't be misled by artificial limitations either because, once accepted, they become yours to keep. As Mr. Spock of Star Trek fame once said way back in 1970, "Once we are convinced of the reality of a situation, we are bound by its rules." Beliefs about reality are not necessarily the truth about reality, however, so try and distinguish the difference. Is it belief, or fact? Also remember that most claims of, "I can't," are self imposed and sometimes people do get themselves in situations where their choices are limited or no longer exist but again, as a reminder, they need to realize that originally they created the situation they are in, either in the present lifetime or set it up before entering into it. In the end that becomes one of life's bigger challenges and the average person is capable of achieving far more than they do in terms of personal development. And, most importantly, you don't need anyone else to validate your existence and give it meaning. The universe has already done that for you.

BIBLIOGRAPHY

Escape from Evil   Earnest Becker 1975
Mysteries From Forgotten Worlds Charles Berlitz 1972
The Divining Hand   Christopher Bird 1979
Honoring The Self   Nathaniel Branden 1983
The Seventh Sense   Lyn Buchanan 2003
The Cosmic Blueprint   Paul Davies 1988
Space & time in the modern universe P.C.W. Davies 1977
God and the New Physics   Paul Davies 1983
Are We Alone?   Paul Davies 1995
The Fifth Miracle   Paul Davies 1999
The Eerie Silence   Paul Davies 2010
Teaching A Stone To Talk Annie Dillard   1982
Magic and Mystery in Tibet Alexandra David-Neel 1967
Discover Magazine   March 2014 and March 2015
Ego and Archetype   Edward Edinger 1992
All The Strange Hours Loren Eiseley 1975
The Immense Journey Loren Eiseley 1957
UFO Contact from the Pleides Elders and Welch   1979
Out Of My Later Years   Albert Einstein 1956 & 1984
Man's Search For Meaning Victor E. Frankl 1984
Man For Himself   Eric Fromm 1975
The Airmen Who Would Not Die   John G. Fuller 1979
Earthquake Generation   Jeffrey Goodman 1978
The Genesis Mystery   Jeffrey Goodman 1983
The Self-Aware Universe   Goswami 1993
War Is a Force That Gives Us Meaning C. Hedges   2002
The Intelligent Universe   Sir Fred Hoyle 1984
Gentle Bridges   Hyward and Varela   1992
The Self-Organizing Universe   Erich Jantsch 1980
Darwin on Trial   Phillip E. Johnson 1991
Professional Hypnotism Manual   John G. Kappas 1978
Light Years   Gary Kinder 1987
The Physician Within You G. McGarey & J. Stearn 1997
Final Analysis   Jeffrey Masson 1990
Remote Viewing Secrets   Joseph McMoneagle 2000

Confessions of a Medical Heretic R. S. Mendelsohn 1979
Only a Theory   Kenneth R. Miller
Journeys Out Of The Body   Robert A. Monroe 1971
Far Journeys   Robert A. Monroe 1985
Ultimate Journey   Robert A. Monroe 1994
Life After Life   Raymond A. Moody 1975
Mutant Message   Marlo Morgan 1991
Conjuring Up Phillip   I. Owen 1976
The Edgar Cayce Handbook   Harold J. Reilly 1975
Seth Speaks   Jane Roberts 1972
The Nature of Personal Reality Jane Roberts 1974
The Unknown Reality   Jane Roberts 1977-79
The Nature of the Psyche   Jane Roberts 1979
The Individual & Nature of Mass Events J. Roberts 1981
Dreams, Evolution and Value Fulfillment J. Roberts 1986
The Early Sessions   Jane Roberts 1997-99
The Mind Body Prescription John E. Sarno 1998
Healing Back Pain   John E. Sarno 1999
The Divided Mind John E. Sarno 2006
UFO Contact from the Pleides Stevens 1989
Beyond the Quantum   Michael Talbot 1986
On The Wing   Alan Tennant 2004
Beyond The Time Barrier   Andrew Tomas 1974
Conversations With Seth (2 volumes)   Sue Watkins 1981
Lifetide   Lyall Watson 1979
Supernature   Lyall Watson   1973
Beyond Supernature   Lyall Watson 1987
Dreams of Dragons   Lyall Watson 1987
Gifts of Unknown Things Lyall Watson 1991
The Secret Life of Inanimate Objects Lyall Watson 1990
An Essay on Morals Philip Wylie 1947

www.ingramcontent.com/pod-product-compliance
Lightning Source LLC
Chambersburg PA
CBHW051949090426
42741CB00008B/1324